D1304761

Leading Your Church Through Conflict and Reconciliation

Library of Leadership Development

Leading Your Church Through Conflict and Reconciliation
Renewing Your Church Through Vision and Planning

Library of Leadership Development

Leading Your Church Through and Conflict Reconciliation

30 Strategies to Transform Your Ministry

Marshall Shelley, General Editor

BETHANY HOUSE PUBLISHERS
MINNEAPOLIS, MINNESOTA 55438

Leading Your Church Through Conflict and Reconciliation
Copyright © 1997
LEADERSHIP/Christianity Today, Inc.

Cover design by Eric Walljasper

Published by Bethany House Publishers
A Ministry of Bethany Fellowship, Inc.
11300 Hampshire Avenue South
Minneapolis, Minnesota 55438

Printed in the United States of America.

Library of Congress Cataloging-in-Publication Data

Leading your church through conflict and reconciliation : 30 strategies to transform your ministry / Marshall Shelley, general editor.
    p.   cm. — (Library of leadership development)
Includes bibliographical references.
ISBN 1-55661-940-5
1. Church controversies. I. Shelley, Marshall. II. Series.
BV652.9.L39   1996
253—dc21   96–45869
                                                        CIP

Contents

Part 1
Anticipation

Part 2
Prevention

Part 3
Confrontation

Part 4
Redemption

Foreword

You have leadership potential. That's the working assumption of this new series, the Library of Leadership Development.

The theory that you must have certain traits to be a leader, now passé in academic circles, still dies hard in our minds. Management consultant Peter Drucker says, "There may be 'born leaders,' but there surely are far too few to depend on them. Leadership must be learned and can be learned. . . ."

Yet too often we measure our skills against the "born leaders," the superstars who build large organizations. We compare our style of leadership to someone else's, always coming up short. If the apostle Paul were writing today to his mentoree Timothy, he might say, "Don't despise your potential; your leadership is unique."

Potential requires effort to realize. And some pain. Church leadership may be learned, but to learn it, you may have to fail. After being forced to resign from a Colorado congregation, a pastor friend said, "I will never again make a controversial issue a referendum on my leadership."

Thankfully, he survived the ordeal with his calling intact and is now effectively serving another congregation. My friend will admit that today he is a much better leader because of his mistake.

The volumes in the Library of Leadership Development aim to give you practical help before you need it. I think you'll appreciate the candor of our authors. I also believe you'll appreciate the tone of their writing: They use few "you shoulds"; instead, they say, "This is what I've learned." They tell the good, the bad, and the ugly aspects of ministry and allow you to learn from their experience.

Leadership can be learned. We hope this series emboldens you

and provides you with practical help to develop your God-given potential.

—David L. Goetz
Senior Associate Editor,
LEADERSHIP

Introduction

*Wherever two or three are gathered, conflict is
in the midst of them.*

—Edward Rowell

I was nursing a bad case of Monday morning blues.
    Angry homeowners around the church were threatening to sue over unkept promises made by the previous pastor. A key lay leader and I mutually agreed that the church wasn't big enough for both of us; but he had tenure and influence. Even more threatening was an ongoing difference of opinion over style and strategy with a denominational official who controlled the lion's share of our financial support.

I went to the Monday pastors' luncheon to get away from my own bad company. As I shoveled my food, I marveled as my peers told of Sunday statistics and stories of glorious fulfillment. I didn't buy it; I walked out at the earliest opportunity. As I did, I was surprised to see Joe following me. Joe was one of the most respected pastors in our association.

"Ed, let's have breakfast together tomorrow," he said.

The next morning, Joe listened to my epic of woe. When I finished, instead of sympathizing with me, he congratulated me. He said the trials of my ministry showed that God wanted to make a spiritual man out of me.

"The only pastors who don't experience regular, character-building periods of conflict," he said, "are either bullies who walk all over everyone or cowards afraid to stand up for what God wants to accomplish." Pastors between the two extremes, he said, were destined for a lifetime of learning how to lead in spite of and amid conflict.

I went to work more encouraged than I had for months. Over the next year, Joe taught me some valuable lessons in conflict management and team building.

There's no getting around it: Conflict is. Wherever two or three are gathered, it is in the midst of them.

Leading Your Church Through Conflict and Reconciliation, the first volume in the Library of Leadership Development, helps church leaders understand, prevent, and redeem conflict. Its authors, who've survived *and* thrived in church conflict, tell their stories, and explain the principles that have helped them treat congregational infections. They offer the help that Joe gave me—honest, practical, hopeful.

—Edward Rowell
Assistant Editor,
LEADERSHIP

Contributors

Jim Amandus is pastor of Highlands Community Church in Renton, Washington. Prior to his seven years at Highlands Community, he served as pastor in Ventura, California, and in Corvallis, Oregon.

LeRoy Armstrong is associate pastor of Concord Missionary Baptist Church in Dallas, Texas.

Stuart Briscoe has been pastor of Elmbrook Church in Brookfield, Wisconsin, for more than twenty years. Before entering the ministry, he was a banking official in England. He has also ministered with Capernwray Missionary Fellowship of Torchbearers. He has authored numerous books, including *Fresh Air in the Pulpit*, and co-authored *Mastering Contemporary Preaching* and *Measuring Up*.

Daniel Brown is founding pastor of The Coastlands in Aptos, California. He has written *Unlock the Power of Family*.

Donald Bubna is pastor-at-large for the Christian and Missionary Alliance and is a member of the editorial advisory board of *Leadership*. He has authored two books, *Building People* and *Encouraging People*.

Andre Bustanoby is a marriage and family therapist in Bowie, Maryland. He is a member of the American Association for Marriage and Family Therapy and past president of the mid-Atlantic division. He is the author of numerous books, including *But I Didn't Want a Divorce* and *Just Talk to Me*.

Edward Dobson is pastor of Calvary Church in Grand Rapids, Michigan. Before that he served as vice-president for student life at Liberty University in Lynchburg, Virginia. With Jerry Falwell and others, he has written *The Fundamentalist Phenomenon*, and with Ed Hinson, *The Seduction of Power*. He is also the author of *Starting a Seeker Sensitive Service*.

David Goetz is senior associate editor of LEADERSHIP. Before coming to *Leadership* he served as associate pastor of Mountain Christian Fellowship in Golden, Colorado. He also served as interim pastor of Hope Congregational Church in Elgin, North Dakota.

Jack Hayford is pastor of Church on the Way in Van Nuys, California. He is the author of many books, among them *Worship His Majesty* and *Rebuilding the Real You*, and is a co-author *Mastering Worship* and *Who's in Charge?*

Bill Hybels is founding pastor of Willow Creek Community Church in South Barrington, Illinois. He is the author of, among others, *Descending into Greatness* and *Rediscovering Church*, and co-author of *Mastering Contemporary Preaching* and *Fit to Be Tied*.

Doug Jackson is the pastor of the Second Baptist Church in Corpus Christi, Texas. He is the author of *The Fountain*.

Wayne Jacobsen is director of BodyLife Resources in Visalia, California, a ministry to encourage spiritual intimacy and Christian community. He also serves on the leadership team of Living Water Christian Fellowship, and has written *A Passion for God's Presence* and *Tales of the Vine*.

Speed Leas is a senior consultant at The Alban Institute in Boulder Creek, California. He is a member of the Society of Professionals in Dispute Resolution and the Religious Research Association. He has written *Moving Your Church through Conflict* and co-authored *Understanding Your Congregation as a System* and *Mastering Conflict and Controversy*.

Kevin Miller is editor of LEADERSHIP and executive director of editorial development at Christianity Today, Inc. He is the author of *Secrets of Staying Power* and co-author of *More Than You and Me: Touching Others Through the Strength of Your Marriage*.

Bob Moeller is contributing editor of *Leadership* and interim pastor of First Baptist Church in Elmhurst, Illinois. Previously he was director of communications at Trinity Evangelical Divinity School and has served as a senior pastor in Arizona and Minnesota. He has written *For Better, For Worse; Love in Action*, and *The Stirring*.

Larry Osborne is a senior pastor at North Coast Church in Vista, California, a suburb of San Diego. He is author of *The Unity Factor* and co-author of *Measuring Up*.

Ben Patterson is dean of the chapel at Hope College in Holland, Michigan. Before that he pastored Presbyterian congregations in New Jersey and California. He is contributing editor to *Christianity Today* and *Leadership*, author of *Waiting: Finding Hope When God Seems Silent*, and co-author of *Mastering the Pastoral Role* and *Who's in Charge?*

Michael Phillips is pastor of Riverside Alliance Church in Kalispell, Montana. He is the author of *To Be a Father Like the Father*.

Douglas Rumford is pastor of First Presbyterian Church in Fresno, California. He is also the pilot pastor for Chapel of the Air and author of *SoulShaping: A Guide to the Care and Feeding of Your Soul* and *Sacred to Life*.

Norman Shawchuck is president of Shawchuck & Associates, a management consulting firm serving religious organizations and a member of the Religious Research Association. Previously a pastor, he has worked in management consulting for such organizations as the Vatican and the Pentagon. He has written numerous books, including *How to Manage Conflict in the Church*, and has co-written *Benchmarks to Quality in the Church* and *Leading the Congregation*.

Marshall Shelley is editorial vice-president at Christianity Today, Inc., and senior editor of LEADERSHIP. He is author of *Well-Intentioned Dragons* and *Helping Those Who Don't Want Help* and co-author of *The Consumer Church*.

Fred Smith, Sr. is a business executive living in Dallas, Texas. He is a recipient of the Lawrence Appley Award of the American Management Association. He is a contributing editor to *Leadership* and serves on the board of directors of Christianity Today, Inc. He has written *You and Your Network* and *Learning to Lead*.

Chuck Swindoll is president of Dallas Theological Seminary and speaker of the radio broadcast *Insight for Living*. Before that he was pastor of First Evangelical Free Church in Fullerton, California, for twenty-two years. He has written more than forty books, including *Growing Strong in the Seasons of Life* and *Laugh Again*.

R. Steven Warner is founding pastor of Maranatha Chapel in Evergreen Park, Illinois. He is also currently serving as Presbyter of the Chicago Central Section of the Illinois District of the Assemblies of God. Before that he served as vice-president of Chicago Christian Television, which later became Channel 38.

Charles Wellington is a pseudonym for a pastor living in the Midwest.

PART 1

Anticipation

1

Wiring Yourself for Lightning

I can't serve God and play it safe.

—Ben Patterson

There she sat, nervously but methodically making her way through two pages of typewritten, single-spaced criticisms of our church office operation. To her credit, she met with me face-to-face, which is more than many critics are willing to do.

As she rehearsed the failures of the staff (and seemingly, everyone else born after the Spanish-American War) I felt increasingly melancholy. From improper procedures in answering the phone, to conflicting announcements in the bulletin, to secretaries breaching confidences, she had meticulously kept track of every offense. She had no less than fifty indictments.

When she was through, I did what pastors are supposed to do. I thanked her and affirmed her concern. After she left, I seriously considered conducting tours of the Holy Land for the rest of my career.

Why is it pastors so often serve as the lightning rod for the highly charged complaints and grievances of church members? Why do we attract criticisms that pulsate with gigawatts of negative energy? How do we protect ourselves from ecclesiastical electrocution? Can we transform these painful experiences from lethal discharges into spiritual energy and light?

High pressure systems

Upper air turbulence and the clash of competing weather fronts often produce violent and dangerous storms. In much the same way, unstable patterns and changing seasons in the church can produce high voltage criticism. Some conditions in church life predictably produce more lightning.

Transitions. When I began my ministry in a church that had been two years without a pastor, I noticed immediately how uncertain people seemed. If they were leaders in the old system, would they be trusted by the new? If they were good friends with Pastor Harry, would they enjoy the same relationship with me? In one way or another, all these insecurities became focused on me.

It wasn't long until twenty-five people joined another church, unhappy or uncertain of their place in the new order. I was blamed for their departure, though I didn't have a clue why they left. All they said was, "I don't think I fit in here anymore." What it felt like to me was, "Something is the matter since you've come."

I was a new pastor: I didn't know them; they didn't know me. And they knew I didn't know them. That's unsettling. It can produce sudden storms and foul weather before I even have the opportunity to unpack my furniture.

Financial difficulties. When giving is down, trouble is usually up. Financial problems raise insecurities or frustrations that have been lying just beneath the surface of a church.

The most common result is the blame game, and the most logical "blamee" is the pastor. Blamers reason that people have quit giving because something is wrong, and it's up to leaders to keep things from going wrong, and therefore, what's wrong must be me. In its worst forms, angry parishioners will use a type of blackmail to get rid of the minister: they stop their giving, hoping to force the pastor out.

Projections and dependency. For some people, I become a Rorschach inkblot: they see in me whatever it is that is troubling them.

A psychologist friend suggests that people's unresolved issues with their fathers make pastors a prime target for criticism. Either irrational anger or an inappropriate clinging is the tip-off. When someone clings, I instinctively retreat, and that makes the clinging individual angry.

At one church, one man began this pattern with me. He had been orphaned as a child. His mother had left him when he was young, and his father eventually passed him off to people who adopted him.

When I first met him, he had no beard. But within a couple of weeks of becoming friends, he began to grow one (I have a beard, too). Initially, he was my best friend. He was talented, intelligent, and loyal, and I was grateful for his acquaintance.

Over time I became uneasy about the demands he placed on me. We were having more lunches, breakfasts, and get-togethers than I could handle. Frankly, he became a nuisance. I attempted gently to put some distance between us, and he immediately picked up on it.

Something changed inside him. In less than a year, he went from ally to adversary. Soon he was opposing me on various issues, on any grounds he could dig up. The flip-flop was so obvious it was embarrassing. My two-cent Freudian analysis suggests that my backing off, however slight, made him feel orphaned once again.

Consumer mentality. Churchgoers today often think of the pastor as performing a service for them. They are as demanding and particular as if they had bought a suit from a clothing store and didn't like the cuff length. If something doesn't meet their standards, they want to see the store manager and file a complaint. The result is a critical and demanding spirit. The woman with the two pages of complaints acted like a customer who was pointing out the faults in our service.

High-voltage pain

When I was younger, I believed my ego strength could protect me from the pain of criticism. As I've gotten older, I've come to admit how much this stuff hurts. I wish I could become what some call a "non-anxious presence," but public and private criticism still unsettles me. When I'm criticized, I am subject to a variety of emotions.

Of all the jolts you take in the course of your ministry, perhaps none hurts more than having your character called into question. A pastor friend was confronted by a man who had a mile-long list of criticisms. My friend had tried previously to reconcile with the man over a few meals, but all he had to show for his efforts was heartburn.

My friend interrupted the attack: "Clearly, you think I'm doing everything wrong. But do you trust my heart?"

There was a long pause. The man looked at my friend and said, "No, I think you're trying to ruin the church." My friend was stunned.

Several months later, in a meeting with elders, this man appeared before the church elders with the same grocery list of complaints against the pastor. My friend asked him the same question, "Do you think I'm trying to destroy the church?"

To the man's credit (at least he was honest), he said yes. Now the board sat astonished and speechless.

Even if I'm sure the person is wrong, when people question my character, it hurts. Character and motives are two of the main things we offer a congregation. If character is questioned, the foundation of ministry is threatened. Frankly, I don't think anyone except a sociopath can take that type of heat from people and remain indifferent.

Though few people in my life have had the candor (or perhaps the audacity) to tell me I don't belong in the ministry, when it has happened, it has left me with a feeling of shame, mingled with anger.

If I'm tired and under stress, I can begin feeling like a failure. I doubt the very thing I've given my entire adult life to. I wonder if I'm losing it as pastor. The Enemy jumps on those situations to whisper, "Your critics are right, you know. You have no business being here. Cut your losses and get out before you're humiliated big time."

If you're not careful, your mind can begin racing and creating frightening scenarios: *What if I have to move my family again? What if I can't get another job or provide for them? What if I end up on an ecclesiastical blacklist?* You begin imagining yourself ten years from now lying in an alley near a rescue mission, dead drunk, having lost your wife and family!

Then I can begin imploding. I blame myself for all that has happened. If only I had done this or that differently.

I don't know how common the emotion of rage is among pastors, but I struggle with it. When I've been told that my ministry is bogus, I want to shout my defense. Yet, because of my professional and family responsibilities, I'm not allowed to do that. And the anger inside me just keeps building.

What I need to do is forgive, to bless those who persecute me. But sometimes their actions eat away at my soul.

Vital circuit breakers

Building codes require special electrical devices that prevent a surge of energy from overloading the circuits and leading to a meltdown and fire. These circuit breakers interrupt the dangerously high level of electricity in the line by providing relief from the excessive load.

In the same fashion, I've found I need emotional and spiritual circuit breakers to protect when highly charged criticism is directed at me.

Accepting who you are. When a woman told me that I always wanted to do things my way, I had to agree with her. Knowing myself, my gifts and convictions, and God's call for my life has been absolutely essential to carrying me through the deep waters of ministry.

At age 50 I can say things with certainty about my life that I could not have said, nor should have, at age 25. There's a peace of mind that comes with twenty-five years of learning who you are. I possess reasonably good self-evaluation skills and a good deal of self-knowledge. I've come to know my deepest passions in ministry.

Furthermore, if I know God has called me to a particular place, I can be assured that what I bring is what the church must need. Is that outrageous? Arrogant? If I *didn't* believe that, I would call the moving van every time I'm struck by lightning.

(The corollary, of course, is also true. If I find I can't do ministry the way God has called me to do it, then I must go elsewhere. And this for me is one test I use in determining when it's time to move on.)

The necessity of rest. When fatigue creeps on you, it isn't long before your instincts start failing you. As Vince Lombardi said, "Fatigue makes cowards of us all." You start to lose focus. You begin to make unwise decisions. I say things in meetings when I'm tired that I would never say if I was refreshed and well-rested.

One annual meeting came at the end of a long week and full day. I remember thinking to myself, *I just want to get this stupid thing over with.* When people began throwing verbal tomatoes at the staff, I showed little patience. My answers were short and curt, with an edge of sarcasm. What the people saw that night was a tired, touchy, frustrated pastor. I think they would have seen someone entirely different if I had taken a nap that afternoon.

Can we be gentle and sensitive when we've worked 60, 70, or 80 hours that week? I no longer trivialize the importance of getting adequate rest. It's a cheap and simple fuse that can save me a great deal of trouble.

Keeping perspective on the 5 percent. I'm amazed at what 5 percent of the congregation can do to my perception of ministry. In the calm light of day, I can see that the overwhelming majority of the church is happy, contented, and sailing down the highway on cruise control. Yet, if I'm not careful, I can let the one nasty look or the one vindictive letter change how I see everything.

Several years ago psychologist Albert Ellis said that it is irrational to believe that every significant person in your community must like you before you can feel good about yourself. He is right, particularly in a church setting.

The power of a prayer journal. The biggest mistake I've made through the years is to turn my feelings in on myself, allowing them to implode. I now turn them into dialogue with God, and I do that with a prayer journal.

I use the journal to record the feelings and thoughts that are stirring in my soul. I lay them out before God where I don't have to hide anything. When I feel betrayed, or my anguish is overwhelming, I'll mirror that before God.

I often allow the Psalms to become my discussion with God: "Contend, O Lord, with those who contend against me." My feelings are transformed into dialogue with God. That's so much better than talking to myself, or even laying it all on my wife. Later, when I've resolved a particular crisis, I like to go back and read the chronicles of my struggle. Seeing how I navigated heavy weather two years earlier helps me weather my current storm.

Memorizing comfort. When I was young, I never won any awards for Sunday school Scripture memory contests. Someone else always rode away on the ten-speed bicycle at the end of the year. But in the last three years I've discovered that Scripture can give voice to things I don't know how to express. It transforms the things churning inside me and brings real healing to my soul.

One summer I memorized the twelfth chapter of Hebrews. At the time the entire chapter seemed autobiographical: running the race set before us, remembering Jesus, who endured the cross, who didn't lose heart though scorned by men. The chapter reminded me that pain is a discipline God uses in my life: I was in training, and the pain caused by criticism was my coach.

Finding Aaron and Hur. Every pastor needs an Aaron and a Hur, the two men of Israel who held up the arms of Moses in the battle against the Amalekites (Ex. 17:8–13).

When I arrived at one church, I met two men who introduced themselves by saying, "We're here to pray for you." From that point on they were up at six o'clock every Saturday morning to pray on my behalf.

The Aarons and Hurs in my life have seldom, if ever, been aware of the machinations going on within the church, but their prayers for me have helped me weather many storms.

The support of family. When one presidential candidate announced his withdrawal from the race, he was asked if he was deeply disappointed.

"No," he replied, "but my ten-year-old daughter is. She said she believes if people knew how wonderful her dad was, they'd certainly vote for him."

That's the type of support every pastor needs. And I have no better supporter than my wife, Loretta. I'm reminded of a cartoon in which a minister is sitting in his living room on a Sunday afternoon sucking his thumb. His wife, obviously attempting to comfort him, says, "Yes, honey. Your sermon was just fine." I turn to my wife for comfort when I'm feeling overwhelmed by the insecurities and anxieties the pastorate produces.

Once during a particularly difficult time in our ministry, we took a trip that covered a large portion of the northern United States and Canada. We were driving through a marvelous wooded landscape. It was late in the afternoon, and the sun was low, setting the horizon on fire with shades of purple, red, and orange.

We were listening to a tape by Garrison Keillor. He described a scene in which a husband and wife are sitting across the breakfast table from each other. The husband is a mess; he has the flu. The pressures in his life are making him sick. The story ends by Keillor telling how the man's wife reached across the table, took his hand, and said, "You know, I care for you." In his deep baritone fashion, he concluded by saying, "And you know, sometimes that's enough."

Loretta and I were feeling the burden and the sorrow of having served as lightning rods for so many months at our church. We reached out and held each other's hands as the story ended. It was a wonderful moment.

Harnessed energy

The same water that, unchecked, uproots trees and floods a town can, when channeled, light a city. As frustrating and difficult as it is to serve as the lightning rod for a congregation, it does have its useful side.

We ought to worry, in fact, if we never receive a zap now and then. If I can't remember the last time I was criticized for something, chances are I'm not doing anything significant. If my goal is simply to keep all the cattle mooing softly in the corral, I'm failing as a leader. But if you are moving them out on the trail toward Dodge City and points beyond, you can expect an occasional stampede or two. It comes with the territory of leadership.

But I try to listen to Balaam's donkey. It was the nineteenth-century pastor and writer George MacDonald who said, "Truth is truth, whether it's spoken by the lips of Jesus or Balaam's donkey." In the midst of even the most withering criticism, I need to stop and listen for the grain of truth. Granted, it may come across as unfair, judgmental, and cruel, but underneath the rough exterior there may be something of value.

This is especially true if an issue keeps surfacing. If people say repeatedly, "We feel you don't care about us pastorally," it likely indicates people are feeling lonely and in need of spiritual support. That doesn't mean *I* have to become more pastoral—make more hospital calls, arrange more counseling sessions. But I better make sure that somebody is doing that sort of thing.

Sometimes, of course, there's nothing better I can do than simply apologize. At my last church, I suggested that we add a third service to our Sunday morning schedule. Although there wasn't much enthusiasm for the idea, my attendance projections indicated we could support a third service. I enthusiastically pushed the new schedule through staff, elder, and congregational meetings.

After a few months on the new schedule, attendance continued to sag. Finally, a good friend told me the truth: "Ben, the numbers just don't support that type of change. You really should have done your homework first." I was angry at him, but I was forced to be more thorough about my original calculations. Sure enough, he was right. I remember distinctly the emotion I felt at the time: stupidity.

I began to see all the administrative pain I had caused choirs and church school teachers. I felt like quitting and entering a remote desert monastery. But that was not the time to flee. Instead, I simply admitted to the board that I had blown it and began taking administrative steps to return to two services.

After one horrible defeat, in which he lost thousands of men, General Ulysses S. Grant was seen going into his tent that night to cry uncontrollably for nearly an hour—he'd made some strategic blunders that needlessly cost men their lives.

But the next day, his men saw him emerge with the determined look of a general. He calmly mounted his horse and continued on with his campaign.

That is the type of resolute courage I want to have even when I've deservedly been struck by lightning.

Diploma of Pain

My seminary degree and my years in the pastorate don't authenticate my ministry, at least not according to the apostle Paul. He believed his apostleship was validated by the sufferings and hardships he had endured: shipwrecks, beatings, hunger, and rejection. In some ways pastors are called to a ministry style that invites confrontation and criticism. It's the nature of our calling.

I don't want to rationalize insensitivity or poor leadership as prophetic ministry. Yet, as I look back, I've often been placed in situations where new foundations needed to be laid. That often involves shaking things up.

I can't serve God and play it safe. The risk of criticism and misunderstanding is the price of a pastor's life, a life filled with dreams and visions of what God wants to do next. It's a risk I'm willing to take.

2

Standing in the Crossfire

*The popular concept of unity is a fantasy land where
disagreements never surface and contrary opinions
are never stated with force.*

—Bill Hybels

At Willow Creek, we expect disagreement—forceful disagreement. *Unity* isn't the word we use to describe our relationships.
The popular concept of unity is a fantasy land where disagreements
never surface and contrary opinions are never stated with force.

Instead of unity, we use the word *community.*

We say, "Let's not pretend we never disagree. We're dealing with
the lives of 16,000 people. The stakes are high. Let's not have people
hiding their concerns to protect a false notion of unity. Let's face the
disagreement and deal with it in a godly way."

The mark of community—true, biblical unity—is not the absence
of conflict. It's the presence of a reconciling spirit. I can have a rough-
and-tumble leadership meeting with someone, but because we're
committed to community, we can still leave, slapping each other on
the back, saying, "I'm glad we're still brothers." We know no one's
bailing out just because of a conflicting position.

Community is bigger than that. But developing community, true
biblical unity, does not happen naturally; it must be intentional.

Non-negotiables

Because of my commitment to community, there are several issues for which I'll go to the wall.

First, we at Willow Creek will not tolerate biblical infidelity, a discounting of the clear teachings of Christ.

Second, we insist on the enforcement of Scripture, the living out of the teachings of Christ. We'll defend not only the inerrancy and authority of Scripture, but also the indisputable importance of applying biblical teaching to our daily lives in practical ways.

Someone told me of a woman who is terrorizing a local congregation with her slanderous tongue. She's doing so in a church that holds high the Word of God. But the church leaders don't enforce it. They'll permit a loose-tongued woman to poison the body of Christ. They get an *A* for inerrancy and an *F* for enforcement. We want an A in both.

Third, we expect lay and staff leaders at our church to be on board with the basic vision of Willow Creek. We had a leader who, after several years of service, concluded that he could no longer agree with our vision. When we were a small church, he believed in our mission. But when we passed the 4,000-attender mark, he thought we should start satellite churches and decentralize. The rest of us, however, didn't sense God's leading in that direction.

We had an oil-on-water mixture. He made a high-integrity move and voluntarily resigned from his leadership position.

The last non-negotiable is verbal discipline. Years ago, I took to heart what Scott Peck had to say about conflict resolution. Often what undermines the conflict resolution process, he says, is the lack of verbal discipline. When we attend a piano concert we expect the pianist to offer a disciplined performance, demonstrating that thought, skill, and practice were part of the preparation. A concert is not a "whatever I feel like" event.

In confrontation, however, too often our verbal discipline goes out the window. People make *always* and *never* statements. They exaggerate the truth or get careless with facts. Volume levels increase. And then we wonder why we're unsuccessful in finding resolution.

Through the years, I've reminded our church continually about disciplined verbal expression. If in a debate someone is losing verbal control, I'll call a time-out so people can settle down. Then we'll come back together for a discussion that is controlled, accurate, and constructive.

Preferred risk

Verbal discipline is one facet of a commitment to fighting fair. There are several other ways that we teach people how to handle conflict in a Christian, redemptive way.

First, we acknowledge that conflict is inevitable. Then we go the next step and say, "When your nose does get bent out of joint—not *if* but *when*—you have a biblical responsibility to take the high road of conflict resolution."

That means going directly to the person with whom you're having this conflict rather than building a guerrilla team to ambush this person later.

We also teach a kind of reverse accountability. In staff meetings or in front of the congregation, we say, "If someone whose nose is bent out of joint comes to you for a 'Won't you join my cause?' conversation, you have a biblical responsibility to interrupt mid-sentence and say, 'I think you're talking to the wrong person. Please go to the individual with whom you're having this conflict and seek to resolve it in a God-glorifying way.' "

By expecting people to fight, and teaching them how, we have created more conflict in our ministry, but most of it stays above ground. Conflict that goes underground poisons the soil and hurts everyone eventually. We would rather have conflict within community than a mask of unity.

At Willow Creek we experimented for a couple of years with publishing a magazine, but the time came that we needed to shut it down. We didn't communicate that in the best way possible to those who had been working on the magazine, though.

In the aftermath several people asked, "Do you have any idea how hurt the volunteers were when you decided to close the magazine?"

That's a fair question, but when one person asked me that in a public forum, the edge in the voice made me uncomfortable, so I said, "You're probably one of those volunteers who's deeply hurt over losing your ministry, aren't you?"

"Yeah."

"I feel terrible that you made the sacrifice and then it fizzled. Let me explain the original purpose of the magazine, why it folded, and the steps we took to close it graciously. If we can learn from the way we handled it, we're open to suggestions."

After several months had elapsed, one of the magazine's writers and his wife attended a management team meeting and said, "I'd like to give this management team four or five ideas on how to shut a ministry down in a less painful way."

And we listened. We were humbled, and we learned from their suggestions.

That kind of positive resolution can happen only in an atmosphere where conveying threatening or negative information is okay.

Fighting fair

But while communicating that disagreement is okay, I invite people to speak openly with me. After speaking at a weekend service, I may receive fifteen high-octane letters the next week, saying, "When you said thus and so, it wounded me deeply for the following reasons."

On the surface, that can be discouraging. (For me, the 10-to-1 rule applies here: ten complimentary letters are needed to get over one missile.) However, when I'm feeling wounded, I always say to myself, *Aren't you glad this person expressed his frustration to you rather than calling fifteen people and holding a town meeting at your expense?*

And so when I write these people back—which I do—I always begin the letter by saying, "Thank you so much for the courage it took to express your displeasure with me. I don't take lightly your willingness to follow the biblical injunction to come straight to me." Then I delve into the issue at hand.

Once a month I stand in front of the whole congregation and emcee an open question-and-answer time for half an hour. People can ask anything and everything—financial questions, personal questions, rumor questions. If people feel hesitant to ask a question publicly, they can submit it in writing before the session. I address every question.

No matter how well you have coached people in the past, teaching people to fight fair is an ongoing process. Before one of these meetings, I reminded the congregation, "When you stand and ask your question, remember pastors have feelings, too. So, if you're going to come after me, remember my heart is as fragile as your own."

Sometimes, though, someone will ask a question that has an edge to it or that is mean-spirited. If that happens in a public meeting, I ask the person to restate the question in a more gracious manner. In a private setting, I'm more direct: "Is there a spirit of love behind that question? What's going on in your spirit right now? Are you only upset about the specific question, or is there something deeper you're concerned about?"

Often someone will respond, "I'm filled with rage." Or, "I'm so angry." Or, "I'm just upset about a lot of things."

If a question is mean-spirited, it's usually because another issue is interrupting the relationship. I've learned to deal with the underlying problem first.

Our congregation is learning. The people have even developed the habit of hissing—when I tell a joke they don't think is funny or make a statement they don't think is tactful. On occasion, they've hissed a careless questioner. It's their lighthearted but firm way of saying, "That's not the way to fight fair."

Preempting the unnecessary

Certain people are more prone to create harmful conflict. People who are emotionally unhealthy are more likely to create the kind of conflict that is difficult to resolve.

Emotionally healthy people are less likely to internalize differences of opinion and less likely to assume the worst. For that reason, we are committed to placing healthy people into key leadership roles, both on a staff and lay level.

Of course, you can never be sure you're looking at a healthy person, but a person who has never wrestled with how his upbringing affects his adult relationships is a sure bet for a barrel of conflict.

In our interviewing process, we often ask, "Were you raised in a perfect family?" Most often, of course, the answer is no. Then we probe deeper. "How did your parents let you down? Have you worked through that?"

If someone says, "My family wasn't a safe place growing up," we'll ask, "What have you done about it? How have you worked through that?"

We're looking for self-aware individuals who are coming to grips with their pain and their woundedness. If someone says, "Actually, my family was just perfect. There were no problems," or, "My dad was an alcoholic, but it didn't affect me much," we know there's cause for concern.

People on the journey toward health generally can answer yes to two important questions: (1) Will you admit that you have baggage from your past? and (2) Will you do honest work on it so it doesn't distort your relationships and work around here?

A person's emotional health tends to express itself in hundreds of small ways. For example, we're in a leadership meeting and I'm passing out assignments. If I say, "Tom, can you handle this project for me?" I expect Tom to give me an honest "Yes, I can" or "No, I can't."

Let's say, however, that Tom doesn't do that. Tom's plate is full; he's buried in work. But he's afraid to say, "Bill, I can't handle it right now."

Though he told me yes, in reality the extra work overwhelms him. So he spends the next eighteen evenings trying to finish my project and winds up feeling angry at me.

Then through the grapevine, I learn that Tom is busy telling people that I overwork him, that I'm not sensitive to his family.

I have a problem with that kind of behavior! If I've asked an honest question, I should be able to expect an honest answer. Often, an unhealthy person will say yes when he should say no.

We look for people who have the emotional health to say, "I'm swamped right now. I won't be able to get that assignment done by the due date. Can we discuss how the assignment can get done another way?"

Another tip-off that something might be amiss emotionally is when a person cannot subject himself or herself to loving, constructive evaluation. Obviously, if we're evaluating with Uzi's, then the process is the problem. But around here, we have a carefully thought out and regularly scheduled evaluation process that is normally done with sensitivity and tenderness. In a situation like this, if people are terrified of the evaluation process or hostile to it, there's usually an underlying issue that needs to be explored and understood.

Another way to avoid unnecessary conflict is to sidestep anything that breaks trust.

Once a denominational executive called me, asking if he could bring a large group from his denomination for our presentation on seeker-oriented ministry. His only available night was a Tuesday. Our senior high ministry uses the auditorium on Tuesday nights.

I resisted the temptation to say yes and then deal with the logistical problem later. Instead, I called the director of the youth ministry and explained the situation.

"You make the call," I said. "How do you feel about our using the auditorium that night? Can you make different plans for that evening without disrupting your program?"

He said, "No problem. With this much advance notice, we can easily work around that evening. Thanks for checking with me."

Had I said yes before calling him, he would have felt devalued and taken for granted. It would have broken our trust.

Around Willow Creek we also talk about having "check-ins." If we sense tension with someone, we sit down and say, "I just need to check in with you. Is everything okay between us?"

Once a month, we also have a question-and-answer time with the staff, and in addition, we have regular talk-back sessions with those who work in the sub-ministries.

The more interactive we are, the more we preempt serious conflict, because we get people talking before conflict goes underground.

Answering the personals

Not long ago someone questioned my motivation for being a minister. "The reason Bill is in ministry," this person said, "is because of Willow Creek's size and all the perks that go with being its senior pastor."

I was surprised how hurt I felt. I was devastated. I also felt defensive, which bothered me. After journaling and mulling over the criticism, I realized that part of what upset me was that the one making the accusations had been around Willow Creek for only two years. He was unaware of the years I worked with no salary, when my wife and I took in boarders to make ends meet, when we paid for the birth of our daughter because the church couldn't afford medical insurance.

In that case, I had to process his accusation, to figure out why it hurt me so deeply, not just accept or reject it. I also realized that in order to be freed in my spirit toward that person, I had to explain to him why his accusation hurt and why I felt it was unjust.

At other times, conflict energizes me. If someone doesn't like a new venture I'm suggesting, I can respond as a competitor. *When the final gun sounds*, I think, *we'll see who's right*. It can make me work even harder. Or if it's clear the other person has a better idea, I can jump on board. Conflict, I've learned, can be a constructive part of the creative process.

The difference between these two reactions is the difference between being attacked personally versus having my ideas attacked. About my ideas, I've always been able to say, "You got me. I was wrong; I blew it." But when my motivations are questioned, I feel wounded, helpless. How can I prove the sincerity of my motives?

I think most people feel this way. When conflict reaches the level of personal attack—suspicion about integrity, trustworthiness, purity of motivations—it's hard to handle.

Trying to convince people that our heart's in the right place isn't futile, but the conversation will require an enormous level of maturity—for the accuser *and* the accused. The person making the accusation has to be mature enough to sense the gravity of what he's doing. And the one feeling stung has to be mature enough not to lash out in defense. Each has to enter into that discussion with a high degree of vulnerability.

Once someone questioned my motives in launching a new ministry at Willow Creek. I arranged a time when I could express my hurt and openly explain my vision for this new program. He received it beautifully and apologized for his broad accusation. He then brought up several legitimate points we discussed at length.

Some people say a pastor should never defend himself, but obviously I think differently. When the apostle Paul felt that the church of Corinth was not understanding his role, essentially he said, "Excuse me. Pardon what I'm going to do here for the next few minutes, but I'm going to tell you the price I've paid to carry out my apostolic calling." And Paul proceeded to recount his shipwrecks and beatings for the sake of the gospel. I see that as a way of defending himself.

Sometimes we have to do that to keep our heart pure. At times certain accusations take root in my spirit. If resentment grows, I have to go to the individual and say, "As hard as I'm trying to ignore what you're saying, you're hurting me, and you need to know that."

Many years ago, I heard from reliable sources that a local pastor had commented repeatedly that Lynne and I were unhappily married,

headed for divorce. Included in his charges were accusations of unfaithfulness. Needless to say, Lynne and I were deeply saddened by
these false reports.

After much discussion and prayer, Lynne and I drove to this pastor's church and walked into his office, unannounced, and introduced ourselves.

"The things you've been saying are ripping our hearts out," we
said. "They're not true. We're wondering why you're saying what
you're saying."

"I thought my information was accurate," he sputtered.

By the end of the conversation, he was apologetic. He appreciated that we had come to him and spoken the truth in a loving way.
I think we all learned some valuable life lessons that day.

The toughest skill for me to learn in handling conflict is hearing.
Not just listening, but really hearing. Recently a colleague and I experienced a serious break over a complex issue—philosophical and
personal. We spent three, two-hour sessions attempting to resolve
our differences. Though both of us had prayed and submitted to the
Holy Spirit, we couldn't put the issue behind us. Neither of us felt
completely heard.

Finally, the other person asked if I would be willing to go to a
Christian counselor to resolve our differences. I readily agreed. We
spent two sessions with a Christian counselor who gave us tools to
work through the issue more effectively.

I discovered I was listening only to 90 percent of what this person
was saying. There was 10 percent I didn't want to hear. The counselor
helped me go the last 10 percent to get the issue fully exposed so we
could move toward resolution.

Since then, I've worked on that skill in my marriage, with my children, and with friends in my accountability group. I'm becoming a
better person for it.

Swimming with sharks and guppies

A man at our church once told me: "When you swim in the ocean,
you get attacked by sharks and guppies. Don't worry about the guppies."

Over the years, I've concluded that some of the potshots I take
from the Christian community are guppy problems. If a Christian

leader criticizes me for allowing drums in the church, I'm not going to worry much about it. Someday we'll reach across the table at the marriage supper of the Lamb and say, "Wasn't that silly? Those were guppy things."

When our church was struggling in the late seventies, the outside attacks felt like shark attacks. We were renting a movie theater then, doing an unusual style of ministry that some considered liberal and others called fundamentalist. Many vocal critics never took the time to figure out who we were and what we were all about.

Careless media coverage, in which we were called a cult and linked with everyone from Reverend Moon to Jim Jones, threatened our viability at times. Many people became suspicious of us.

It was a frustrating and scary time. But we converted our anxiety into earnest prayer energy. It forced us to examine our motives. We asked ourselves a hard question: "Are we really doing what God called us to do?"

Such attacks forced us to become even more committed to pursuing God's specific will for us, even if that meant being criticized or persecuted. We said, "Let's quit complaining about the attack and get on with the ministry."

Redeeming criticism

My response to criticism has definitely changed through the years. In my early years of ministry, I rebutted people who wrote to me and said I had offended them or hurt their feelings. For years, I'd write back and say, essentially, "I'm sorry you took it wrong, but there really wasn't anything wrong with what I said." But then they'd write back, doubly hurt. They knew what I really meant was, "I'm sorry you're so sensitive that you get upset about petty things."

After several years of this, I thought, *What if I just said, "Thank you for writing me and expressing your hurt. I'm sorry. I didn't intend to hurt you. Please forgive me."*

Soon after implementing this approach, I began receiving letters saying, "Thank you for your letter. You don't know how much that meant to me."

Many people, I discovered, just want to know if their pastor is a safe person. Can he respond to hurt with compassion? Does he care as much about relationships as he does his sermon material?

I don't mean that I apologize if I truly believe I have nothing to apologize for. But often the source of offense is a flippant remark or an insensitive stab at humor—something I thought was harmless, but that ended up being offensive to someone.

During Christmas vacation several years ago, my family and I visited a church where for special music the pastor played a song on an accordion. That was so contrary to the culture in which my children had grown up that they were choking back their laughter.

When I returned to Willow Creek the following week, I enjoyed the first half hour of our service so much—the orchestra, the singers, the drama—that in my pre-message remarks I said, "It's so good to be home. Last week I was in a little church where the only thing besides the pastor's message was the accordion solo." Most people laughed. I went on to thank the people who planned and presented the music and drama that morning.

But then came the letters. Some were angry because they felt I had belittled pastors who don't have staff and music programs. Then I received notes from people who played accordions.

I knew I had crossed a line. So after writing ten or fifteen apology notes, I decided the situation called for a public apology. So, at each of the weekend services, I said, "I really didn't intend to make a disparaging statement about limited church staffs or accordion players. I just felt thankful for the people God has provided to minister so creatively here. But the way I phrased my comments was careless and conveyed negative values. I was wrong. I am sorry. So please forgive me."

Such a response doesn't hurt my credibility; rather, it builds credibility. People have sought me out, saying, "Knowing that you'll apologize makes me feel safer accepting your leadership."

Our people already know we make mistakes. What they want to know is whether or not we have enough integrity to admit them.

Kinder, gentler leader

Handling conflict well is essentially an issue of maturity, and leading a church to community, to true biblical unity, begins with its leader.

Due to my upbringing, one way I have handled hurt is to clench my teeth and say, "I'm not going to let that get to me." I'd buck up, power through, put it out of my mind, and keep going. The problem was that each time I did that, my skin became a little tougher, my heart a little harder, my feelings deeper below the level of my awareness. I became another step distanced from the people around me.

With the help of my wife, Christian counselors, and other trusted friends, I'm learning a more constructive way to negotiate conflict. I'm learning to admit to the person involved that what they said or did hurt me, and slowly I'm learning to feel that hurt inside. I'm learning to say "Ouch" and talk about what that ouch means, rather than discounting relational wounds and powering past them.

As I get better at acknowledging the hurt that conflict causes me, I also become more aware of the hurt that conflict causes others. This has led me to approach conflict resolution with a much gentler spirit, both for my sake and for others' sake.

That kind of vulnerability in relationships did not come naturally to me. But I believe it's a necessary part of obedience to Christ.

3

Why I Expect Conflict

You can't rock the boat if you are rowing.

—Ben Patterson

Oakland A's manager Billy Martin had a formula for managerial success, which he expressed in *Sports Illustrated*. "You'll have fifteen guys who will run through a wall for you, five who hate you, and five who are undecided. The trick is keeping the five who hate you away from the five who are undecided."

There have been times in the past four years, four months, and twenty-two days—precisely the period of time that I have been a pastor—that I have felt like a graduate of the Billy Martin School of Church Management. To be honest, trying to write this article on conflict has been a bit like not having enough time to read the marvelous book on time management I bought six years ago. I feel that I must know a lot about conflict because I have been so involved in it. But I can't seem to get out of it long enough to reflect on what I think I must be learning. As the saying goes, "When you're up to your posterior in alligators, you don't think about draining the swamp."

This may be more true of a small church than a large church. Large churches may have all kinds of different groups and individuals in conflict with one another, but they often have a way of absorbing it all; so as some would say, they can co-opt conflict. Like old man river, they just keep rolling along. Small churches, on the other hand, have too many opportunities for the conflicting parties to keep meeting one another, or colliding, as the case may be. And their conflict has much greater potential to rend the tender fabric of the body. For the small church, it is much harder to keep the five who hate you, or the church, away from those who are undecided.

How then is the small church to regard conflict?

Protracted theology

My Old Testament seminary professor once suggested that some-. one should attempt to write a theology of conflict. At the time his suggestion sounded foolish and superfluous to me. But not now. What follows will hardly qualify as a theology of conflict—it's those alligators again—but perhaps it will serve as a little pump at the edge of the swamp.

First, what do I mean when I use the word conflict? I mean a protracted struggle, clash, fight, or opposition between personalities, ideas, and interests. Key here is the word "protracted." Differences, even clashes, between parties in a church do not in themselves constitute conflict of a destructive kind. They can be signs of vitality in a congregation. It is when they defy peaceful resolution and become protracted and entrenched in the life of a church that they become sinful and destructive. It is in this latter sense that I use the word conflict.

Second, why is there church conflict in the first place? It's because we church people are sinners. "What causes wars, and what causes fightings among you?" asks James. "Is it not your passions that are at war in your members? You desire and do not have; so you kill. And you covet and do not obtain; so you fight and wage war" (James 4:1, RSV). Church conflict will always find its roots in our passion to make ourselves—our needs, our opinions, our group, our goals, our theology—the center of the universe.

Clarence Jones, a basketball player for Tulane, recalled a high school basketball game against Darryl Dawkins of the Philadelphia 76ers. "We were lined up for a free throw and Darryl turned to me and said, 'If you get the ball I'm going to smash your head against the backboard.' I didn't get the ball," said Jones. There's a childlike simplicity in Dawkins' straightforward statement. It gets right down to theological basics. We have all approached God and other people in the same way Dawkins went for the ball; some of us perhaps more subtly and symbolically, but nevertheless in ultimately the same way. The wages for that style of play may be high in the NBA, but they mean conflict and possible spiritual death in the church.

The roots of conflict are also planted in our cultural soil. A significant part of that soil is our demand for instant gratification and the
immediate solution of problems. As we American Christians have
been reminded *ad nauseum*, we live in the "now" generation. At
McDonald's we buy fast foods and at Sears we buy microwave ovens,
or television sets whose weekly programs pose great human dilem-
mas and mysteries, all to be solved in sixty to ninety minutes, ex-
cluding commercial breaks.

All of our buying can be done on little plastic cards that promise
instant credit, instant gratification, the satisfaction of all needs, the
killing of all boredom. And lest we feel a little tongue-tied in the face
of all this, there are signs telling us "Just say, 'Charge it.' " To all this
the media adds its weekly opinion polls and 45-second "in-depth"
analyses designed to evoke instant responses and quick decisions.

Behold now the local church with its garden-variety mixture of
sinners saved by grace, all representing various needs and points of
view that must be brought into the harmony of the Spirit and the unity
of the body of Christ through committees, commissions, boards, and
sessions. Real-life conflicts here, as elsewhere, are not solved by just
saying "Charge it," nor will they be solved in ninety minutes. On the
contrary, such a mentality ensures that the conflicts will not be solved
but will be exacerbated. The perseverance and tenacity required to
resolve differences will be just another irritant in the already irritating
situation.

As American as apple pie

Many American Christians respond to this situation by loving it or
leaving it, shutting up or going to another church, or better yet, starting up their own church. "We sleep in separate rooms, we have dinner apart, we take separate vacations," said comedian Rodney Dan-
gerfield. "We're doing everything to keep our marriage together."

That seems more and more to be love, American style; and it certainly characterizes Christian unity, American style. As loyalties narrow and our capacity to tolerate pluralism diminishes, new Christian
groups proliferate. Ours is the age of single-issue politics and single-
issue churches. Here in Southern California, it is a buyers' market in
churches. What are you "into"? Look long enough and you'll find a
congregation "into" it too. If your tastes are extremely discriminating

you can start a house-church in an 800-square foot condominium. It's sure to be big enough. Conflict? Who needs it? Just move out West, young man.

In the space of one week last fall, I met with one person who was leaving the church because I was too liberal, and another who was leaving because I was too conservative. I suggested that both start carrying shopping lists in their Bibles when they go church hunting. While I am convinced that I'm doing something "radical" by staying in a so-called mainline denomination, splitting off and forming another group when differences arise would be as American as apple pie.

Servant's posture

What we need is a new mindset toward conflict. Paul calls it the *mind of Christ.* What he is referring to is not so much an intellectual system on how to deal with conflict or a manual for church fights; he exhorts the church to look at what Christ did when he laid aside his rights as God's equal, emptied himself, and lived the life of a servant in our midst. Paul writes, "So if there is any encouragement in Christ, any incentive of love, any participation in the Spirit, any affection and sympathy . . ." (Phil. 2:1, RSV).

What the apostle is saying to these people is that the next time they find themselves squaring off in a fighter's stance they should switch to a servant's posture. For that is what the mind of Christ is more than anything else—a posture, kneeling and washing one another's feet. It's loving and giving as we have been loved and given to.

Paul clearly thinks that this will do wonders for dealing with conflict in the church. For if they are trying to outdo one another in servant love, they won't be doing one another in over differences of opinion or lifestyle.

We American Christians need to hear this at least as much as did the Philippians. But since we are so suspicious of anything that smacks of kow-towing or slavery, perhaps the best way to approach the subject is by way of negation.

There are at least three things this attitude of a servant does not mean. It does not mean that conflict is resolved in a Christ-like manner by one party becoming the doormat for the other. To be a servant

like Christ presupposes that you have a high view of yourself. He was
by nature God. He knew it, but did not regard equality with God a
thing to be clung to. Instead, he let go and poured himself out and
became a servant, even to the extent of dying. It was because of this,
not in spite of this, that God so highly exalted him. The resurrection
and ascension of Christ were not simply God's reward for a dirty job
well done, but were his supreme *vindication* of the things that Christ
did. God gave his stamp of approval. He said, in effect, "This is the
way I get my work done!"

Christ's ministry was a living demonstration of his teaching that
the man who loses his life is the one who finds it. The point here for
us is that in a conflict situation we need not fear that we will be swallowed up if we adopt a servant's posture, and perhaps relax our grip
on our point of view. In this we may achieve the larger end of pre-
serving the unity of the church or to encourage a brother or sister to
love Christ more deeply. We serve as Christ served from a position
of strength, not weakness. "We who are strong ought to bear with the
failings of the weak," says the apostle Paul. "Let each of us please his
neighbor for his good, to edify him" (Rom. 15:1–2, RSV). I wonder
how many conflicts in churches are never peacefully resolved due
simply to the basic insecurity of the parties involved?

Ego set-aside

The attitude of a servant also does not mean that the truth of the
gospel be compromised. Paul, after having urged the Philippians
toward the unity of mutual servanthood, speaks of the Judaizers and
says, "Look out for the dogs, look out for the evil-workers, look out
for those who mutilate the flesh" (Phil. 3:2, RSV). Those are hardly
kind words, but they are the words of a servant; for to be a servant
of Christ and his church must mean to preserve the integrity of the
gospel. The trick for us is to know when to cry "Look out for the
dogs" and when to keep our mouths shut and let sleeping dogs lie,
so to speak. I am afraid we have historically been paranoid about
dogs. "Unity in essentials, liberty in nonessentials, love in all things,"
reads the dictum. Could it be that our list of essentials is longer than
the New Testament's?

To have the attitude of a servant is not to be afraid of differences
of opinion. Indeed, it is servants who can most tolerate differences

because their potential for conflict has been diffused. To adapt a phrase by Henry Steele Commager: Churches, like democracies, must have criticism to flourish. To function, they must have dissent. The alternative is cultism. For many Christians "one mind" has been the *group-think* of Orwell's *1984*. The one mind Paul speaks of is the mind of Christ, who laid aside his prerogatives in order to be a servant. You can't rock the boat if you are rowing. But you can speak out in dissent as one wholeheartedly committed to the boat and to the integrity of its course, and stop rowing only as a last resort.

I think it's significant that one symbol for the church is that of a ship. It is a ship much bigger than its individual passengers, bigger even than the sum total of them. It belongs to its captain, and it is ultimately his responsibility to bring it safely into port. That ought to help us all relax a bit and stop thinking that our opinions and determinations are all that important. It's presumption to do otherwise. It's hubris of the first magnitude to take our response to the gospel and begin to confuse it with the gospel itself.

Well, can this be done? Is it possible to "be angry but not sin" (Eph. 4:26)?

Last year I sat across the room from one of the elders of the church I pastor. We were glaring at one another, and I was trembling with rage. We had disagreed and disagreed. During the session meetings we slipped automatically into adversary positions toward one another. That evening I had gone to his house to try to improve the situation. But our talk quickly degenerated into another verbal sparring match, and I was ready to turn it into a physical one.

What could be done? There seemed no place to go but to start the First Church of Ben Patterson, corner of Sectarianism and Schism. I don't remember which one of us asked the question, but it was like a shaft of light in a dark cave. "Can we set aside our egos in order to serve the Kingdom?" The tension began to drain out of my body. Bruce Larson is right. He says we people in the church are like porcupines in a snowstorm. We need each other to keep warm, but we prick each other if we get too close. But there is One who can stand between us. Bonhoeffer is also right. He said Christ is the mediator between not only God and man, but between man and man; and, I would add, man and his opinions. He has taken upon his own body the wounds we would deliver to one another. In Christ I no longer have immediacy with anything or anyone, not even myself. The

blows and hostility I deliver must pass through his heart before they
reach my brother. The opinions I cling to so tenaciously must be in
him, through him. Is anything worth rending the body of Christ, his
church?

Unity call

Were it not for his presence in our midst, the call to peace and
unity, to "do nothing from selfishness or conceit," would be an intolerable burden to bear. In the musical *The Sound of Music*, Maria
teaches the children how to overcome their fears in the midst of a
violent thunderstorm. She tells them to remember their favorite
things, things like "raindrops on roses and whiskers on kittens, bright
copper kettles and warm woolen mittens." When she does this, she
loses her fear and her sorrow. It works for the children too. Later on,
Maria leaves them because she is frightened and confused over her
love for their father. The children are inconsolable. One day they try
to cheer themselves up by singing once again their "favorite things."
They get a few lines into the song and the smallest girl speaks up. "It
only makes me sadder to sing without Maria here."

So it is with God's call to unity in Christ. Passages like Philippians
2 and First Corinthians 13 are lists of God's favorite things. And were
it not for him with us, they would drive us to despair. As Lewis
Smedes puts it in *Love Within Limits*, the love of God is not an ideal
but a power. He would enable us before he obligates us.

4

The Ten Most Predictable Times
of Conflict

*Pastors are better prepared for church conflict if they know
when it's more likely to come.*

—Speed Leas

P astors have learned not to be discouraged the week after Christmas or the week after Easter. Those Sundays are traditionally the
lowest in attendance. Coming as they do immediately after high
points in the church year, the unprepared pastor sets himself up for
despair if he doesn't recognize the pattern.

In the same way, pastors are better prepared for church conflict
if they know when it's more likely to come. Certainly, pastors know
that church conflict is coming—it has been part of the church since
day one. Knowing *when* it's apt to come is a different matter and one
that pastors are wise to be alert to.

1. Easter

During Lent and just after Easter, the number of calls for help received by the Alban Institute rises substantially: up 28 percent over
the normal number of calls per month.

Easter is usually the busiest time of year—even outdoing Advent
and Christmas. Usually during Lent, a church offers more programs
and worship services, and attendance is up. All that creates more
stress and tension, and any underlying or submerged conflicts more
easily surface.

In addition, when Easter arrives, church leaders realize that there are only a couple of months, before the summer slow-down, to take care of problems that have developed in the program year.

Perhaps the youth sponsors have been sporadic in their efforts with the high school group. The associate pastor doesn't want to ignore this problem until the fall—otherwise he may end up letting it go another year. Better to nip it in the bud and start the next year's program in a fresh way.

So he asks another couple to become youth sponsors and encourages the present sponsors to retire when summer comes.

The present sponsors are hurt and use the occasion to complain about the work of the associate, about which they've not been happy for some time. Pretty soon, the problem of high school sponsors becomes the entire church's problem—another Eastertide conflict.

2. Stewardship campaigns/budget time

In November and December of each year, I receive several calls from pastors and/or lay leaders about what they discovered during their annual stewardship campaign: when the church callers spoke with the members of the congregation about their pledges, they not only received less money than was expected, they also learned that members were unhappy. The every-member canvass has uncovered some deeper problems in the church, and the problems may have little to do with money.

In a Michigan congregation, giving had dropped off markedly, and the position of some staff members was in jeopardy. So the board decided to call on all of the members of the church to request their financial support. They trained a cadre of leaders to visit every member: they wanted to listen to each member's hopes and concerns for the church and then tell them what the church was doing, inviting them to increase their pledges.

When they asked for volunteers to make the calls, few people at first responded. When they finally did get enough callers and made the calls, the board was surprised at the response: the callers heard a great deal of dissatisfaction from the members—about the pastor's preaching, the staff's sloppy work in religious education, and the general dreariness of the worship services.

The board had been unaware of members' feelings because, in general, church members usually did not speak directly to one another, let alone the board, about their dissatisfaction with the church. The every-member canvass provided a channel for their complaints.

3. Addition of new staff

The most frequent type of conflict in congregations is between the pastor and key leaders in the church. This is particularly true when a new pastoral staff member is called. New staff means not only changes in relationships and procedures but also changes in directions and priorities.

I worked with one congregation that had two interim pastors during its two-year search for a pastor. The interims were passive leaders who seldom interfered with the leadership of the church. As a result, eight laypeople emerged to carry the church through the interim.

These eight people were delighted when the new pastor arrived—at last they wouldn't have to spend so much time at the church; they would get a rest as somebody else handled all the details.

But when the new pastor started to handle the details, the eight leaders found themselves sorely disappointed. The pastor made decisions all right, but differently than they would have. What was worse, he tended to listen to the views of others more than he did theirs!

4. Change in leadership style

In another congregation, the pastor was introverted—quiet, reserved, bookish, but thoughtful and caring. The problem was he followed a highly extroverted pastor who loved being with people in the church and in the community.

Members felt awkward having to take the initiative in conversation with the new pastor, and they became impatient for the new pastor to warm up to them. In fact, the pace of his interaction was simply different than what they were used to, and that took some adjustment.

When a congregation hires, either deliberately or by mistake, a pastor whose leadership style differs from his predecessor, conflict is a near certainty.

Leadership problems are often "followership" problems. For a leader to lead effectively, people must follow effectively—people must actively cooperate with the pastor's style of leadership.

For example, some families experience more turmoil when their children become teenagers. It's not that the parents have changed, but that the children, now teenagers, have. They no longer want to follow the style of leadership their parents have been exerting for years. Leadership is only as effective as its followers.

Often congregations will choose a new pastor with the express intent of picking someone who offers a style of leadership different than the previous pastor—let's say the last pastor was an authoritative leader and the new pastor is participatory (a not unusual occurrence in congregations).

In this scenario, things may go well until there is a congregational crisis or major decision. Then people become anxious, and they revert to old patterns of behavior—and they expect others, like the pastor, to follow suit. They want the pastor suddenly to become decisive and bold. At this point, everyone becomes confused.

5. The pastor's vacation

While the pastor of one Presbyterian congregation was away on his honeymoon, the session (church board) met to discuss his leadership. They decided it was serious enough to phone him in the middle of his honeymoon; they told him a delegation was being sent to the presbytery to ask help from the committee on ministry.

Ouch!

Is this typical? No. But if serious problems are festering in a church, it's not surprising that the dissatisfied group will gather to discuss them while the pastor is away.

Also, some churches depend unduly on their pastor, so that when he or she does take a vacation, the people subconsciously panic. One group begins squabbling with another, or the associate says something offensive from the pulpit ("If you're not giving a tithe to this church, you're not fully committed to Christ!"), and people react. Before long, someone feels compelled to phone the vacationing pastor to tell him things are falling apart.

6. Changes in the pastor's family

Often changes in a pastor's family, even for the better, will cause conflict in the congregation.

One pastor for years devoted his primary energy and attention to the congregation. The congregation got used to his seventy- and eighty-hour weeks.

When the pastor's daughter reached her teens, he and his daughter began quarreling more. She began to get into trouble at school. The pastor was concerned.

So he started to spend a great deal more time at home, and he began attending a weekly therapy session with his wife and daughter.

Well, the church started feeling neglected. Even though the pastor still put in some fifty hours a week, the congregation complained about his flagging interest in the church.

7. Introduction of baby boomers into the church

Over the last ten years, a new generation of churchgoers has begun to participate in congregational life. These so-called "baby boomers" tend to be more liberal than previous generations, and they live significantly different lifestyles: typically both parents work full-time, they have little free time, they hold only short-term commitments, they tend only to support programs that meet their needs, and they tend to be more forthright and outspoken.

This has presented many a problem to churches. Women's groups find it difficult to attract working women; program planners are annoyed by the baby boomers' unwillingness to make long-term commitments; committees are aggravated by baby boomers' commitment to excellence, especially when it comes to programs and facilities for children, because excellence is a lot of trouble!

All this can be aggravating to the older generation.

8. The completion of a new building

When the Alban Institute researched pastoral firings, it discovered that after the completion of a new building, clergy were vulnerable to firing. Several factors are involved:

The leadership (including the pastor's) has centered on a focused and specific task. Once completed, a new kind of leadership is required—usually leadership focused on program.

If the transition is not made, the church, which had experienced itself as successful, now feels it's drifting. It wants the kind of energy and focus it had during the building project. Unless it finds a new focus, the frustration gets directed into a conflict.

9. Loss of church membership

Conflict is more likely when a church endures significant drops in membership. Membership is a scarce resource for many congregations; as resources—money or people—dwindle, tension increases.

Members of declining congregations often pin the blame for their problems on a person or group, even though the people they blame may have done little if anything to contribute to the difficulty.

In upstate New York, a downtown parish had suffered a slow, regular, and significant decrease in attendance for ten years. The pastor, who had been with the church for fifteen years, knew that part of the decline was due to urban renewal, which had removed much of the housing near the church. In addition, two new congregations of the same denomination had been started not far away in the suburbs.

Still, he was convinced that the *real* reason the church had been losing members was because of three older women of the congregation: They had controlled the church for twenty years. They resisted everything he tried. They were hostile and forbidding. They intimidated anyone who wanted to try something new, whether it was a new church school class, a program for the homeless, or innovations in worship.

While many of the members agreed that the problem was this formidable troika, an equally large group thought the problem lay with the pastor: he didn't pay enough attention to the older members, he didn't call on the members frequently enough, and he was too involved in controversial social issues about the poor.

Which group was "right"? Both and neither. But the pain of membership loss was so great, each felt the need to blame someone.

I pointed out to both sides that although the women and the pastor could each improve how they worked in the church, the membership problems were largely caused by factors beyond the control of any individual or group. Consequently, I encouraged them to identify ways they might strengthen their church's work in their community and discouraged their attempts to improve each other.

10. Increase in church membership

On the other hand, an increase in church membership can also trigger conflict, because as congregations grow, their personalities change. People happy with the old personality usually don't like the new personality that emerges.

As do others, I classify congregations into four sizes: family, pastoral, program, and corporate.

Family size. These congregations average less than fifty on Sunday morning. They tend to be single-cell organizations with only one dominant leader—usually not the pastor, rather a long-term and active member of the congregation. Family-size congregations tend to look to the past, to what has or has not worked, to guide their decisions.

Pastoral size. These churches average 50 to 150 people on Sunday morning. They have several cells, or primary groups. These cells tend to relate to each other through the pastor.

The pastor links the congregation. Usually it is the pastor who calls on newcomers and acquaints them with others in the congregation. He orients them to congregational life and helps them find a place to land—a committee, a Bible study, the choir. Furthermore, the pastor is about the only person who attends every church function.

The pastor, then, wields more authority in a pastoral-size congregation than in the family-size church. People look to the pastor for information and advice.

Planning in pastoral-size congregations is still determined by what has happened in the past, although not as much as in the family-size congregation.

As a church moves into the pastoral-size category, the matriarch or patriarch will lose his or her power to the pastor, and this transition will not be easy.

Also, as the congregation swells, it begins functioning in distinct groups. Those who formerly liked the unified, family feel of the church are likely to complain.

Program size. These congregations have from 150 to 350 on Sunday morning. Since duties exceed the physical capabilities of a single pastor, the church hires other staff and delegates more work to boards and committees.

Not everyone in the congregation works directly with the senior pastor, but some relate to the music personnel, others to the Christian education director, and others still to the associate pastor. Thus, to some the congregation feels like an "organization" rather than a church.

Exigencies often determine planning. Members get in trouble with one another for scheduling two events in the same room on the same day, or attempting to take the young people on a weekend retreat on the Sunday of the all-church picnic. Planning worship is more complex, since the interests of the music personnel, the preacher, and the worship committee all have to be coordinated.

(Actually, congregations with more than 150 on Sunday morning can function like a pastoral-size church. Such a church usually has few committees and offers few programs. The church essentially revolves around the Sunday morning worship service.)

The shift from a pastoral-size congregation to a program-size congregation is likely to be more disquieting still. The changes will be more visible, thus threatening to more people.

For example, changing from one worship service to two will likely be the most disturbing change for the church: "The church will no longer be unified." "We won't be able to see our friends if they attend another service."

Usually congregations restructure their boards when they move from pastoral- to program-size congregations. The governing board no longer works as closely with all aspects of the congregation's life. Some committees report less and some not at all to the governing board, and consequently many people feel increasingly alienated from church leadership.

The pastor restructures his schedule as well. He or she can no longer visit everyone who is sick and shut in, or meet with every committee. That is felt as a real loss to everyone, including the pastor.

Corporate size. These congregations, with more than 350 people on Sunday morning, are even more hierarchically organized than program-size churches. The pastor now relates only to program staff, certainly not all staff. Often the pastor focuses more on his unique ministry (usually preaching), and others have the administrative and program responsibilities.

Often cadres, groups, special ministries, or even pastoral-size churches emerge within the corporate-size congregation. The pastor becomes a symbol who holds the entire congregation together.

Planning is now more complex, but in addition to responding to the needs of the moment, corporate-size churches have the time and staff to base their decisions on future contingencies.

Many of the same tensions experienced in the previous size change are felt here as well.

What can be done to better deal with these predictable times of conflict?

Knowing the stages of grief helps; after all, nearly all of these occasions have something to do with letting go of something past.

Also, knowing that conflict and stress, at low levels anyway, are helpful for congregations, helps reduce some of the tension brought on by these transitions.

But in any event, just knowing what may come helps.

A football receiver often knows he's going to be hit immediately after he makes a catch. Knowing that doesn't lessen the impact of the hit, but it does help him to hold on to the ball and sometimes even maintain his balance, elude the tackler, and gain some extra ground.

Likewise with pastors, if they know when the church is likely to be hit, they'll more likely be able to turn up-field for a few extra yards.

5

Why Peacemakers Aren't Popular

True power—and peace—come through humility and obedience. That's a price few are willing to pay.

—Fred Smith

Nothing I know starts fights faster than the subject of peacemaking. In principle, of course, everyone is for it. But it's amazing how defensive and hostile people get trying to make peace.

The situation reminds me of when the current interest in small groups was just beginning. Speaking at a gathering that included many small-group fans, I mentioned I felt the dangers of small groups outweighed any potential benefits. Many wouldn't speak to me afterward.

To me, this demonstrated what I was trying to prove: those particular small groups, at least, weren't based on love but fear. People weren't there for what they could give, but for emotional security. By saying, "I love you," they were trying to ensure their own protection, hoping talk of love would keep people from hurting them. They were really expressing a fear of, not a love for, other people. Relationships were based only on a negotiated nonviolence.

So when a foreigner came in and expressed a different view, they joined together in hating him because "he wasn't for love."

Later I told them I was actually doing an experiment—to prove they really weren't as loving as they thought. The Bible says if you love those who love you, so what? Pagans and publicans do that.

They were still angry with me, and maybe rightfully. Likewise in peacemaking, ideals are preached, but pragmatics often reign.

One of the reasons peacemaking in churches isn't a popular item is because some people have a vested interest in conflict. Like union bosses and management negotiators, ending the war means they lose their jobs. I'm afraid some religious leaders also need conflict. They carry their greatest power in leading the fight to purify the church. They claim they're defending the faith; they act as if they're defending God. Personally, I don't think God needs defending, especially by those who are basically hostile.

We've been so imbued with the idea we must fight Satan that we get the notion faith involves lots of fighting. But rather than personifying the purity of Christ, more likely we're trying to establish our self-righteousness.

Any time I'm arguing with a brother, I need to check my attitude carefully. If I'm enjoying it, if I feel righteously glad to be in the dispute, then the war is probably not justified.

Part of our problem is our desire to be seen as successful. For example, many evangelicals are almost gloating over the decline of the liberals. They're acting as if their spirituality somehow contributed to the liberals' downfall. No—our attitude must be one of humbly offering assistance, water to the thirsty.

One famous evangelist exhibited this spirit recently when he was planning a campaign in a large amphitheater. Six liberal ministers, who didn't deem it worthwhile to participate, somewhat arrogantly invited him to defend his position before them. With a gentle spirit, he went. Immediately they told him, "We admire you as a person, but your message is just too simple for us."

He responded softly, "What happens when you preach? Do prostitutes become virtuous? Do murderers become converted? Do thieves become honest?"

"We don't know what happens after our sermons," they said.

The evangelist continued, "I would like to be an intellectual. All my life I've envied intellectuals, but when I try to preach that way, nothing happens. Only when I have used the simple message of the gospel have these things happened. Now, do you feel I should change?"

He didn't condemn them. He took time to meet with a half dozen skeptics and say, "Hungry, guys? Here's where I found the nourishment." To me, that's the spirit of peacemaking.

This is different from mere tolerance. This is what I call "objective acceptance." It's burying the hatchet but not burying the issue.

If we have differences, I think we must define them very sharply. In fact, my wife criticizes me at times for pressing my friends so hard to find out where they stand on issues. I do it because I think surprises hurt friendships. If we press each other and discover exactly what we believe and what we're going to do, then there are few surprises. And we can accept our difference.

We must learn to be comfortable with both similarities and differences. Our tendency is to hide differences and focus only on areas where we're alike. That's a mistake.

I was asked to speak to the annual meeting of Christians and Jews in a large city. After I accepted, I got a call from a Protestant minister who nervously said, "Mr. Smith, I would like you to agree not to embarrass our Jewish attenders by mentioning Christ."

"Are there going to be blacks there?" I asked.

"Yes, of course."

"Would you like me to come as a black?"

There was silence for a moment before he said, "You can't."

"It's going to be just as difficult for me to come as a non-Christian," I said. "If I'm introduced as a Nashvillian, does that mean I can't mention Nashville? If you're going to introduce me as a Christian, can't I mention the source of the name? That doesn't make much sense.

"Let me put it another way," I continued. "Suppose I'm walking down the alley behind my house at night, and I see a Hell's Angel standing next to his motorcycle, and I start saying, 'Hi, friend. We're both human, we both live in Dallas, and we're both seeking meaning in our own way.' What do you think is really on our minds—our similarities or our differences?"

So I told this story at the meeting. It helped establish communication. Intelligent, realistic people want to understand differences.

This is true also of peacemaking. We don't do away with differences; we define them with great clarity—but also with objective acceptance. We don't say, "You're polluted because your thoughts are different from mine."

Condoning or converting?

Objective acceptance and tolerance are two different things. Tolerance is satisfied with the status quo; it too often is merely a euphemism for apathy.

Objective acceptance doesn't mean you never try to change people's views. Sometimes you should. But you admit to the people involved you're trying to change them. You don't manipulate them.

I know an avowed nonbeliever, for instance, who's a professor at a Christian school. I would have no compunction about sitting down with him, praising him for his scholarship and intellectual abilities, but also saying, "In my opinion, you shouldn't be teaching in a Christian school." And if I got enough agreement in the administration, I'd have no qualms about removing him—not as though he were some kind of cancer, but because I don't think that position should be filled by that man.

You can't fill an engineering department with people who aren't engineers. I'm not for witch-hunting. I'm simply saying that objective acceptance allows you to accomplish your purposes but in an honest, fair way. The process must be as Christian as the result.

That's the spirit of peace, not merely of tolerance.

Defending faith or living it?

Among Christians, perhaps the greatest temptation is to defend the faith but not personify it. If you do that, you cannot make peace.

This tendency to say one thing and be another is one of the problems with our society. Teachers used to be models; now they want to be instructors. They know the responsibility of living as an example is very, very heavy. As mere instructors, they can refuse the burden of responsibility for exemplary personal integrity.

Likewise in the Christian world, we have no shortage of those willing to join the fighting squad, to be Christian marines. But we don't have too many willing to personify the love of God. Those who personify Christ rarely get into fights. I don't find Mother Teresa doing anything but helping the poor; she seeks no recognition. She's personifying the spirit of Christ, and who wants to start a fight with her?

I have a friend who's a top executive and one of the most profane men I've known. Some time ago he was working on a major acquisition and phoned me. "I need someone's objective thinking," he said. "Can I come down and spend the weekend with you?" I hesitated. He's a brilliant man, a Ph.D., but so profane. Should I expose my family to him? After a quick prayer, I said, "Sure, come on down."

He came and was a perfect gentleman. On the way back to the

airport, he said, "Fred, I want to thank you. You didn't change me, but you didn't let me change your family life either. You still prayed and read the Bible. I appreciate your accepting me that way."

A few years later, he showed up at our laymen's institute and the next day told me he wanted to become a Christian. Why? "I've dropped into churches for years looking for what I found last night," he said. "I've never felt such joy, such love, and I want to be a part of it." So he accepted Christ.

Unfortunately, I suggested he visit a denominational leader in his home state who also was an outstanding businessman. The two had lunch, but it was during a time of tension in the denomination, and the leader spent most of the time castigating the opposition. To this day, my friend has never been back to church.

I think we're losing a great many people because they see the fighting. They want joy and peace. As little as they know about Christianity, they look at squabbling Christians and say, "This can't be it."

In the middle of it

What if you're already involved in hostilities? The responsibility of the Christian is to turn up the light and turn down the heat. We must look at every situation redemptively.

We don't redeem situations by changing organizational structures. We redeem them by bringing in a different spirit—the spirit of Christ—even if it means we'll lose. As difficult as this is for me personally, it's still true: If I can't win in the spirit of Christ, I should lose. It's God's will for me to lose.

If I've got to maneuver or manipulate or go behind someone's back, it's not God's will.

Peacemaking is an action that springs out of an attitude. We'll have differences, but they mustn't make us mad at one another in the body. When you're angry at a fellow believer, you raise the temperature, and I don't know any time when you're supposed to bring fever to the body of Christ.

The spirit of Christ, when truly exhibited, can actually reduce the inflammation.

One of my few firsthand experiences with this truth happened in a small-town church when I was young. I asked to be the song leader, and the pastor said, "Will you make me one promise?" I was so eager for the job I said yes.

"Promise me you will not say one bad thing about anybody in this church for as long as you have the job."

It was contrary to my nature, but I made the promise. And kept it. Never since have I received the love I received in that place.

Years later I began wondering about that and went back to the pastor. I reminded him of the promise and told him how amazed I was at the results.

"It's very simple," he explained. "If you never say anything bad about someone, you're never afraid to face that person. If you've spoken against someone, something inside tells you that person shouldn't like you, which raises a spiritual wall. Plus, if people never hear you say anything bad about anyone else, they'll believe you never say anything bad about them. And they'll love you for it."

I saw the sheer practicality of it, and it worked! But I must admit I haven't always practiced it since.

Power source

It's amazing that with the nearly universal desire for peace, very few people are willing to pay the price it requires. Like the rest of the traits mentioned in the Beatitudes, peacemaking is admired as an ideal and ignored as a reality. Too many of us prefer power to peace.

What Christians must remember is that power does not come by vanquishing someone else. Power doesn't even come by defending the right causes or by the purity of our theology.

No, true power—and peace—come through humility and obedience. And that's a price few are willing to pay.

6

Identifying a Dragon

Dragons can drive pastors crazy . . .
or out of the church.

—Marshall Shelley

C an you draw out Leviathan with a fishhook? Or press down his
tongue with a cord? . . . His breath kindles coals, And a flame
goes forth from his mouth (Job 41:1, 21, NASB).

Dragons, of course, are fictional beasts—monstrous reptiles with
lion's claws, a serpent's tail, bat wings, and scaly skin. They originate
in the imagination.

But there are dragons of a different sort, decidedly real. In most
cases, though not always, they do not intend to be sinister; in fact,
they're usually quite friendly. But their charm belies their power to
destroy.

Within the church, they are often sincere, well-meaning saints,
but they leave ulcers, strained relationships, and hard feelings in their
wake. They don't consider themselves difficult people. They don't sit
up nights thinking of ways to be nasty. Often they are pillars of the
community—talented, strong personalities, deservingly respected—
but for some reason, they undermine the ministry of the church. They
are not naturally rebellious or pathological; they are loyal church
members, convinced they're serving God, but they wind up doing
more harm than good.

They can drive pastors crazy . . . or out of the church.

Some dragons are openly critical. They are the ones who accuse
you of being (pick one) too spiritual, not spiritual enough, too dominant, too laid back, too narrow, too loose, too structured, too dis-

organized, or ulterior in your motives.

These criticisms are painful because they are largely unanswerable. How can you defend yourself and maintain a spirit of peace? How can you possibly prove the purity of your motives? Dragons make it hard to disagree without being disagreeable.

Relationships are both the professional and personal priority of pastors—getting along with people is an essential element of any ministry—and when relationships are vandalized by critical dragons, many pastors feel like failures. Politicians are satisfied with 51 percent of the constituency behind them; pastors, however, feel pain when one vocal member becomes an opponent.

Sightings of these dragons are all too common. As one veteran pastor says, "Anyone who's been in ministry more than an hour and a half knows the wrath of a dragon." Or, as Harry Ironside described it, "Wherever there's light, there's bugs."

Job one is to know a dragon when you see one.

Dragon varieties

Before looking specifically at two of the most common tactics of dragons—personal attacks and plays for power—it might be helpful to catalog some of the varieties inhabiting the church. All of the following have been reported by working pastors.

The Bird Dog. Four-legged Bird Dogs point to where the hunter should shoot. The two-legged Bird Dog loves to be the pastor's eyes, ears, and nose, sniffing out items for attention. "If I were you, I'd give Mrs. Greenlee a call. She has some marital problems you need to confront." Or, "We need more activities for the youth." Or, "Why doesn't the church do something about . . ."

Most pastors respond to Bird Dogs by saying something like, "The Lord hasn't said anything to me about this, but it sounds like a good idea. Obviously you're concerned, and that's usually a sign that the Lord is telling you to do something about it." Those who are genuinely concerned will take up the challenge. Genuine Bird Dogs, however, will grumble, "That's *your* job, Pastor. I'm just calling your attention to something important."

Of particular bother is the Superspiritual Bird Dog. This purebred strain is more likely to point out things that always leave the pastor feeling defensive and not quite spiritual. "The Lord has laid on my heart that we need to be praying more for renewal." Who could argue otherwise? Or, "We need to develop more discipleship and maturity within this congregation, wouldn't you say, Pastor?"

These people like to give the impression that they have more spiritual perception than anyone else. "It's more irritating than threatening, but it always shakes my confidence," says a pastor in Virginia. "I find myself questioning whether I really have the mind of Christ, whether I'm fulfilling my pastoral responsibilities as I should. Especially when I'm tired and feeling overwhelmed already, this kind of person really gets me down. I don't need more Bird Dogs. I need more shooters."

The Wet Blanket. If you've heard the phrase "It's no use trying," you've probably spotted the Wet Blanket. These people have a negative disposition that's contagious. They spread gloom, erase excitement, and bog down the ministry. Their motto: "Nothing ventured, nothing lost."

A pastor in upstate New York describes one such obstructionist couple, who live next door to the church. Since it's a yoked parish and the pastor lives twelve miles away, this couple informally oversees building maintenance. "Last winter I called them each Wednesday afternoon to turn on the heat in the church building for prayer meeting that night," the pastor recalls. Inevitably, the couple would refuse. "We don't need heat," they would argue. "It's too expensive, not enough people will show up, and those who do can sit for an hour in their coats."

In business meetings, they exhibit the same attitude toward any step of faith. "We tried that before, and it didn't work" is a familiar refrain. Because of their intimidating personalities, people are reluctant to vote against them.

The Entrepreneur. Just the opposite of the Wet Blanket, the Entrepreneur is enthusiastic. He's the first to greet visitors at the church and invite them to his home. Unfortunately, in addition to being enthusiastic about the church, he's equally eager to sell them vitamins, bee pollen, or car wax.

"We were losing people because they felt victimized," says a minister in Wisconsin. "It got so bad I had to mention in a sermon that we can't make each other the objects of our enterprises. We also had to put a notice in our church directory that it was not to be used for business activity."

Captain Bluster. This is the person who comes from the union steward school of diplomacy and speaks with an exclamation point instead of a period.

He (or she) is right, and everyone else is wrong, and he doesn't mind saying in the middle of a church business meeting, "I don't like what you said."

"All our salaries are out of line; pastors are paid too much these days!" said one such dragon in a business meeting with the pastor's entire family present.

This kind of person is a steamroller who flattens anyone in his way with his overwhelming certainty that his is the only way to do it. Negotiation is a dirty word; compromise unspeakable.

If this person is on a church board that has settled a sensitive issue privately, but he wasn't completely satisfied with the decision, he's likely to bring it up again in a congregational meeting because he enjoys the fireworks.

The Fickle Financier. This person uses money to register approval or disapproval of church decisions. Sometimes he protests silently by merely withholding offerings.

"I can always tell when I've made an unpopular decision," says one Maryland pastor. "Missions-giving goes up, the general fund scrapes bottom, and it's usually right before the quarterly business meeting. They think they're punishing the pastor."

Others however, because of the amount of their giving, realize their money means clout, and they directly manipulate people and programs.

In one small church in Oregon, the owner of the local school bus company and his family represented 50 percent of the church's income. When the new pastor went in for his first haircut, the barber said, "Oh, you're at the church Mr. Peabody owns." The pastor couldn't tell if he was joking. He later discovered he wasn't.

Mr. Peabody expected the pastor to keep regular office hours and managed to find some excuse to call almost every morning at 9:00 and again shortly after 11:30 to find out if he was there.

"That was just one symptom of the control he exerted," says the pastor, who has since left, though the calls continue with his successor. "It was a hardship, but there's no solution unless you're willing to stand up to him and risk losing half your funds, a loss I didn't feel the church could survive."

On the other hand, a Georgia pastor faced a similar situation.

"In my first church of thirty members, the largest contributor threatened to move his letter if such-and-such wasn't done. I said, 'I'm sorry you feel that way, but you don't judge this church—God judges all of us.' The church wasn't for sale. It cut the ground out from under him."

These are just a few of the dragons ministers encounter. There are many others too numerous to mention in detail:

The Busybody, who enjoys telling others how to do their jobs.

The Sniper, who avoids face-to-face conflict but picks off pastors with potshots in private conversation, such as the cryptic "Be sure and pray for our pastor. He has some problems, you know."

The Bookkeeper, who keeps written records of everything the pastor does that "isn't in the spirit of Christ."

The Merchant of Muck, who breeds dissatisfaction by attracting others who know he's more than willing to listen to, and elaborate on, things that are wrong in the church.

The Legalist, whose list of absolutes stretches from the kind of car a pastor can drive to the number of verses in a hymn that must be sung.

Any of these can inhabit a given congregation.

How do you know a dragon if you see one? You can't tell by looking. Dragons can be as friendly and charming as nondragons. Sometimes you can't even tell by listening . . . at first. People can criticize, voice dogmatic opinions, tangle with others, and yet not be dragons.

The distinguishing characteristic of a dragon is not *what* is said but *how* it's said. Even though these people are well-intentioned, sincerely doing what's best in their own eyes, they aren't quite with you. Often they have a spirit that enjoys being an adversary rather than an ally. They have a consistent pattern of focusing on a narrow special interest rather than the big picture, which leads to tangents rather than a balanced church life.

Theirs is a spirit quick to vilify and slow to apologize. Dragons usually cannot bring themselves to accept responsibility for something that has gone wrong, and hence, they resist asking anyone's forgiveness.

This spirit, of course, is difficult to discern. It can only be judged by observing the person's effect on the larger ministry of the church. As First Timothy 5:24 says, "The sins of some men are obvious . . . ; the sins of others trail behind them."

Perhaps the greatest damage done by true dragons is not their direct opposition. It's more intangible. They destroy enthusiasm, the morale so necessary for church health and growth. People no longer feel good about inviting friends to worship services. The air is tense, the church depressed, and everyone aware of "us" and "them."

Their effect on pastors is equally serious. They sap the pastor's energy and, just as damaging, goad them into *re*acting instead of acting.

"The real problem isn't so much their overt actions," observes a veteran pastor. "But they divert your attention and keep you off guard even if they never openly oppose you. You find yourself not planning, not thinking of the future, not seeking a vision for the church—you're just trying to survive."

If pastors become preoccupied with dragons, afraid to challenge them or at least too concerned about "fighting only battles that need to be fought," they often lose their spontaneity and creativity. Change is stifled, growth stunted, and the direction of ministry is set by the course of least resistance, which, as everyone knows, is the course that makes rivers crooked.

If the first casualties in dragon warfare are vision and initiative, the next victim is outreach. When a pastor is forced to worry more about putting out brush fires than igniting the church's flame, the dragons have won, and the ministry has lost.

Dragon habitations

Where are the places dragons are most likely to emerge?

The following warnings are not intended to arouse suspicion or distrust of potential friends. They're offered simply to help clarify some of the dynamics of potential conflict.

The worst dragons may be, in the beginning, the pastor's strongest supporters. Often the opposition seems to develop from among those responsible for calling the pastor.

One pastor, now in his fifth church, says, "A wise old minister told me the person most likely to become your severest critic is the person who picks you up at the airport on your candidating visit. So far he's been right three out of five."

They're not always members of the pastoral search committee, but dragons often seem to emerge from among the people influential in calling the pastor.

Why? Perhaps their expectations are greater. Perhaps they are more emotionally tied to the church and feel more of an ownership. Perhaps they feel their leadership threatened by the pastor. Perhaps they're simply the stronger personalities. Whatever the reason, they often become the loyal opposition, or in some cases not so loyal.

Another pastor, a church planter, observes a similar tendency even in situations without a search committee. "The people who were part of the core, the first four families, were among the first to become disenchanted with me. They saw me as *their* pastor, and as the congregation grew, one of them told me, 'These new people don't love this church like we do.' And when I inevitably spent less time with the charter members to concentrate on growth, they became sharply critical of me, too."

Dragons often work overly hard initially at befriending you. If you list the people who make an appointment to see you in the first month of a new pastorate and another list of those unhappy with your ministry a year later, you'll be amazed at the overlap. Often when they first come, they want to "share a personal concern" or let you know "the *real* situation in the church." They really want, of course, to co-opt your allegiance for their special interest.

Other times, certain individuals will give overgenerous gifts. "One man in my congregation took me aside and gave me $100 every month. Another offered to buy me a new suit each year," said a pastor in Des Moines. "I didn't refuse at first, but then I realized they had a political end in mind. I felt they were trying to own me. I've since turned down these gifts."

People who try overly hard to be friends are sometimes genuine, but other times they just want to be in the inner ring, to gain the pastor's ear, to increase their influence in the church.

Dragons usually compare you to their former pastor.
Dragons have invariably had previous church experience, either at
another church or in the present church with the previous pastor.
Dragons are virtually nonexistent among those for whom you are the
first pastor.

One small-town pastor in the Midwest, who counts among his
congregation the widow of the former pastor, was confronted by her
one Sunday morning.

"I tried to call you this week," she said. "Your wife told me it was
your day off. I'll have you know my husband never took a day off in
twenty-three years of ministry." The pastor stifled an urge to point
out that her husband had also died at age forty-five.

The prior experience of a congregation affects churches of every
size and denomination. Unless the congregation has been without a
minister for a *long* time, the spirit of the former pastor is very much
present. Whether the former pastor was loved deeply or intensely
disliked, the congregation's priorities certainly have been shaped by
the predecessor. Some will want a clone; others will want a sharp
contrast.

Interestingly, just because people praise their former pastor does
not mean they're going to become dragons. In fact, they are probably
not as dangerous as those who've developed a habit of criticizing
past ministers. They may be revealing their respect for the pastoral
position.

"When I first came to Birch Ridge Presbyterian," says the current
pastor, "I got so tired of hearing how wonderful my predecessor,
Reverend Becker, had been. They called him Old Brother Beck, and
they adored him. But when I had been there four or five years, their
loyalties shifted my way. It just took a while to be accepted as their
leader."

If they brag about the former pastor, it may be cause for thanks,
not irritation. It's safer than the members skinning him alive. Members' attitudes about their former pastor can, in time, transfer to you.

**Dragons thrive when the church's formal authority
and informal power structure don't match.** Whenever the
church office holders, elected or appointed, are different from the

unofficial but widely recognized power brokers in the congregation, dragons seem to multiply.

One Minneapolis pastor who teaches a seminary course in practical theology asked his students to draw a chart of the lines of authority in their home churches. The students all drew neat boxes for various committees and boards with lines running cleanly from one to another. Then he asked them to diagram the *real* decision-making process. One student turned in a sheet with lots of small circles around the edge connected to one large egg-shaped circle filling the center of the page. The large circle was labeled "Ralph."

No polity is perfect. Dominant personalities may not be spiritually qualified for church leadership. And no church structure can ever perfectly fit the changing human relationships within a congregation. But stress will come to the extent of the mismatch between formal and informal leadership. One inevitably must adjust to the other.

Dragons are often bred in counseling. Those you've counseled, or their family members, frequently become either eternally grateful for your help or infernally gravid with hate since you know too much.

People often seem to resent those who become too familiar with their intimate struggles. In counseling, if the problems are not completely solved, counselees are often uncomfortable facing the counselor later—not only does he know their problem, he knows it hasn't been solved. When this happens with a pastor, often the persons withdraw from the church physically or emotionally, or else they begin working to oust the pastor.

Even if the pastor maintains a good relationship with the counselee, sometimes family members resent his involvement.

"The wife of one of my deacons came to see me about their marriage difficulties. Her husband refused to admit there was a problem, but his relationship with me became tense because he knew what his wife had been telling me. Eventually he became one of the individuals instrumental in demanding my resignation," says the pastor, who was forced to leave. "I can't help but think at least part of the breakdown in our relationship was due to his discomfort knowing I was aware of his marriage problems."

Dragons often sensed a call to the ministry at one time. Surprisingly, most pastors indicate they do not have as many problems with those currently in Christian work as they do with those who should be in ministry and aren't.

"I have several parachurch workers, preachers' kids, and retired ministers in my congregation, and they're my most supportive members," says an Illinois pastor. "I've learned to lean on them when I need to. They understand ministry and appreciate what the church is doing.

"The problems come from those who've sensed a call and haven't followed it. It's the frustrated, armchair pastors who want to run the church."

Another pastor reports his dragon is a former missionary who took a job in the home office and is suddenly away from a direct people ministry.

The only solution? Finding a place where these people can minister directly to needy people.

"We had a young couple who'd committed themselves to going overseas during a missions conference, but they never went," says the Illinois pastor. "They were a source of dissension until we identified what they were feeling and put them in charge of tutoring some inner-city kids. Now they feel great about the church."

The old adage "If they have a problem, give 'em a job" isn't bad if the job is meaningful, and especially if it's in an area where God has called them before. If you can tap the cause of the frustration, help them recognize it, and love them in spite of their abrasiveness, they can be transformed from dragons to highly motivated allies.

These are by no means all the situations conducive to dragons. Nor do these conditions mean dragons will necessarily appear. Many pastors are able to minister effectively in all of these situations without arousing the wrath of their people. It does help, however, to understand the factors at work.

Dragon understanding

How do dragons get that way? Rarely is it a conscious choice to become beastly. Hardly ever are dragons so bad that they see themselves as dragons. Other than the pathological sadists, not many people in human history were mean because they enjoyed it.

"I have never met a man who wanted to be bad," writes George

MacLeod. "The mystery of man is that he is bad when he wants to be good."

In the church, most dragons see themselves as godly people, adequately gracious and kind, who hold another viewpoint they honestly believe is right.

Unfortunately, sincerity without self-examination is no excuse. Remember the old joke about the proud mother who thought every member of the marching band was out of step except her Freddy? Even with intense self-examination, not all the factors are self-evident. In dealing with dragons, it's helpful to understand some of the underlying causes of their behavior.

First, people do battle because they *feel* so strongly. Emotions are often more powerful than logic. In an ideal world, people who differ would sit down together in faith and good fellowship, and after some friendly debate reach an agreement based on Scripture, sound theology, and calm reasoning. But we know that doesn't happen. If a person is argued into submission or politically subdued in one area, but the underlying emotional need isn't met, he'll simply create another headache somewhere else.

When a person complains, "I'm not being fed," or, "You're not meeting my needs," sometimes it's out of frustration, as mentioned above, or out of a sense of neglect or isolation.

"I used to have very little patience with these people," says a Nazarene pastor, "until I noticed I do the same thing. Another pastor, a good friend of mine, accepted a denominational position, and I began to resent him because when he was in town he always seemed to have time for other pastors but not me. I found myself criticizing him, but I wasn't *judging* him, I was *mad* at him."

In a similar way, the criticism of a dragon may spring more from anger than differences over the immediate subject. And sometimes the anger is not specifically directed at the pastor but at the situation.

"The guy who's overlooked in his company and has been passed over for promotion five times can make the dirt fly in the church," says a pastor in Alabama. "I've struggled most with people who resist all types of authority, not just pastoral leaders. They've never met an executive they liked, and they see the pastor as an executive. They don't have much control in their jobs, but they're determined to exert some power in the church.

"It's taken ten years to get close to these people, and it's happened as a result of their seeing my failures."

Second, despite their sincerity, people cannot overcome their human nature. All of us sometimes act out of sheer cussedness, even while justifying our actions to ourselves. In John Miller's *The Contentious Community*, he compares the church to a children's choir gathered in the sanctuary to sing praises to God. "Innocence and guile are perched on the edge of the platform, waiting to burst forth in song or shove some unsuspecting freckle-faced being to an ignominious landing three feet below. And it isn't that Bonnie is innocent and Bobby is full of guile; it is that innocence and guile, the ideal and the real, are coursing through the veins of each."

Or, as Saint Augustine pointed out with barbed wit, "The innocence of children may be more a matter of weakness of limb than purity of heart."

The church, indeed every Christian, is an odd combination of self-sacrificing saint and self-serving sinner. And the church, unlike some social organizations, doesn't have the luxury of choosing its members; the church is an assembly of all who profess themselves believers. Within that gathering is found a full range of saint/sinner combinations. Ministry is a commitment to care for all members of the body, even those whose breath is tainted with dragon smoke.

PART 2

Prevention

7

Stopping Conflict Before It Starts

There is no guarantee that spiritually mature people will work well together.

—Larry Osborne

When I entered the pastorate, I had a good understanding of original sin. Six months later, I had an excellent understanding of original sin.

I had arrived only a few weeks after the departure of the founding pastor. He was well-loved and had left on the best of terms to pursue a doctorate and a career in seminary teaching. We were just a small group meeting in a high school cafeteria, but I thought we had great potential. I was particularly impressed by the unity and quality of relationships I found. My call had been unanimous. It looked as if we were ready to roll.

There was just one problem.

I had failed to take into account the simple fact that when no one wants the previous pastor to leave, no one really wants the new one to come (no matter how unanimous the vote). I was, at best, their second choice. At worst (at least, whenever I tried to change something), I was a barbarian invader.

Needless to say, my honeymoon was short. People were literally leaving as fast as they came in. In a six-week period, we gained ten new families—only to lose ten families that just months before had voted for me to become their pastor.

I was devastated. I worried a great deal about being fired. I often asked myself, *What will I do when the ax drops? Will I give the min-*

istry another shot—or more important, will anyone give me another shot? I didn't know.

Fortunately, that never happened. Now, nearly fifteen years later, a church that was once a battleground has become known for its absence of conflict. That's a testimony to the Lord's redemptive power and grace. But on a human level, some important changes helped make a difference.

No monolith

One important change was that I stopped treating the church as if it were a monolithic organization. Like most churches, we are made up of three distinct groups, and each is prone to its own conflict. Each needs a unique strategy for preempting conflict (or to put a more positive spin on it, for building and maintaining unity). These three groups are:

1. the congregation
2. the governing board
3. the staff

Early on, I missed this. I thought unity was something the entire church either lacked or enjoyed.

I didn't realize I could have a brewing disaster on the board despite a happy congregation and staff; or that a few disgruntled staff members could sabotage the unity within the board and congregation; or that a congregational uprising was possible even if the staff and board were on the same page.

I now know better. As a result, I try to keep tabs on the health of each group. In addition, we've developed specific tools and guidelines to help preempt conflict within each of the three groups.

Preempting congregational conflict

The most effective tool I've found for preempting congregational conflict is what I call a "Front-Loaded Pastor's Class."

It is not a membership class. The typical membership class is designed for those who have been around long enough to decide they want to join the church. A front-loaded pastor's class is designed for those who are new to the church and simply want to find out what it's about. We describe ours as a look at "why we do what we do the way we do it." Those who come have been at the church only a short while; they are far from ready to commit to membership.

Especially for people who transfer from another church, the class is our most effective tool for preempting future conflict. Here's why.

When most people change churches (for example, due to a move or a problem in a previous church), they bring to their new church expectations and assumptions. If they like the new church's preaching, worship, and people, they settle in, assuming the new church uses the same compass as their old church. But such is not always the case.

I think of a church that grew from 300 to 1,200 in five years. But at least two-thirds of the growth was transfer growth fueled by internal strife at three other churches in the area. When I talked to the pastor, he was ecstatic over the influx of people already eager to serve and willing to give. He felt he now had the type of people he could build a ministry upon.

Perhaps he did. But he also had a large group of people with their own ideas of what his church should be—and the assumption that he shared those notions. For a while, that was no big deal. Then came the day when he recommended the church hire a music director who happened to be previously divorced.

The pastor and those who had been around from the beginning lined up on one side. For them, the divorce issue had been settled years before when a divorced-and-remarried man was appointed to the board. The pastor had clearly addressed the issue when he candidated for the position.

But for the folks who had transferred in (especially those who had come from one of the churches), accepting a divorced leader was tantamount to denying the faith. They came from a background in which divorce permanently disqualifies a person from ministry.

When these people came to the church, it never dawned on them that this new church could see it differently. And no one told them.

Eventually things got so bad, the pastor left. Looking back, he now realizes that in his desire to enfold people who had transferred, he understated or ignored the differences between his philosophy of ministry and that of the churches they came from.

It would have been better to candidly inform people of the differences up front. Sure, some would have left. But they would have left before they formed the webs of relationships that eventually made their leaving a tearing apart of the ministry.

That's why one primary goal for our pastor's class is to let everyone know what we are about. Rather than avoid controversial issues in fear of losing people, I hit the issues head on, in hopes of weeding out those people who are most likely to pick a fight in the future.

It sounds like the strategy would threaten new believers and seekers. Surprisingly, it doesn't. Nearly 50 percent of our first-time visitors have little or no church background, but they aren't turned off by my explanations of controversial issues. Why? Because whether we discuss worship style or lifestyle, political involvement or non-involvement, Calvinism or Arminianism, they don't see it as a controversial issue. Only longtime Christians see these as controversial issues. New believers want to know what we believe; it's only the folks from other churches who want to debate.

So I tell everyone up front, "Here's what we believe, and here's how you can expect us to behave in the future."

For a front-loaded pastor's class like this to succeed in preempting conflict, it has to get a high percentage of the new folks to attend. We do several things to make the class attractive to them.

The senior leader teaches the class. New folks always want to meet the head person. Those who have been around churches a long time aren't too interested in another class on the church. They'd prefer to send a letter of transfer and get on with it. But if I teach the class, they'll come, because they usually have a high need to know and be known by the pastor.

Many people have suggested I pass off the pastor's class. I've resisted. I realize that it's my presence that gets folks there, and no matter how tiring the classes might be, it's a lot less exhausting to weed out "problem people" on the front end than to deal with them in the middle of a major conflict.

It's held in a home. A second way we make the class more attractive is by holding it in a home. The home environment sets an informal, relational tone that disarms those who come with a strong agenda. In a home, people let their guard down. I'm no longer a pastoral figure on a platform; I'm a human being. That makes it easier for me to say something that goes against what a person has heard in another church. I've often watched in amazement as someone who came across as contentious in the lobby turned into a pussycat in our living room. The old adage says, "We fight with strangers and discuss with friends," so I make the environment as friendly and relational as I can.

It's held as often as possible. We hold the class often because I want people to take the class before they develop significant relationships. That way, no one settles in only to find out we are not the church he thought we were.

Surprisingly, few people who start the class leave the church. When they get a clear explanation, many who might have balked at differences climb aboard. They do so with a clear understanding of what they're getting into. The simple concept of the front-loaded pastor's class has virtually eliminated the conflict that arises when differing assumptions unexpectedly collide.

Preempting board conflict

Stopping conflict on the governing board requires a somewhat similar approach. We have to "guard the gate." It's too late to try to build unity after we've allowed a contentious or divisive person on the board.

Guarding the gate is delicate and dangerous. To pull it off, some key questions need to be answered.

1. What is the board's primary purpose? Is the primary purpose of a church board representation or leadership? Our answer significantly affects our potential for unity.

Many churches have opted for the representative model. It fits well with our American democratic principles, as well as one of our most cherished doctrines, the priesthood of believers. It insures that everyone has a chance to be heard, not just those who are powerful or well-connected. And it is one way to guarantee the board stays in touch with the needs of the congregation.

But in a board of representatives, the emphasis on representing various interest groups makes it difficult to justify keeping anyone off the board. From a representative perspective, any church member, no matter how divisive, has a right to lead.

It's also harder to come to a consensus when faced with controversial issues. By definition, a representative board seeks to protect minority opinions; this often results in a stalemate rather than a solution.

Finally, members of a representative board can start to see themselves as lobbyists. Jack may become the champion of traditional worship, while John defends the youth. Meanwhile, Susan fights for the rights of the Sunday school. Forgotten in the fray can be the most important thing: finding and carrying out God's will.

For these reasons, and others, I've become a strong advocate of a leadership-oriented board. Rather than figure out what everybody wants them to do, the members of a leadership board have only one focus: finding the best course of action and following it. When faced with a difficult decision, they ask first not "how will people react?" but "what does God want us to do?"

We help to preempt board conflict when we establish the board not as representatives but as leaders.

2. What are our minimum qualifications? In many churches, anyone who faithfully supports the church and works hard eventually finds himself or herself rewarded with a seat on the board. But passages such as Acts 6, 1 Timothy 3, Titus 1, and 1 Peter 5 make it clear there are spiritual qualifications, and they don't stop at being born again. They go way beyond to issues of character. That's not so much a matter of what a person knows as who he is.

Some of the most self-centered and divisive people in the church are highly gifted, know the Bible inside out, and exhibit a zeal that puts most people to shame. But when they get on your board, watch out!

As important as spiritual maturity is, though, to build a harmonious and effective leadership team there are other qualifications to look for:

—Is this person in basic agreement with our current philosophy of ministry?

—Will this person fit the leadership team we've already assembled?

If the answer to either is no, we've found it is a mistake to add the person to the board, no matter how spiritually mature he might be. There is no guarantee that spiritually mature people will work well together. When their convictions are strongly held and mutually exclusive (as were Paul and Barnabas's plans for dealing with John Mark), terrible things can happen. That's why it's important to have philosophical and relational qualifications as well as spiritual ones.

Imagine a pulpit committee deciding that the only qualifications necessary in a pastor were spiritual maturity and pastoral gifts. If they failed to consider the importance of a good fit with the congregation, they'd be asking for trouble. It seldom works, for example, to bring a blue-collar pastor into a white-collar congregation. Any wise pulpit committee, wanting to see a long and successful ministry, would obviously take these things into consideration. Is a good fit any less important when it comes to selecting lay leaders?

The more fully our qualifications are thought out, and the more strictly they're held, the greater will be our chances of experiencing a harmonious and healthy board.

3. Who should guard the gate? Every church has gatekeepers, the folks who nominate. Unfortunately, even churches that are careful when choosing a governing board can be casual when deciding who will control the initial selection.

I was in one church when an announcement was made asking anyone who wanted to serve on the nominating committee to show up the next Tuesday night in the fellowship hall. Other churches throw open the process to anyone willing to come to an all-church business meeting a month before the election. Those methods will never help preempt board conflict. Why? Because no matter how out of line a nomination may be, hardly anyone will be willing to speak out against it in a public meeting.

Choosing leaders is a very selective process. The nominating committee may be the most important committee in our church, because it serves like the headwaters of a river. If there's pollution upstream, it will eventually defile everything downstream.

One person, I believe, should always be involved in the process: the senior pastor. I realize that in some polities the pastor isn't allowed to take an official role in the nominating process, but even in those situations, a pastor can exercise a great deal of informal influence. By definition, a healthy and effective leadership team demands a good working relationship between the pastor and the board. It seems foolish to knowingly put someone on the board with whom the pastor is at personal or philosophical odds.

I'm not suggesting the pastor hand-pick board members. But I am suggesting the pastor be given the opportunity to speak out against the nomination of someone who will cause nothing but conflict.

That opportunity will do us no good, however, if we lack the courage to use it. I've talked to many pastors who served as an ex-officio member of the nominating committee but felt it was inappropriate to offer input. If I'm not willing to speak up, why be there? And if I'm there and stay silent, I'm not sure I have a right to complain later about the people on the board. The nominating committee is like a wedding: speak now or forever hold my peace.

I remember the first time I vetoed a nomination. A godly man, with a totally different philosophy of leadership than the board's, had been put forward by numerous members of the congregation. When our nominating committee came to his name, there was an uncomfortable silence. Everyone knew he wouldn't fit the leadership team. The problems would be philosophical, not spiritual, but problems nonetheless. After what seemed like an eternity, I swallowed hard and spoke up: "I don't think we should have him run; we'll spend all our meetings going around in circles." A couple of others were quick to agree. It was obvious that others felt as strongly as I did, but no one had said a word until I broke the ice.

Obviously, my decision to get involved in the process holds some risk. As one friend keeps asking, "How can you do that without being killed?" Actually, it has never created a problem, because we keep strict confidentiality. And in case members of the nominating committee forget that, I remind them before every meeting!

But I'll admit that getting involved in the selection process can be risky for a pastor. Secrets are hard to keep, and a pastoral veto has the potential for creating hurt. So I'm always careful with what I say and how I say it. I hope things I say won't be repeated, but I make sure I can live with them if they are.

My decision to become an outspoken member of the nominating committee didn't come easily. It went against the advice of some of my most trusted mentors. But, after prayerful and careful consideration, I figured I had little to lose. I'd witnessed the results of silence too many times.

Preempting staff conflict

A church staff, the third area, calls for yet another approach. It's essential to preempt conflict in the staff, for a divided staff can easily sidetrack a ministry.

When I met Ted, he was pastoring a rapidly growing church. The congregation seemed united and highly committed. Members were quick to bring friends and freely gave their money and time. Ted appeared to have close relationships with his board. In short, he had the kind of ministry that can make the rest of us struggle with jealousy.

There was just one problem. His staff was rife with conflict. Worse, he was unaware of the problem until it erupted in a coup attempt while he was away at a conference.

The coup failed. The instigator was fired, along with a couple of staff members who took his side. But the damage was done.

Shortly after the disaster, Ted admitted he had hired the wrong people. When it came time to add staff, Ted had hired helpers and "gofers" rather than leaders and co-workers.

A high-energy, hard driver, Ted loved much of the ministry, but like most pastors, he disliked parts of the job. Not wanting to waste time on those areas, he hired staff members. That took a load off his schedule, but it did nothing to build a ministry team.

By hiring helpers and gofers, Ted failed to bring aboard people he could respect and relate to. From the beginning, there was a large social and emotional distance between him and his staff. The thought of rooming with any of them for a week-long conference was depressing. They simply weren't his kind of people.

I made this same mistake with my first hire. As soon as we had the money, I hired someone to do all the things I no longer wanted to do. Then I wondered why I had a hard time connecting with him. I didn't realize that, by definition, anyone willing to do all the tasks I hated was not the kind of person I would draw close to.

If asked, I would have said I wanted a ministry team. But my actions showed that what I really wanted was to get out from under the load. It's no wonder that, over time, we grew further apart. Eventually, our distance turned into enough conflict that I had to let him go.

I now look for leaders or co-workers. At times, that has meant I've had to hold onto tasks I would rather jettison. But the trade-off for a ministry team of peers and co-workers is well worth it—as is the absence of conflict that comes when I am leading a team instead of a work crew.

Even with the best of people, conflict can still arise, of course. But there are things I can do to lessen the likelihood. The key one is to share not just the work but also the perks.

As the church's primary up-front leader, I receive a great deal of affirmation. It begins with the social status of the position. As a senior pastor I'm asked, "How is the ministry going?" As a youth pastor and associate, I was asked, "When are you going to get your own church?" As a senior pastor, everyone wants me to sit at the head table. As a youth pastor, few cared if I came.

Consider the traditional division of tasks between senior pastor and staff. Weddings, funerals, and preaching God's Word all bring attention, appreciation, and gratitude. But administration, visitation, recruitment, counseling, and youth ministries often suffer from a lack of notice by any except those directly involved in the program.

All of this can generate resentment and foster rapid turnover of staff. Some of this is just the way life is. But there are a number of things I can do to make sure the perks of ministry are more evenly divided.

In our case, it begins with titles. I'm no longer the only senior pastor at North Coast. Three other members of our staff have proven themselves qualified and able to carry out the work of a senior pastor, so we call them senior pastors.

I still function as the captain of the team, but the change in titles has been significant. Titles help define role, self-image, and social status. By calling the other senior-level staff members "senior pastors," I send a strong message both to them and the congregation.

Another area I watch is the working environment. Providing myself with a special parking space, a better computer, or nicer furniture would be culturally acceptable. But it would send a message I don't want to send.

I also allow others to have a prominent role (or the leadership role) in highly visible and rewarding events like weddings, baptisms, and funerals. I don't even preach all the time. Three out of ten Sunday mornings will find another of our gifted pastors in the pulpit.

What's been the result? In the last ten years, our turnover has been practically nil. More important, so has any significant staff conflict.

I had come to the church thinking that conflict and disunity were aberrations, that good people would get along if I could get them to sit down and work through the issues. But that's not what happens in the real world.

Conflict is inevitable, but it can be preempted and lessened in both its intensity and frequency. And that's well worth the effort.

8

Controlling the Flow of Information

*When God calls us to control information in the best
interest of others, he can also be trusted to
control the situation.*

—Jack Hayford

Several years ago we entered into a purchase agreement to buy a church building and property that also happened to house a private school. The purchase agreement specified that we would assume operation of the school and pledge to keep it open for at least a year and a half, giving the faculty and administration ample time to relocate. We were hoping to begin a school ourselves at some future date, so the agreement appeared to work to everyone's benefit.

The agreement stipulated that once we began making deposits to an escrow account, we were legally and financially in charge of the school's operations. All was going smoothly when disaster struck.

Routine inspections that had accompanied the standard closing procedures revealed a significant amount of asbestos in the school building. The previous owners had known that some asbestos material existed but had no idea of the extent or severity of the problem.

Our church leadership faced a serious dilemma: If we kept our word and opened the school on schedule, as the purchase agreement specified, we would risk endangering the health, and possibly the lives, of school children. If we backed out, citing the potential for high-risk health hazards from the asbestos, we could throw the faculty out of work in mid-August and break our pledge. The projected expense of removing the hazardous material exceeded one million dollars. It looked like a lose-lose situation.

It was an agonizing decision, but we could not in good conscience open the building for a new school year and expose the children to a significant health danger. We decided to slow down the purchase of the school. With the start of school only a few weeks away, the faculty stood between a rock and a hard place. And so did we. To outsiders, it looked as if a good deal had gone bad because we were fickle and untrustworthy.

When our actions were relayed to the school faculty by representatives of the other church, for whatever reason, the asbestos problem was never mentioned. The teachers were simply told the hard realities; we were backing out of the agreement, and they were losing their jobs.

Soon I began receiving scathing letters from disaffected (and unemployed) faculty members. Their correspondence reflected a mixture of confusion and astonishment. Why would a church such as ours, with a reputation for honesty and integrity, suddenly break our word and eliminate their jobs? They were unaware of the asbestos problem, so the only conclusion they could reach was that we lacked basic integrity.

I faced a crucial decision regarding confidentiality and the control of information.

Should I extricate our church from this messy situation by going public with the asbestos problem, and so publicly embarrass the other party? Or should I maintain confidentiality and wait for the other party eventually to explain the whole of the situation? The longer things dragged on, the worse the local press treated us.

I mentally rehearsed how to get out of this dilemma. I could simply call the faculty together and say, "Look folks, let me tell you the whole story. There is a high level of asbestos in this building. We didn't know that when we entered escrow, and apparently neither did your employers. We can't run a school that might cause children health problems now, or even fifteen or twenty years from now."

Had I done that, I suspect the majority of teachers would have supported our decision. I also suspect that the other church would possibly have been torn within by the anger our unexpected revelations would have produced, with the faculty confronting the church and demanding answers: "Why didn't you tell us about this problem?"

As I said, as if to add insult to injury, we were taking a thrashing in the local press. But whatever temptation I may have felt, it was never a serious option to break our silence and go public.

Instead, I met with the school faculty. I urged each of them to continue to trust our integrity, though circumstances suggested they should do otherwise. "We haven't changed character, though we have been forced to change course," I said. I believe they saw the pain on my face and heard the hurt in my voice. I never mentioned the asbestos problem.

In the following days, we gave each teacher a month's severance pay, though we were under no obligation to do so. God honored our actions in a remarkable fashion. Even though a new school year was nearly underway, every teacher secured a contract in another setting.

All in all, we took a beating at the time, but I'm glad I didn't say anything more than I did.

This situation was extreme, but the issue at stake wasn't all that unusual. Pastors are privy to the secrets of member's lives, secrets that often affect congregational life. We worry about how much to reveal to the entire congregation about individual staff salaries, or how much detail we should report to the church regarding a dishonest building contractor. Church leaders fail morally, and we wrestle with how specific to be with the congregation.

Sometimes these situations seem insoluble.

As we consider the control of information, what hazards should we be aware of? What information should we divulge and what should we restrict? How do we handle the pressure personally?

Dangers, toils, and snares

Controlling information is a process fraught with dangers, but it is vitally important to a ministry characterized by wisdom and integrity.

The first danger of secrecy is that it tends to carry in it the seeds of pride and power. I can control others by choosing what I will and will not tell them. If I know the board is going to cut one of two staff members, I could play them off one another: in separate conversations, I could see which one would be more willing to take a pay cut or shoulder more responsibilities—and then encourage the board to let the other one go.

Another destructive side of secrecy occurs when you are privy to information long before anyone else. As a public announcement is being made regarding a matter you knew about long ago, it's tempting to sit back and think, *I'm way ahead of everyone else. I'm important.* It gives you a temporary sense of significance, but something devious is happening in your soul. Pride is seeping into the deep wells of your personality.

Or I can manipulate people and wield extraordinary power by leading individuals to believe I'm sharing privileged information with only them. I simply have to call in one staff member and say, "Bill, I think so highly of you, let me tell you what's happening with . . ." and then drop the juicy tidbit. Then I could call in the next staff member and say essentially the same thing, assuring each person he or she is favored, creating a sense of loyalty based on a lying manipulation. That is evil.

Not all secrets are evil in and of themselves. Some are simply points of privacy, such as those that exist between a husband and wife. Even though our family is open, we don't tell our children everything. The dynamics of intimacy and deep relationships require some holding back.

The key is to search my own motives. Am I controlling information for the purpose of controlling people, or am I withholding information for the purpose of serving their best interests?

In guarding against the sinister use of secrets, I make sure I use no intrigues. If I share something with one member of the executive team, I share it with all the members of the team. That way, there are no hidden intrigues to divide the group.

For example, I once was faced with a decision as to how much to tell the staff when a particular staff member resigned in anger.

When this man first submitted his resignation, I called him in and said, "I'm not going to accept your resignation. That doesn't mean you can't resign, but I'm not going to accept your letter at this time. I'd like you to think it over for a few more days." He looked bewildered but agreed to follow my advice. A few days later I received a letter in which he reaffirmed his decision to leave.

This time I honored his wishes, and we set a date for severance. But just a week before he was to conclude his ministry with us, he unexpectedly withdrew his letter. The family circumstance that initiated his resignation had changed, so he reverted to my earlier offer to reject his resignation.

Yet, just six weeks later, he *again* gave notice he was resigning. He was disappointed that we did not dismiss the person we trained to take over his position. Even though we tried to work out an amenable integration of the two positions, he was unhappy, feeling somehow diminished (even though we had not demoted him). Now he was leaving, and not without bitterness toward the church, and I guessed sooner or later people would question why he left.

Our executive pastoral team (7 persons) is responsible for the overall flow of information in the church. We wrestled with the question of how much to tell the rest of the pastoral staff (20 additional persons) about his reasons for resigning.

We opted for sharing the facts with the whole pastoral team, not to defend ourselves but to avoid confusion. We explained the person's reasons for leaving, being sure to be forthright but gentle. I asked the pastoral team to hold this confidence, yet I was as candid as possible regarding the man's disappointment with the church. It helped lay the matter to rest.

I also try to develop a staff mindset. When I ask staff members to keep a confidence, I'm not being secretive. We're no clandestine cult where only the "initiated" know the inner workings of the group. Nor do I believe that the congregation is "too dumb" to be trusted with sensitive information.

Rather, I want my staff to see information as a trust, and they understand we limit it to reflect the wisdom and gentleness of Christ in dealing with others. My basic concern is to serve people's best interests.

A staff member sometimes will understandably ask, "May I share this with my spouse?" I never ask staff to withhold information from spouses. I have a high view of the oneness and sanctity of marriage. If a spouse volunteers to be exempted from hearing matters of confidentiality, that's his or her choice. If they decide as a couple not to burden each other with certain matters, that's fine. But I will never request—nor would I foolishly attempt to compel them to keep secrets from each other.

These two simple, common-sense steps work to detoxify secretiveness in a staff setting. I believe they also work to create trust and integrity.

Degree and timing

When do I share privileged information or decide to restrict it? When does a church member have a "right to know" sensitive or potentially embarrassing information? Whose permission do I need to go public?

In my twenty-three years of ministry at Church on the Way, I have encountered two episodes of serious moral failure involving staff. In both cases we controlled the flow of information until we were ready to relate the appropriate facts in sequence to the appropriate levels of church leadership.

In the first case, we waited nearly eight days until we were ready to share the tragic news with the congregation. Why the delay? We wanted to protect both the person involved and the congregation from unnecessary harm. Pacing was crucial to assure avoidance of dumping the failure on the body.

Through careful steps we provided differing levels of confidence, according to a person's responsibility in the church. The few who needed to know all the sorry details were told everything. Those who needed to know only the basic outline of the incident learned nothing more than that. We meticulously worked through the process so that by the time we informed the congregation, over two hundred leaders had been informed. We told the congregation that specific sexual immorality was the problem, and the offending pastor confessed it of his own volition. But the details were not elaborated.

There was another case: a report of indiscretions by a staff pastor that stopped short of complete moral failure. In this case, the staff member made a veiled proposition to a woman in the church.

Our lead administrator turned to the guilty but unconfessing pastor and said, "You're not telling us about the day you were sitting in a car with another woman." Our administrator specifically described the location of their meeting, the content of their conversation, and the color of the woman's clothing. Since the administrator had no prior knowledge of the incident, I concluded that the Holy Spirit had revealed the information to him. The guilty staff member literally collapsed and tearfully confessed his sin.

This was an awkward situation, yet we neither removed the pastor nor informed the congregation, but we did bring him under strong discipline. We were able to deal with the problem before his weakness led to a total moral failure.

We were able to correct another situation before it reached the general congregation. Our church ethos encourages hugging one another. Several people noticed that the embrace between one of our leaders and a woman in the congregation often seemed intimate rather than brotherly-sisterly. When it was brought to our attention, we informed only the executive committee, one elder and his wife, and we confronted the pastor privately. Why? Because the pastor hugging the woman had not yet crossed a line of transgression requiring public rebuke. Both love and wisdom demanded in this case we protect his reputation and guard his ability to minister in the future. Love covers a multitude of sins.

Does that imply we should hide transgressions? No. Love never glosses over sin. Love doesn't sweep things under the rug. My congregation will attest that when something demands public disclosure, we lead toward that in an open yet gracious way.

Controlling information in many cases is an act of love. "Covering" people in that case is not the same as a cover-up, but an act of nurture and protection.

Financial truths

Financial information is a particularly delicate area to talk about publicly. Here's how we deal with two such issues.

Salaries. Do church members have the right to know anything they wish about the operation of the church, including individual staff salaries? Does their giving to the church imply an ownership granting them free access to any and all information?

My answer to both questions is no.

Not everyone wants to know the yearly salaries of individual staff members. It's silly to force information on people who don't care to know what the youth pastor earns.

Rather than share salary information in a shotgun fashion, I use a need-to-know test with two parts. First, do people need to know this information because the staff member's salary is raising serious questions? Second, is this information pertinent to a leadership issue and being requested by an appropriately positioned leader in the church? If individuals meet either of these two criteria, I will consider sharing privileged salary information.

Generally, though, there's no compelling need or right for people to know how much a pastor takes home each month. First, in the workplace this is private information, and the church should be at least as courteous. Second, many people cannot appreciate the various considerations that went into this final package. Thus, I opt to keep the information confidential (and I'm supported by our church elders in doing so).

The average median income in our city for a family of four is approximately $35,000 per year. Naturally, many in our congregation make somewhat less. The church pastoral staff, however, is composed of highly trained, capable, and qualified professionals, and their remuneration reflects it.

Individual salaries made a matter of public record could easily provoke envy or bitterness. Few would argue they don't deserve their salaries, but those making significantly less could be tempted toward jealousy. To avoid that and other problems, we lump salary figures in one budget item in reporting.

When I report that figure at our annual business meeting, I often do so lightheartedly: "I'm sure all of you noticed that the staff salary line item exceeds a million and a half dollars this year. Half of that is my salary alone!"

Once the laughter subsides, I explain, "Though the figure looks enormous at first glance, keep in mind it supports over 100 families." I then detail the salary components, including our medical, dental, retirement, and other benefits. Once people understand the various costs, they agree our salaries are equitable.

I did on one occasion, however, reveal my own salary figure to a sizable but select group within the congregation. It was during the televangelist scandals of the late 1980s. To ensure people of my integrity, I felt at least a few key people should know what I earned.

I scheduled a series of backyard desserts at the parsonage. We invited about thirty people at a time (a total of 300), selecting these people based on how they served in the body and how vital it was they have full confidence in our financial dealings. They hadn't had doubts, but they were greatly reassured.

On one other occasion, we made pastoral staff salaries a public matter. During the depths of a recession, our pastoral team asked not to receive a salary increase that year, expressing a concern for many in the church who were losing jobs. I shared that piece of information from the pulpit during a morning sermon. You could just feel the appreciation of the people. It confirmed in their minds the shepherding, servant spirit of these men and women, and that the pastors existed to serve, not exploit the church.

In no other business does everyone know what everyone else is paid. Why, then, require church staff to divulge something so intensely personal? Justice, equity, and fairness demands that church employees receive the same considerations members of the congregation enjoy.

Financial records. When an individual in the congregation *demands* access to financial records but has no basis for an accusation of mismanagement of funds, I know I'm facing a spiritual, and not managerial, battle. In such cases, the inquiry is not usually a quest to affirm integrity but to gain control.

I keep such unreasonable requests to a minimum by focusing on the basics. I occasionally remind the congregation that the Holy Spirit controls the church, not any one person or group of people—and certainly not me. I reiterate that we conduct our affairs on a biblical model of conferred authority. When the church elects deacons and leaders, the people authorize them to use their office to distribute funds as best they see fit.

That doesn't mean individuals can't raise legitimate questions. We have an open-door policy.

"Never feel that asking a question insinuates you lack trust in the leadership," I assure our members. "In fact you may ask any question you wish of our financial administrator or other staff members." At most three or four people take us up on that invitation in a year, and they are received with courtesy and trust. Almost always they inquire not out of doubt but out of a desire to investigate ways to help.

Confidence-keeping loneliness

As I mentioned at the beginning of the chapter, withholding information out of a sense of integrity can exact a high price. We will be misunderstood and misrepresented. During the crisis of closing the school, about a hundred of our people seemed to "evaporate" by starting to attend one of our "daughter" churches.

Watching that exodus cut deeply into my soul. Though few ever said so directly, I knew they questioned our fidelity. They were bewildered. (Sheep are easily scattered when a shepherd can't raise his voice.)

Only my wife knew the deep valley I passed through during those days. Alone, I agonized; I prayed; I wept.

During the darkest of those days, the Lord did a remarkable work in my life. He gave me a dream one evening that began to restore my peace of mind. Then, while I was reading the Psalms one night, a portion of Scripture came alive in such a powerful way I suddenly sat up wide-eyed. I couldn't stop reading. With tears in my eyes I sensed the Holy Spirit saying, "I'm going to take care of this. It's all going to work out." My unanswered questions dissolved in the seas of his assurance and presence.

The asbestos eventually was removed from the building, and we completed the purchase. We did not have to jeopardize the rights and reputation of either congregation.

The other pastor later thanked me for our conduct during the crisis. Almost two years later, word about what really happened leaked out little by little. I received several apologies from those who had misjudged us. I learned that God honors integrity, even when it hurts.

9

Bringing New Leaders Up to Speed

New leaders can change everything.

—R. Steven Warner

In 1975 I served as the pioneer pastor of a new church. From our mother church, a large congregation with a long heritage, we inherited about fifty people and some experienced leaders. Although this was my first pastorate, those leaders and I worked fairly well together. Frankly, I couldn't understand other pastors' complaints about troublesome board members. Working with leaders wasn't so tough!

Four years later, however, all board members, who were now fully experienced, rotated off the board because of constitutional requirements. We started our fifth year with an entirely new set of leaders. Most were fairly new Christians and inexperienced at church leadership.

I felt the difference immediately. The new leaders thought they needed to straighten out what the earlier leaders had done. Leading our council meetings was like driving with the brakes on. There was always an edge to things.

One November day I decided to visit a member's home. I knocked on the door, and when it opened I found not only the person I came to visit but two of our deacons and another lay person from the church. Spread out on the table, I saw to my astonishment, were some of the church books, minutes, and other confidential papers.

I asked what they were doing. After a bit of stuttering and stammering, I was told they had some concerns about the way certain things were going in the church. They told me they had planned to call and ask me to come over to settle a few things.

At that point, it was obvious that settling their concerns was not only a good idea but essential. I called a man in the church to come serve as a witness to our conversation.

That night we talked for several hours, fairly calmly considering the circumstances, but little was resolved. By February, when the church again elected leaders, three of the four board members had resigned. The previous leaders had been off a year, and constitutionally they could again be elected. A serious crisis was averted, but all of us learned from the experience.

I'd learned that *new leaders can change everything*. I decided then to develop a plan to bring them up to speed.

First gear: briefing

People with no experience in church leadership generally have low expectations about their church responsibilities. So to get new leaders up to speed, I must help them understand from the start— not when a problem arises—what I expect from them and what they can expect from me. Here's how I do that.

Interview before nomination. I interview potential nominees to our leadership council before we allow the nomination committee to put up their names for election. And I've learned I need to ask questions I might assume are unnecessary.

In one interview the man under consideration had cleared every hurdle with ease. He had sterling character and ability. For some reason, toward the end of the interview, I asked, almost as an aside, if he had any controlling habits.

To my surprise he admitted that he had been smoking (though had just quit). He had suffered a reversal in his business and reverted to his cigarette habit.

I suggested that this indicated he was experiencing significant stress.

"It might not be a good idea for you to become a deacon this year," I said, "but let's make it a goal for you to stabilize your life and be off cigarettes in a year, and we'll reconsider you then."

In one year he did become a deacon and served effectively for four years, and now as an elder for another four.

Interview candidate and spouse. In our pre-nomination interviews, a senior church leader and I meet with the husband and wife together (if the person is married). By that time we feel they are qualified, and they know the purpose of the interview. The interview lasts from thirty minutes to an hour. We're friendly but serious, because we want to communicate how important church leadership is. We sit around a table at church, not in a restaurant where there will be interruptions.

I slowly read to them the relevant passage from First Timothy and ask if this describes them. I then ask the spouse if this describes his or her partner. I'll ask how stable their marriage is, whether they have prayer and devotions as a family, and how their children are doing. I quiz them about church membership issues, doctrinal matters, personal finances, personal Bible study, and their giving to our church and missions.

"Suppose something doesn't go the way you'd like during a leadership meeting," I'll ask. "What would be your response? Would you be willing to support the decision of the group?"

Then we discuss time commitments. I ask if they are prepared to continue to attend worship regularly, to participate in prayer meetings and other special meetings. One key question: "How much time do you think it will take each week to be a good deacon?"

No one is perfect. But if people are going through a difficult time with their marriage or having more than the usual challenges raising their kids, we do them no service to nominate them as leaders.

This whole process may sound intimidating, but people tell me later that it was at this interview they realized the seriousness of church leadership. Leadership is about servanthood and responsibility, not prestige.

Agree to key principles. Church leaders need to agree on how they will work together. At the first meeting of the new leaders, I present our "leadership covenant," the principles we have followed as leaders in the past. We discuss it point by point, pausing after each to see if everyone can agree to it. I let them know that, just as at a marriage ceremony, I want them to speak now or forever hold their peace.

I say things like, "We need to be acquainted with those in the church, especially with the needs of the widows, the legitimately poor, and those who are out of work. Could we all agree to keep our eyes and ears open for that?

"If I'm going to be out of town, I will always notify you. You won't come to church and find I delegated the service to an assistant pastor. I will always let you know well ahead so that you will not only appear informed but also be informed. I'm asking you to do the same. If you're going to miss a service, I would like you to call me and let me know. Can we agree to that?"

This covenant is not a surprise. Most of this has been covered in our pre-nomination interview, so they have had plenty of time to consider whether they can agree. If anything, I want to overstate my expectations.

Occasionally someone says he can't fulfill one of the points. Two of our men, for example, commute a long distance to our church, and getting to our 8:00 A.M. Saturday prayer meeting is hard. Given those circumstances, I encourage them to come as often as they can.

Second gear: performance

It's not enough to agree to the covenant. Once the agreement is made, I have to monitor performance.

Take note of broken promises. One summer, about every fourth Sunday, a deacon called one of the other elders and said, "Tell the pastor I can't come tonight." Supper had burned or he was taking a motorbike trip or he got caught meeting his daughter's boyfriend's parents or . . .

At first I let it go. I have a saying: Once is a mistake, twice is a coincidence, and three times is a pattern.

Finally I picked up the phone. "I missed you Sunday night," I said. "I need you here. You're my right-hand man. You've got to quit taking off whenever you want."

We had a good talk. He was honest; I was honest. I wasn't heavy-handed, and he seemed to understand. (By the way, this man is now one of our most committed leaders.)

If our leaders' covenant is going to have any meaning, I have to confront people in love and with understanding when they fail to follow through. If I don't, that pattern probably will never be broken.

Pace the performance. We assign an elder or deacon of the week. Like doctors on call, leaders work hard and invest extra time for a week, but then they are off, so they don't get burned out.

We have five deacons, so they're on one week and off five. The week they're on, I brief them on what they will be doing on Sunday and any other tasks I'm aware of for the week ahead.

On Sunday they have responsibilities in each service, such as leading in prayer or giving the announcements. They arrive thirty minutes before church on Sunday morning, work with me and the staff until the end of the second service, and help close the building. Then they help in the evening service. Having leaders up front enhances their office in the eyes of the congregation.

During the week, if I make hospital visits or see a shut-in, I'll often take them with me. They may also handle other emergencies that arise. Not only are the deacons helping to minister, we get to know each other better, and they can see what ministry is about.

Third gear: team spirit

The greatest danger facing new leaders is to fall into disunity. I tell new leaders that unity is job one; if we don't have it, we won't get any other job done. Here are some of the ways we help new leaders pick up on our team spirit.

Give weight to a leader's vote. In general, new leaders will learn to seek unity when the decision-making system rewards unity. At the outset I say our aim is for full agreement in all decisions. If even one leader feels strongly against something, we wait for a month. If the leader still has objections, we wait another month, or however long it takes until we have a unanimous spirit.

Does that give new leaders too much power? Can one person be an obstructionist? Yes, but I tell them, "If you feel strongly about an issue, God may be speaking through you; but if God is not speaking through you, you could be holding up what God wants to do today. So you better pray hard about it."

I've never seen anybody use the vote merely to hold up the rest of the group.

Warn of initiation rites. One older man in our church doesn't believe in tithing. He buttonholes every new leader when he starts and drills into him his opinion on tithing.

His aggressiveness upsets some of the new leaders. "I always thought this guy was such a wonderful man," some have said.

Every church has dissenters. We tell them the confrontation is standard. In fact we've kidded about it: "Have you gotten initiated yet? If he hasn't gotten to you yet, you aren't really in."

Other behind-the-scenes happenings can disconcert a new leader. I warn them ahead of time that people will disappoint them, that they will not be able to come to church with the bliss of not knowing so-and-so has a marital problem or another person is vigorously critical of some church policy. Conflict can knock new leaders for a loop.

It's like a tourist who visits Disney World and then gets a job there and goes behind the scenes. Enjoying the show at the Magic Kingdom is totally different from seeing workers putting on their makeup and memorizing lines.

So I discuss Matthew 18 with leaders. "Here's my promise to you," I say. "If I have a problem with you, you won't hear about it through somebody else; you'll hear it straight from me. I want you to do the same for me. And I will give you the benefit of the doubt because I'm probably the one who didn't understand or who miscommunicated."

Sometimes people will come to me with a complaint about a leader. I will always stand up for the leader. I may later talk to the leader in private about something, but I will support the person in front of others. If I expect leaders to support me, I've got to support them.

I coach new leaders that when people come to them to criticize the pastor, they should not accept it. They should interrupt a detractor and say, "Excuse me, but you're talking to the wrong person. You need to go talk to the pastor. I guarantee you he will give you a good hearing. If he doesn't, I'll go with you next time."

Be sure to minister to leaders' spouses. During a leader's first year, I try to keep abreast of how things are going at home. I can't compete with the last voice an elder or deacon hears every night. If the spouse isn't on our side, we're in trouble. A leader's spouse makes significant sacrifices, so I'm careful to tell the spouse things like "I want you to know how much we appreciate your loaning your spouse to us."

In a recent leaders' meeting at my home, we invited all the

spouses, and I gave a gift to each one. "I'm giving you this gift," I said, "to show you we appreciate the sacrifice you make for your spouse to serve as a leader. If his serving in the church ever causes a family problem, come and see me, because we don't want to do anything that will hurt your family."

Fourth gear: experience

The chairman of a bank was retiring, and a young man he had mentored asked him, "In a nutshell, how did you become a success in the business world?"

"That's easy," the retiring chairman said. "I made good decisions."

The young man nodded. "But how did you learn to make good decisions?"

"Experience," replied the old man.

"Where did you get the experience?"

The old man paused a moment, pursed his lips, and said, "I made bad decisions."

New leaders in church will never get past second gear if they aren't given the opportunity to make mistakes and learn from them.

One way, then, that we speed the growth of new leaders is to be patient as they try new responsibilities and keep giving them jobs even after they have failed.

One of our new leaders gave announcements during worship. He did great in the first service. But in the second service, he could hardly remember his own name. Afterward he told me, "It was easygoing in the first service, but I got nervous as all get-out in the second. Will I get over that?"

"No," I said. "I've been doing this for twenty-five years, and I still get butterflies. But you learn how to think straight even though you have butterflies. It'll come to you. Don't sweat it; you did okay."

I once took a young leader with me to the hospital to visit a woman who had cancer. She was a real character who had been taking chemotherapy and had lost all her hair. She had five wigs sitting on foam heads in her room. Another wig was askew on top of her head.

As we walked in, she said in her best show-and-tell voice, "Oh, Pastor, have you seen my colostomy bag?"

I said, "No, but I'm sure Bob would like to." Before I could say
another word, she ripped back the sheets and showed him her bag.

Bob grabbed his mouth and ran into the hall.

He never came back.

The lady kept asking, "Where's Bob?"

"He's new at this," I said.

When I finished my visit, I found Bob in the lobby. "Is it always
like this?" he moaned.

"Every day, Bob, every day. Let's go, buddy, we've got another
visit to make."

Bringing leaders up to speed isn't always pretty, but it's always
interesting. And it's an essential part of building the church.

10

Rooting Out Causes of Conflict

Conflict doesn't usually emerge from a single cause.

—Speed Leas

One California pastor found himself at odds with two men in his congregation. The problem was—well, that *was* the problem—this pastor couldn't figure out what exactly the problem was.

Certainly, a host of issues divided the pastor and the two men: They thought he preached too much on sin; he thought they lived by cheap grace. He thought clapping for the choir was inappropriate in worship; they, as choir members, thought clapping was a contemporary way of affirming the choir.

But some personal issues were involved as well: The pastor preached a sermon about homosexuality only to discover later that one of these men, who had a homosexual son, was hurt by the pastor's "insensitive" comments.

And then there was politics: These men had wielded a great deal of power in the church's short history. For some twenty years, they had set the tone for the church: it would be an urbane, liberal, theologically diverse church. The pastor, however, was calling people to a more personal and Bible-centered faith.

The differences erupted one evening in a personnel committee meeting, of which these two men were a part. They lambasted the pastor, and the pastor tried to defend himself. Neither side budged an inch.

For weeks afterward, the pastor tried to repair these relationships, but he couldn't figure out where the main problems lay, in theology, personalities, or politics.

What this pastor slowly realized was a basic truth of church conflict: conflict doesn't usually emerge from a single cause, and understanding the variety of causes is crucial to dealing with conflict.

As I've worked with congregations over the years, I've found that conflict has its roots in, among other things, personal shortcomings (of people and pastor), unsolved problems, and congregational patterns of behavior.

Individual shortcomings

We often assume that the church's problems are caused by the shortcomings of certain people—and that's all there is to it! This may not be entirely correct, but there certainly is a degree of truth to it: many times it is cantankerous or ornery folk who make church life miserable.

I've found three shortcomings in people that cause church conflict.

Fear. Many church conflicts begin when people become anxious about what is happening (or not happening) in the church. When anxiety, a certain level of which is healthy in organizations, turns into worry and fear, people begin to lose perspective about what is actually going on; *then*, you get conflict.

In such cases, fear begins to act on the church as does pollen on a person with hay fever. Hay fever sufferers are hypersensitive to certain allergens. When these substances enter their bodies, their immune systems react so strongly that they become miserable. Their bodies' devices, intended to protect them, end up harming them.

So it is with fear. When we become aware of a problem, we sometimes overreact, and the problem becomes worse than what we feared in the first place. We act in fear and lose our ability to think clearly and understand circumstances accurately. We make decisions or act in a way that we later regret.

I worked with one pastor who had gotten wind of dissatisfaction among some of the elected church leaders. He assumed they would try to remove him from his position.

His response was swift and massive: he talked to many in the congregation, organizing groups to support him; he spoke with his bishop; he did not reappoint perceived opponents to positions of influence.

His reaction, however, was overkill given the level of concern brought by the "dissenters," and his response merely aggravated the dissatisfaction in the congregation.

Fortunately, two things happened that radically changed this pastor's reaction.

First, his bishop assured him that he would not allow the church to fire him. The bishop said, "You are guaranteed this position; there is virtually nothing they can do to remove you from the church. Don't worry about it."

Second, the pastor and the dissatisfied members sat down together, and under the guidance of a skilled denominational official, discussed their cold war. The pastor learned that these people did not want him to leave the church; they simply had concerns about worship and administration.

Needs. Sometimes our needs conflict with the needs of others, and that's when church conflict can begin.

Such conflict nettles all relationships. Recently, I was in the dumps because a church training program I had organized for a congregation had floundered. At the same time, my wife, a writer of computer manuals, had just been asked to write a sizable manual for a large computer company.

She was high and wanted to celebrate; I was low and wanted attention. Needless to say, we didn't meet each other's needs.

In a church setting, because of the variety of needs, such conflicts become complex. Some people are desperate for Christian education for their children. Others need the church to offer more recovery groups. Some people find themselves struggling to keep their marriages together; others can't understand why the church isn't doing more for blacks in South Africa. Some want more praise, others more silence, still others more sermon—all in the same worship service! And on it goes.

In most instances, if the church is large enough, people go off and "do their thing," satisfying their needs in one segment of the church. But sometimes churches find themselves having to play one need off of another; they lack the money, people, or time to please everybody. In such cases, I suggest congregations ask themselves:

—Is it possible for one group to defer getting its needs met?

—Is it possible to compromise? Perhaps each group can get some or most of what it needs.

—Are relationships strong enough to weather the possibility of one group not getting their needs met?

In one Illinois church, some leaders felt the worshipers were suffering because of a deteriorating organ. Others felt children were suffering because of poor classroom facilities. In this case, the worshipers got their organ, and the others got the promise of new educational facilities in the future.

This situation also had political and theological dimensions, obviously, which needed to be addressed. But at the heart of the conflict also stood human needs: to worship, to learn. To ignore those needs would have been to ignore one dimension of the problem.

Sin. Although many books on the psychology of conflict omit this category, in my experience, it's a principle cause of church dust-ups.

I don't have to read the apostle Paul's words on the sinful nature to know that from time to time a voice within me screams that *my* needs and values are the most important, no matter what! Others can fend for themselves! I readily see how others act selfishly, but I am oblivious to my own selfishness. This attitude only intensifies conflict.

In the case of the California pastor, he clearly saw the judgmental attitude and greed for power in the two men who opposed him. What he didn't see for months, he admits, was his own arrogance and self-righteousness.

The only way to deal with sin, of course, is through repentance. Often that's difficult to do in the middle of a conflict. But if each party can at least recognize the likelihood that their own sin is probably contributing to the conflict, it brings a measure of humility to the process, which helps keep conflict from mushrooming beyond control.

"Out there" problems

Individual shortcomings come from within people, but problems to solve come to the church from "out there." Problems to solve include such things as how much money should be given to missions, whether to buy a photocopy machine, or what stand to take on abortion.

Such problems fall into various categories, each of which suggests a different approach to finding a solution.

Issues. In your garden-variety problem to solve, the disputants have alternatives. They're not stuck with an either/or dilemma but have a variety of choices. For example, in answer to the question "What shall we do with the $10,000 donated to 'upgrade the church office'?" there are many options: buy a new computer, buy a new photocopier, buy new office furniture for the pastor's study, redo the reception area, and the like.

Further, each option has its own issues: What type of computer, and how large? Which style of furniture? What color paint for the walls?

Basic problem-solving techniques are usually the best way to deal with this form of conflict:

—Clearly define the problem.

—Agree on the problem's definition.

—Explore alternative solutions.

—Develop criteria for selecting one of the alternatives.

—Choose one of the alternatives either by collaboration or by negotiation.

In a *collaborative choice*, both or all of the parties essentially agree. Each party's needs are fully discussed, and solutions are sought that address each party's concerns.

In the example above, $10,000 won't go far enough to get the secretary a new photocopier *and* the pastor a new office *and* the church treasurer a new computer. So in a collaborative choice, the secretary gets the photocopier and the pastor new office furnishings. In addition, the pastor trades his new office computer for the treasurer's (the pastor only uses the computer for word processing, and the old computer does that well enough for him).

This is often called a "win-win solution." However, it may be that not all of the parties fully "win," but only that everything possible has been done to arrive at a mutually satisfactory solution.

In a *negotiated choice*, the parties agree on a solution, but there is less commitment to finding solutions that fully satisfy the needs of each party. In negotiation, parties assume they will have to give up one thing to get another.

In the Illinois church that decided for the new organ, the Christian education people were able to get the church board to see the gravity of their needs, but they had to delay for three or four years any improvements in the church school wing.

Dichotomies. In a dichotomy, the possible solutions are limited to two. The choice facing the congregation absolutely excludes the possibility of satisfying both sides of a controversy.

Typical dichotomies: Should the church change locations? Should the church leave the denomination? Should the organist be replaced?

The answer in each case has to be either yes or no. Sometimes it is possible to soften the decision by throwing in something of value to those who "lose," but with truly dichotomous questions, there is clearly a winner and loser.

In one church of about 1,800 members, the dichotomy centered around the work of the youth pastor, who was about to be fired. He had made a personal impact on a number of high school youth, but overall attendance was down. Naturally, those parents whose kids were being helped, although small in number, were happy with his work and were stunned to learn that his job was threatened. Other parents could see in the young man only a lack of organization and drive.

The personnel committee had tried to keep the problem from becoming a dichotomy: at first they had called in the youth pastor and told him the concerns most parents were expressing, encouraging him to make changes. But the youth pastor wouldn't or couldn't. He finally had to be let go (with three months severance pay to soften the blow to him and his supporters).

Dichotomies are much more difficult to deal with than issues. Losers can become angry, and they tend not to be committed to the decisions. Sometimes they sabotage agreements or leave a church when they don't get their way.

Actually, anyone who is sensitive to relationships—that includes most people in a church—doesn't like the tension dichotomies cause. We don't like to see people alienated from one another.

There are two ways, though, to lessen the fallout.

1. You can convince. Leaders can make convincing arguments that cast a new vision of the problem and so entice the disputants along.

Or leaders can convince the opposing group to go along by taking seriously its objections and concerns. When there is a modicum of trust in a church, leaders can help people explore and discuss the issues, and sometimes this process unearths the specific needs of the opposition. Once these needs are expressed openly, the impact of the final decision may be muted; the group may still disagree, but it knows it has been heard.

2. Pay attention to jots and tittles. The pastor of one church was given informal authority to approve infant baptisms. He would interview the couple who wanted their infant baptized, determine if it was appropriate, and then set a date. Later he would get the board's official permission, but that was a mere formality.

One time, however, a young couple who didn't attend church and were merely living together asked him if he would baptize their child. The pastor balked, but the man was on the church rolls as a member; according to church law, he had the right to have his child baptized.

The pastor knew, however, that the final decision for baptisms rested in the hands of the board—only it could refuse the man his right. Rather than exerting his informal prerogatives, the pastor decided to do everything according to the church constitution.

He took the decision to the board, explained the facts, made no recommendation, and asked for the board's decision. The board voted against the baptism, and the pastor relayed their decision to the man and his girlfriend.

The couple was not pleased, but they couldn't fault the pastor or church for anything other than disagreeing with them. If you have to make a decision and you can't get full agreement, at least proceed according to civil and church law.

Value Differences. Value differences are not seen as often in churches as are issues and dichotomies, because congregations are experts at making sure that these types of problems do not come to the fore. Congregations instinctively know that a values conflict is tortuous to work through and the likelihood of finding agreement low.

Some church members, for example, might object to any divorced person being in leadership positions; others believe that forgiveness of divorce extends to letting people lead the congregation. Or some members might believe that a minimum of 10 percent of the church's budget should be designated for overseas missions; others believe local missions should be the first priority.

It's not easy for people to dispute about values. First, people's identities rest on their deeply held values; so they do not change easily.

Also, especially in churches, people are admonished to maintain their values, to refuse to compromise what they hold dear; we regularly hold up for admiration the great martyrs of faith who remained true to the faith.

So with values, much is at stake. If values come up, people are not inclined to say, "I am open to listen to your argument; I am ready to change my mind if necessary." People are more interested in getting their way because their way is "right."

When faced with value differences, the church has a few options:

1. Reframe the problem. One church was struggling to decide whether people should be allowed to speak in tongues in worship. The issue distressed the church's leaders because the choices were virtually dichotomous, and they didn't want to split the church over the issue.

A third party, however, tried to help the situation by pointing out that people in the church had become alienated from one another; they were no longer communicating as they had in the past. This group managed to change the issue from speaking in tongues to how people should communicate better.

You can also reframe the issue by helping people to explore their areas of agreement: their common commitment to Jesus as Lord, their love for the church, their deep respect for the contributions made by their opponents. Then, looking at what holds them together, they can work more irenically on the disagreement.

Frankly, reframing the issue doesn't really deal with the issue. If the issue is not that important, reframing works. But if the issue is a major concern to people, reframing is a short-lived strategy. The problem will present itself again, perhaps in a more vehement form, because the problem has lingered, perhaps festered, without resolution.

2. Partition. To partition means to ensure that the disputing parties do not share the same space at the same time (at least at certain critical times). In the case of the controversy over appropriate behavior in worship, those more charismatic in worship would meet at one hour and those less demonstrative would meet at another.

I have used this technique with budgets as well as programs. A congregation in Iowa had a dispute over how to spend their missions money. One group felt all of it should go to the denomination's missions, mostly hospitals, self-help projects, and education. Another group felt strongly that this money should be used primarily for evangelism.

Since they couldn't agree, we decided that the church should have two missions committees, each with an equal share of the outreach monies of the church, each deciding how it would spend its share of the money. Neither party was fully happy with this solution, but it was better than any other alternative they could think of at the time.

3. Agree not to deal with the issue. Sometimes not making any decision is actually the best decision. As long as the church acknowledges this openly, it's an honest way to deal with values differences.

One church had for fifteen years shared the facilities of another congregation. In that time, about half the congregation became convinced that this was the church's unique identity: a congregation that was a good steward of its resources, a church that was people, not buildings.

The other half of the congregation pined away for a building. They believed the church would go nowhere unless it had its own physical identity.

When a new pastor came to the church, he kept getting different messages about which way to lead the church. He finally organized a goal-setting process in which this issue was discussed—and then dropped. People realized that there was no consensus on the issue, and so they thought it best to leave things the way they were for the time being.

4. Get a "divorce." If all efforts to come to agreement have failed, and the issue is deeply held values, then one group may simply have to leave. It's a solution that is terribly costly, but sometimes it's better for everyone concerned.

The two men who disputed with the California pastor eventually left the church. When they did, everyone breathed a sigh of relief. The issues between them and the pastor were never solved, but the church was able to get back to ministry, and the two men and their families were able to find a church home where they could better serve.

Behavior patterns

Students of family life have noted that behaviors of family members are often practiced apart from the conscious decisions of individuals themselves. Divorce, substance abuse, and suicide are notable examples of repetitive patterns that frequently move in families from one generation to the next. Social behavioral patterns are often subtle. For example, when I was on the debate team in high school, there was an unwritten rule in our debating club, and certainly in formal debates themselves, that personal attack and rigorous challenge of everything the other said and did was fair game. So I found myself often, in the context of the debate team, challenging, attacking, putting others down with relish and abandon. But I certainly never acted that way at home or in other social contexts.

Likewise, each church has unwritten rules about how it goes about disagreeing. In one church, every squabble is immediately taken to the pastor for his adjudication. In another church, disputes are publicly avoided and handled by gossip. But however the dispute is handled, it is not necessarily done consciously. People have learned over the years how to handle congregational conflict, and they may not even be able to articulate exactly what they do.

But often, especially when the pattern of behavior remains unexamined, it terribly damages a church's life.

I worked with a congregation that called itself a "Matthew 18 church." They said they managed conflict by following the guidelines of Jesus as laid out in Matthew 18. Those guidelines spell out a process whereby a person who has sinned is confronted first by an individual, and if the "sinner" remains unconvinced, then by individuals not involved in the dispute, and if still not convinced, then by the entire congregation.

Unfortunately, this "Matthew 18 church" simply used this method to vent anger at one another. An angry member would seek out a person who annoyed him, berate the person for his rude and thoughtless conduct, and then escape from further conversation. People didn't seek to understand one another, let alone compromise. It was simply hit-and-run.

This behavior didn't result merely from people's anger or frustration or personality conflicts. A large part of the problem was "institutional"—this was the way the church had handled conflict for years. No one knew how to do it any differently.

Helping a congregation move beyond their usual patterns is difficult at best. It calls for two courses of action.

Notice the behavior. The people need to see what they're doing and how it's destructive to the church.

Usually groups need help from someone outside their institution to figure out what's going on. The outsider will notice patterns to which an insider is blind.

Learn new behaviors. Once a congregation is aware of how it normally handles conflict, it's less likely to continue the pattern. The game is up; people know what's coming next; they also know that it's an unproductive way to proceed.

Still, learning new behaviors is not easy. I remember when I first learned about active listening (responding to people with word and posture to assure them of my interest), I was thrilled. Immediately, I knew exactly what I was supposed to do, but actually doing it was terribly awkward at first. I needed a good deal of practice, with feedback from a person with a practiced eye, to develop sufficient skill.

If a congregation has learned to deal with disagreement by gossip or attack or whatever, it's going to take some preaching, teaching, and perhaps seminars by outsiders to show people new ways of relating. And sometimes it takes a gentle but direct confrontation of people who continue in the old ways.

One pastor was becoming frustrated with the way his congregation dealt with him about disagreements; people would talk behind his back, and he would have to fish and fish to discover the substance of people's concerns.

So he diplomatically pointed out this behavior in newsletters and in sermons, explaining how much energy and time this behavior wasted, and how many hurt feelings it could engender. He also told his people that if they had a problem with the church, rather than gossiping about it, they should simply write him a note or tell him directly. He admitted that he might not be able to deal with their complaint satisfactorily, but at least he would be aware of what people were thinking, and overall, that would help him be a more sensitive pastor.

Well, the pattern continued, especially by three or four key men in the church. Then one day, the pastor happened to run into one of these men while making a hospital call. He asked the man, thirty years his senior, to have a cup of coffee with him.

After a few pleasant amenities, the pastor came to the point. "Stan, I understand you've not been happy with the change in the order of worship."

Stan was silent.

"And I know you've been talking to John and Jack about your complaints."

Stan squirmed.

"I'm going to be straight with you, Stan." The pastor leaned forward and looked Stan directly in the eye. "I would be helped and the church would be helped if, when you've got a problem with the way I'm doing something, you come to me directly. Complaining to others about my decisions has got to stop. It undermines my ministry and demoralizes the church."

Stan mumbled a weak agreement, and soon after he became a strong, albeit not uncritical, supporter of the pastor. The habit of congregational gossip had been dealt a severe blow.

Church conflict makes a church feel as if it's being swept along by a raging flood. And often it is that way. But if the church can discover the various and sundry tributaries that feed into the conflict, they can turn flood waters that destroy into a river that gently but powerfully moves them downstream.

11

Seven Reasons for Staff Conflict

*When seen for what it is, much conflict can be easily
handled and turned to constructive ends.*

—Wayne Jacobsen

Tension in multiple-staff churches is caused either by the ego of a
staff member or the incompetent management of the senior pastor."

I wish to expose that statement for what it is—a myth. Staff members are just not that rebellious nor senior pastors that incompetent. Assigning blame at either point misses, in most cases, the real issue and only perpetuates conflict.

The vast majority of staff pastors I've spoken with, though they admit the reality of conflict, find it neither overwhelming nor everpresent. Deep joy in ministry and affection for their pastor undergirds their labor. Personally, leaving my staff position was the hardest decision I ever made, knowing how much my relationship with my pastor would change once I was fifty miles down the road instead of fifteen feet up the hall.

No management system or technique can ensure an absence of conflict. In fact, I'm not so sure eliminating conflicts is desirable. Conflict often indicates healthy growth processes are at work. Too often, however, failure to recognize the source of conflict and to handle it appropriately can lead to destruction.

In conversations with pastors and staff members, seven major areas of conflict continue to surface, none of which has anything to do with staff submission or pastoral mismanagement. When seen for what they are, each can be easily handled and the conflict turned to constructive ends.

1. Generational differences

"I've tried to get my pastor to use contemporary choruses in worship with more spontaneity, but he is too locked into old traditions."

"These young kids think they know how everything ought to run. Don't they think we've learned anything after years of ministry?"

"When I was their age, I was pastoring the smallest church in my section and working a second job to pay expenses. They don't know how good they have it."

Generational realities—differences in age, cultural background, and experience—consistently surface as contributing factors to staff conflicts. Failure to appreciate generational distinctives presses minor differences into major conflicts.

These differences shape the way we respond to circumstances and how we make decisions. Many senior pastors came of age between 1940 and the early '60s, a time when society's efforts were successful and the church held a more prominent place. The age of technology brought economic expansion. At the same time, fads came and went. Change almost always meant regression. As a result, many senior pastors generally believe in the value of tradition and working for the kingdom of God within existing structures.

Conversely, many staff pastors came of age in the late 1960s and early '70s, witnessing the limitations of human effort. The West lost prestige abroad and the war on poverty at home. The church lost its place in society. As a result, younger pastors are more willing to tamper with structures. They usually fall on a spectrum somewhere between simple openness and prideful disdain of anything traditional.

When these two generations come together, there is bound to be some conflict. Something I may attempt on a whim might still prove difficult for someone from a previous generation even after months of careful research and prayer. I could misinterpret the caution as closed-mindedness. They could mistake my suggestion as criticism of their experience. In reality, we'd both be wrong.

Background differences are further compounded by recent changes in church life. In the last two decades, people have gravitated to larger churches. In an earlier generation, pastors fresh out of seminary usually took small-town pastorates, where today many begin as staff members. As a result, many senior pastors have never been staff members and can't empathize.

These barriers are not insurmountable. Joel envisioned a community where the visions of sons and daughters would fit side by side with the dreams of old men. His prophecy pictures a community able to draw on the wealth of God in each individual. The idealism of youth can be tempered by the wisdom of experience, and the routine of tradition can be energized by the exuberance of youth. The end product need not be either idealism or cynicism, but biblical realism.

Understanding and respect can diffuse these conflicts. Don't evaluate someone else's actions on your perspective alone. Try to see what they see. Their hymns may be as meaningful to them as your choruses are to you. When you understand why people feel as they do, you are in a better position to work with them. Though this respect must flow both ways, my generation will have to admit that part of our culture has removed from us a respect for the wisdom of age. We must in humility recapture it.

2. Theological disagreements

Differences in biblical interpretation produce conflict even where love abounds. A youth pastor from the Midwest shared his current dilemma. His church had just voted to build a new gym and youth activity center at considerable cost. Though grateful, he was growing in concern for the needy, both for those in the Third World and those across town. Was it right to go to such expense for the recreation of some believers, with others in such need?

It's easy either to support him or to cry "ascetic," but his crisis is real. Theological concerns affect daily ministry.

Certainly each congregation holds theological essentials, and I'm not talking about these. I'm referring instead to differences in applying theology to twentieth-century living. The role of women, divorce, worship patterns, the present ministry of the Holy Spirit, and applied sanctification (legalism or leniency?) all bring struggles. History proves that theological differences among people who seriously study the Word are a virtual given. The only churches I know that are one-minded in all matters of theology are churches where only one mind is allowed to function.

The importance of these differences cannot be underestimated. Yet they do not have to divide people; instead they can become stepping stones to personal growth and biblical enrichment. Growing in theology with co-workers is a great benefit of serving on a ministry staff.

To negate the destructive possibilities of these kinds of disagreements, staffs must cultivate an atmosphere of freedom. I worked on two staffs I would consider exemplary. In our staff meetings, any of our theological concerns (and generational differences) could be discussed and evaluated without people being threatened, hurt, or asked to resign. This freedom fostered growth whether we were discussing how to handle marriages of pregnant couples or what we were learning about worship.

This freedom requires two understandings. First, decision-making authority must be clearly defined. Honest, open sharing cannot be conducted in a political setting where manipulation, compromise, and infighting reign as tools of decision making. The security of knowing who makes the final decision (the pastor or the board) can open the way for free discussion. The most important gift a pastor can give staff members is for him to be secure enough to offer this freedom without being threatened.

Second, differences must never be paraded before the congregation or made an element of corporate contest. Let growing pains be stamped "Staff Members Only." Cooperation even in the face of differences must be the result of such discussions, or freedom becomes destructive. Your personal growth must never become someone else's bondage.

3. Miscommunication

"All conflicts are communication problems" may be a bit overstated, but miscommunication sure accounts for its share. In church offices these are often classics.

We all know staff members who burn with vision as they begin their new vocation, not understanding they were hired simply to perform certain tasks. Conversations before their hiring and the announcements surrounding it may have been laced with phrases like "becoming part of the team," "freedom to carry out your calling," and "it's not what you do but who you are that counts," which always mean more to the hearer than the speaker.

While the pastor sits in the church office wondering why staff members can't settle into their responsibilities, the staff members are frustrated trying to reconcile reproducing tapes or cleaning the kitchen with the ministry they envisioned.

Honesty is the critical element here. The blunter the better. Worry more about your staff members understanding what you will expect of them than trying to make them like it. Perhaps we suffer from "homiletic hangover," but it's easy to make a staff position sound greater than it is. It may help in recruitment, but it leads to trouble in the long run.

Daily miscommunications—not sending the right information or consistent information—create the same potential for conflict. Working together effectively requires lots of communication. Questions. Memos galore. Make sure people understand what is going on, especially when it will affect, no matter how distantly, something in their field of ministry. Get your information from the right sources.

The pastor who on varying issues alternately placates a staff member by giving in and then denies something else to test commitment is not being honest. Neither is the staff member who attempts to manipulate the pastor by not providing all the facts about a decision or hides some pet project for fear the pastor will disapprove.

Miscommunication can also be negated by demonstrating your loyalty. One staff pastor told me how he looks to do things his pastor cares deeply about even though they may matter little to him (picking up a gum wrapper on the carpet). He likened it to bringing flowers to his wife. Find ways to tangibly demonstrate your love and support (a note of thanks or offering to handle some busywork you weren't asked to do). It will cover a multitude of miscommunications.

4. Perspective diversity

I earned spending money in college as an Oklahoma state football official. Most games, I worked with three other officials. On the occasions when I was head referee and responsible for everything that happened on the field, there were six other eyes watching the game with me. Many times we would see a call differently. One would rule a pass complete, another that it had been trapped. My task was to decide who had the best perspective to make the call.

Diversity in perspective is often a major factor in staff tensions. Whether in matters of methodology, facility, personnel, crisis resolution, or budgets, members of multiple staffs view the body from different angles. "How will this decision affect the people and ministries I'm involved with?" That's not wrong. That's being responsible. It becomes wrong when a staff member seeks to compel his perspective over the perspectives of others and expresses dissatisfaction with them, their viewpoints, or the final decision.

My objective as a pastor is the same as that of the referee—to use the perspectives of others to see possibilities from all angles. It's helping the eyes, ears, and hands of the body to work together.

The church is unique in this regard. It must seek to move not by the opinions of people but by the will of God. Listening to many perspectives with a wholehearted search for God's mind is a powerful combination—a process laden with occasional conflict, perhaps, but pregnant with power.

It is a process only for the mature, for those who have lost the need to use pressure and manipulation as tactics for change. It's for staff members who are willing to be only a *part* of the solution, for those who can practice submission, which Richard Foster's *Celebration of Discipline* defines as "the ability to lay down the terrible burden of always needing to get our own way."

At the same time, staff members must avoid self-protectionist tactics like apathy. Withdrawing denies the larger reality of the relationships between various segments of the body. It does not avoid conflicts; it only delays and compounds them.

5. Minor majoring

Society's preoccupation with power often creeps into staff relationships, distracting us from our primary task—serving people—and turning our energies to secondary things such as buildings, budgets, and recognition. When egos become enmeshed in in-house politics, we can miss opportunities to help those in need and to disciple those hungry for the Lord.

In theory, most pastors are eager to let staff members minister. What pastor wouldn't rather have the youth minister lead someone off drugs instead of fighting for a larger budget? But so much of our conversation centers on expenses, record keeping, and maintaining institutional control.

Recently someone told me how snobbish he used to think I was because I would scurry past hurting people on my way to handle some pressing matter of church business. How painful to hear, but how healing to misguided priorities! The parable of the Good Samaritan was pointed directly at me.

Jesus never grabbed for institutional control, either in the Roman Empire or in the Jewish hierarchy. Yet the fire he ignited in eleven men changed the world. Putting too much emphasis on program distracts from personal ministry. What if I don't get all the space I think I need in the new education wing? Does ministry hang so precariously on such externals?

A good test of whether or not you are majoring in minors is to look at what is frustrating you. Does it have to do with institutional questions or serving individual people? Nothing can really hinder the latter. If it's merely an institutional matter, give input where you are invited and defer to the decision makers. Conflict over minors isn't worth whatever you hope to gain.

6. Environment

It is impossible to examine staff conflicts without looking at the environment of staff relationships themselves. What kind of hierarchy allows for both accountability and freedom to minister? A system based entirely on the power of position can't flourish in a setting where the highest order of personal motivation must be the leading of the Holy Spirit.

Is faithfulness to God challenged when you are asked by a superior to do something you don't fully agree with? How can people be freely released when "I felt God wanted me to" is an oft-used excuse of the immature?

These questions complicate the usual employer-employee model. The church isn't just another business, and answers won't be found at the extremes. Freedom to the point of anarchy is destructive. Conversely, authority that chains the church to one person's will may find less outer conflict but breed deeper conflict inwardly.

Obviously the problem calls for more extensive discussion than is appropriate here. The stress between individual conscience and submission to authority, however, does contribute to staff conflict. Until we reconcile these competing values, they always will. The answer lies not in an ideal management system but in compassionate, personal cooperation that seeks to allow Christ to lead the life of the church.

7. Relationship dearth

"I could count on one hand the number of times we as a staff really prayed together other than to cover church prayer requests."

"In six years I have never been invited to my pastor's home for anything but church business."

"I want to share with him what I'm going through, but my struggles are always misunderstood as a lack of personal support."

I've heard these comments from staff pastors who hunger for strong personal relationships. Without them, conflicts become major obstacles to ministry. With them, conflicts are more easily resolved.

Key terms in disarming conflict are *respect, understanding, freedom, submission, deference, honesty,* and *openness.* These words describe personal relationships, not institutional systems. Management systems don't create destructive conflicts; people do. Where conflict destroys ministry, you can be sure that relationships have deteriorated. And preventing deterioration requires maintenance. Here are three principles for building strong relationships.

Relations must be familial. It is easy to let ministry relationships slip into mere professionalism. Relating only on the basis of the organizational chart forces us into an agree/disagree response to each other's ideas and actions. Once that happens, staff relationships become contests of influence, typified by suspicion, hurt, and independence.

The most productive staff relationships I've observed are those in which love was expressed in personal friendship. I'll never forget the morning my pastor came by on his way to the office to sit and talk with my wife and me after our small apartment had been burglarized.

Relationships must be supportive. If our goal is to minister to people and extend the kingdom, then we must work at encouraging one another. As a staff member, can you still support your pastor even if he opts for a different action than you suggested? As a pastor, do you care about helping your staff member go on when you know he or she has been disappointed?

You can't work in God's kingdom with others and ignore their needs. One pastor described the degeneration of relationships among his elders: "Being right became more important than being right with each other."

"You are my friends," Jesus told his disciples. And he cared deeply for their needs. "Familiarity breeds contempt" is a battle doctrine for the world; it has no place in the church.

Relationships must be mature. Being people's friend means saying more than just the things they want to hear. Leadership people must also have enough maturity to accept correction without being hurt or angry.

Jesus' closeness with Peter did not keep him from rebuking Peter when he sought to keep Jesus from the cross. James and John were blasted for wanting to destroy an entire village.

These relationships do not spring up overnight. They are cultivated. Fear of committing time to personal relationships is the greatest deterrent to a healthy staff environment. Maintenance is too time-consuming, some argue. While they do take time to establish, good friendships are not inefficient in the long run. There is no way to measure the time and energy wasted on conflicts that tear people apart, leaving them seething beneath the surface, or requiring endless meetings to resolve.

A local Assembly of God pastor lives out this commitment by meeting twice a week with his four-member staff—once for personal sharing and once for church business.

When you are truly someone's friend, conflicts need not be feared or hidden. They are not seen as the result of incompetence or rebellion but as the natural result of people working together who see through a glass darkly. Even with imperfect people in imperfect environments, the work of God can forge ahead.

12

Toward Better Board Relationships

*If we have areas of disagreement, and we will, let's work
them out face-to-face, courteously and confidentially.*

—Chuck Swindoll

I was playing racquetball with another minister. The score was
close. The serve went back and forth.

Suddenly, as if propelled by a squirt of adrenaline, the guy blew
me away. His serves became powerful, his backhand flawless, his ac-
curacy on those low shots in the corner deadly.

I knew he was good—but not *that* good!

Soundly defeated and drenched with sweat, I took him by the
shoulders and said, "OK, Hercules, what's with you? How did you
pull that off?"

"Well, Chuck," he said, smiling broadly, "I did play beyond my
ability. It started when I began to think about last night's board meeting. I got madder and madder and smashed that deacon's face all over
this court! It's amazing how a bad board meeting improves my game."
We laughed and headed for the showers.

I've thought about that dozens of times since and remembered it
when his church went through a wrenching split that left the ministry
in shambles and him and his family in bitter disillusionment.

Don't misunderstand; there's a lot to say for diffusing hostility in
a game of racquetball or a round of golf. Who knows how many pastors keep their sanity intact because of such outlets. Maybe that's why
we compete so ferociously. But the need for a better relationship between pastors and board members is apparent, and in some cases,
acute.

When conversations with fellow ministers get beneath the surface, this subject is frequently mentioned. And it is not uncommon for board members to contact me about struggles with their ministers. "How can we ask hard questions without leaving the wrong impression?" they ask. "What makes him so volatile and defensive?"

Our situation reminds me of a description of arms talks by former secretary of state Dean Rusk: "We negotiate eyeball-to-eyeball, and each side is afraid to blink." Unfortunately, that is not confined to the political arena.

War zones

Conflicts between a pastor and board don't limit themselves to one or two tension areas. Here are just a few possible war zones:

Confusion about goals. A pastor might think, *I explain where this church is going and often review how we can get there, but my board members don't seem interested.* A member of his board might be thinking, *I wish the pastor would tell us what we are trying to do as a church. I don't see the big picture.*

Broken relationships can blind and deafen us. The words that leave one person's mouth may never enter another's ears or, perhaps worse, may be heard in a twisted manner.

Training and discipleship. Pastors often declare, "I wish my board would take the reins of leadership, but they seem reluctant to accept training, especially from me." To this, some of his board members might silently respond, "Our minister says he'd like us to be more involved in leadership, but he's not just efficient, he's *super*-efficient. How could I ever help *him*?"

Traditional vs. contemporary. A youthful pastor often wants the church to address today's needs in today's terms. With vigor, he presses the issue of contemporaneity, which touches music, style of worship, pulpit terminology, dress, youth programming, and other long-standing "untouchables."

The board, lacking confidence in his leadership and fearing the unknown, balks. "Why can't our preacher just preach the Word, visit the sick, marry and bury, and do the basic stuff? Before we know it, we'll lose our older members."

Desire to know one another. A pastor might sigh, "I realize our relationship would be more productive if I could *really* get to know the people on my board, but somehow it doesn't get done." A lay leader might be thinking, *I would give anything to know my pastor better. But who am I to take his time? He's always so busy, plus he has a lot of other people who need his help. And if he did get to know me, he might not respect me as much.*

Problem roots

Church leaders often clash because they approach situations from different perspectives. A few examples:

Pastors possess a theological or biblical perspective, a problem-solving method they probably picked up in seminary. Board members solve problems more pragmatically, a tried-and-true method they learned in business. It's the idealism/realism rub.

Pastors live in the culture of the church. They wrestle with, think about, pray over, and talk through the issues from the hothouse mindset. But the board members? They live and work in the "real" world and wrestle with church-related problems on the side. In board meetings, the pastor is on familiar turf, the lay person on foreign soil.

Pastors are identified with their ministries, so their egos get intertwined in tough-issue discussions. Board members are often more objective and less sensitive about church matters. It's easy for pastors to feel personally attacked (especially if they are insecure) when board members are determined to solve the problem (especially if they are insensitive).

People with different perspectives are a lot like two ships passing on a foggy night, moving in different directions, not able to see the other. Except for a few flashing lights, the roar of massive engines, and the blast of a loud horn, it's as if they were in the deep all alone. A collision is always a threat.

Perhaps Jesus' periodic struggles with his "board" of twelve were intensified because of this. He described to them a different perspective—the kingdom of God.

Deep need

Jesus committed himself to those men *in depth.* As Mark 3:14 (NASB) states: "He appointed twelve, that they might be with him, and that he might send them out to preach." Before they were sent forth to preach, the disciples were to spend time with him. If I track those words correctly, they really got to know one another. They traveled together, spent nights together, ate together, took time off together, hammered out problems together, evaluated their lives and their mission together.

Robert Coleman, in *The Master Plan of Evangelism*, sums up the idea well: "Frequently he would take them with him in a retreat to some mountainous area of the country. . . . The time that Jesus invested in these few disciples was so much more by comparison than that given to others that it can only be regarded as a deliberate strategy. He actually spent more time with his disciples than with everybody else in the world put together.

Two problems

As I write this, I can almost see your frown. Two problems make us question the possibility of this:

Problem 1: "This is hard." My answer: "You aren't kidding!" I wish I could say I am doing all these things. I'm not, and neither are many others.

The willingness to be candid, available, and confidential is rare. Isolation is more in vogue—especially for ministers. Psychological studies reveal that we tend to be more studious and introverted than the average leader. We may attract board members with similar personality bents. A roomful of introverts doesn't make for an easy, breezy, let's-become-better-friends group.

Further, it takes a lot of time and energy to make friends with eight, nine, or ten people. Peter Drucker says you can't hope to accomplish anything in a meeting of less than forty-five minutes. An intense, forty-five-minute meeting drains the creative juice most preachers would rather pour into sermon preparation and most lay leaders would rather expend on some business deal.

The task is further complicated by such things as personal preference ("I enjoy Russell more than Harry") and turnover (just when you are getting to know Frank, his term expires or he moves out of town).

Problem 2: "This is risky." Both sides must be willing to be rejected and shown to be wrong on occasion. That isn't easy.

A LEADERSHIP survey showed that laymen generally view pastors as more deficient in the area of making friends than pastors think they really are. Such blind spots are painful to admit.

Another obstacle is the pedestal on which pastors are often placed, even though we may work hard to stay off such perilous and unbiblical perches. In the same survey 14 percent of the pastors rated their spiritual life as "excellent," yet 46 percent of the lay leaders thought their pastor's spiritual life was "excellent."

Getting to know each other means phony images must crumble and distance-making formalities must be set aside. A first-name basis and an unguarded, give-and-take style must somehow be encouraged.

Beyond when push comes to shove

How can pastors and boards cultivate better interpersonal relationships?

1. Schedule time together between official meetings, whether one-on-one or with a few. It can be in the pastor's or a member's home for an evening (with spouses), or over lunch.

Tomorrow morning I have initiated a breakfast meeting with five key board members as we work through a matter for our congregational business meeting next Sunday. But sometimes the get-together may simply be for social purposes. I've found I must plan these times well in advance, or they won't happen.

2. Get away for overnight retreats. One of the best decisions we made several years ago at our church was to have pastor-elder retreats at least twice a year. These are great times for getting beneath the surface of one another's lives as well as evaluating our ministry. We eat together, enjoy some needed laughter, and have extended times of prayer with each other. Sharing rooms together overnight also helps us break down barriers among one another. We always come back closer and in better harmony. Start doing this, perhaps on a once-a-year basis, shortly after the annual election of your new board members. It is imperative that *every* member attends these times, by the way.

3. Translate attitudes into actions. You love your spouse, but it sure does help to say so. You enjoy your kids, but a warm embrace

communicates your attitude. Pastors and board members need to tell each other how grateful they are for their time, energy, and commitment.

Written notes are appreciated. A sincere, firm handshake and an eyeball-to-eyeball look never fail to encourage. A phone call is another way of translating our attitudes into action.

4. Support each team member. We all have enough enemies; each of us wrestles with sufficient self-depreciating thoughts. Let's become loyal in our support of one another, especially in each other's absence.

If we have areas of disagreement, and we will, let's work them out face-to-face, courteously and confidentially. Pastors, let's not use the pulpit as a hammer to settle arguments. Board members, let's seal our lips when damage could be done to the ministry by an uncontrolled tongue.

And whenever push comes to shove, play racquetball. Nobody needs to know why you suddenly start playing better.

13

Helping Your Board Listen to God

*An important test of God's leading is spiritual unity, a sense
of peace after a prayerful and thorough
discussion of a decision.*

—David Goetz

I n Texas they call it "kickin' acorns"—when everybody adjourns to
the church parking lot after the board meeting to release their frustrations about the previous two hours.

"That's precisely what's wrong with the way many church boards
are run," says Danny Morris, director of developing ministries for the
United Methodist Church's Upper Room in Nashville, Tennessee.
"Most church boards employ Robert's Rules of Order to make decisions, which often creates animosity among board members.

"RRO is an adversarial system that creates winners and losers,"
Morris says. "And when you deal in an adversarial way, you end up
with adversaries."

But not only does RRO throw up walls between people, it's often
irrelevant. The making and seconding of motions is often done in a
perfunctory manner, not reflecting the deeper mood of the board.

One church board had voted to start a second Sunday morning
service. Six months later, the board wrestled with hiring an additional
music person to help with worship. Finances were tight. After some
discussion, somebody piped up, "I move to drop the second service
altogether," and the motion passed by over 60 percent. Not one person questioned it.

As the meeting wore on, one of the board members said, "I feel
uncomfortable about what we've just done. I think we should pray

before we just eliminate the second service." The rest of the board nodded, and so the service was reinstated until further review.

So much for the vote. Isn't there a better way to "do church"?

God's fingerprint

The answer to the problems of RRO isn't to chuck it. RRO is effective for much of what church boards do—approving minutes and reports, for example. It's quick, clean, and efficient.

What RRO can't do, however, is help explore the deeper issues of church life, such as determining a church's vision. Such issues are the ones over which emotions in God's people run hot and deep. These essential issues have this question at their core: *What is God's will for our church?*

For these issues that matter, God's will can be determined only through a higher level of decision making—spiritual discernment. In short, spiritual discernment is listening for God's will. It's done through consensus, which simply means that in a church board or committee, an important test of God's leading is spiritual unity, a sense of peace after a prayerful and thorough discussion of a decision. (No longer do board members have to adjourn to the parking lot to practice for the punt, pass, and kick competition.)

For more than 300 years, the Quakers have employed this model of decision making. They assume the best of those attending their business meetings: each person genuinely desires the best solution. They also assume that groups, searching together, can reach a better decision than can one person alone.

Consensus doesn't mean that before a decision can be made every board member has to support every point of a proposal. The axiom that true consensus will never occur until a few funerals are conducted is probably still true. But consensus means that despite disagreement, when the group looks at the decision as a whole, they can see God's fingerprint.

"The image we have to get out of our mind," says Morris, "is that consensus means we pastors have whipped everybody into shape. Pastors listening for the Spirit in their congregations take huge risks. Listening creates uncertainty and a new kind of vulnerability between pastor and people, and between people and people."

A change to this model of decision making must be guided by a

powerful vision of pastoring a church where it is normal for the Holy
Spirit to reveal God's will to God's people.

Good or bad vibes?

In many ways, church meetings governed by spiritual discernment look similar to those run by RRO. But there is a qualitative difference, which rests on the shoulders of the person leading the meeting—the chairperson.

Quakers call this person the "clerk," the person whose job it is to
interpret the spirit of the meeting, moving along the agenda while
not controlling or pushing it, someone who guides, not steers, the
meeting.

His or her task is nothing more than good old-fashioned reflective
listening. An item is presented for discussion, and at various intervals,
the chairperson says, "I'm sensing that this is the direction we're
heading," or, "What I'm hearing the group saying is . . ."

What the chairperson (or "spiritual guide") is trying to determine
is a collective thumbs up or thumbs down on the item for discussion.
Is there a pervasive feeling of joy, or feelings of doubt, reservation,
fear? Under the RRO system, the chair would just call for a vote after
the discussion.

Frances Smith chairs the board at Long's Chapel United Methodist
Church. Her forty-year history in the church contributes to her ef-
fectiveness as the board's spiritual guide. She knows well the idio-
syncrasies of each board member.

"A good spiritual guide," says Frances, "knows the backgrounds
of the other board members. If a board member whom I don't know
well begins creating problems on the board, I make it my business
to find out more about him or her."

Informal knowledge of board members is essential, because the
guide must make everyone feel heard, prevent any one person from
dominating, and draw out those who are shy.

Douglas Steere, a Quaker, explained: "[A] good clerk is a person
who refuses to be hurried and can weary out [i.e., endure] dissension
borne of the confidence that there is a way through, although the
group may have to return again and again to the issue before clear-
ness comes and a proper decision is reached."

Of course, the spiritual guide must be savvy enough to know that when ol' John Knecht squashes for the umpteenth time a proposal to give more to missions, that John will always be John. But that's just the point of consensus: ol' John is valued by the board; factions are not permitted to power past him by a simple majority. Besides, there is probably a kernel of truth in his concern, and this is precisely the point of spiritual discernment: to get on the table all nuggets of truth on a particular matter.

"I'm constantly reminding our folks," says Jeff Spaulding, pastor of North Hills United Methodist Church in St. Louis, "they should be listening for God's voice while looking into the face of their fellow board member."

Agreeing to disagree

But doesn't consensus mean one person can derail every good idea that rolls down the track?

No. Not all disagreement is created equal. When the chairperson attempts to wrap up a discussion with, "I sense the group is saying we should go ahead," the board is given the opportunity to register its disagreement on one of four levels:

Level 1: "I am a bit uncomfortable going ahead with this proposal."

This is the softest level, which simply communicates that the way the spiritual guide phrased the conclusion of the group's overall feeling isn't quite right for that person.

Level 2: "I disagree, but I do not wish to stand in the way."

This is typical of most disagreement. By speaking up, the speaker has put the board on notice about his or her concern. But the proposal hasn't been derailed.

Level 3: "Please put me down as opposed."

This slows down the train, stimulating discussion about his or her concern. Other board members may pick up on the objection and let it shape other responses. The meeting is free to proceed, but the comment makes the group cautious, though it shouldn't stand in the way of final action.

Level 4: "I am unable to unite with (or affirm) the proposal."

Now the proposal has been derailed. The person is unwilling to step aside and allow the matter to move forward. There is clearly a lack of consensus. The normal procedure is to delay action until a later meeting. By the next meeting, the individual or group of individuals may conclude that there was a frivolous reason for objecting, or the proposal might be adjusted.

The key is that not all objections are given equal weight. Only when someone officially puts the board on notice (Level 4) does the proposal in its present form lurch off its tracks.

Of course, this method isn't woodenly followed. After a while, boards learn how to disagree with each other, and good spiritual guides gently hold the reins on discussions.

"I've come to learn that everyone doesn't have to be thrilled with every proposal," says John Boggs, pastor of Long's Chapel United Methodist Church at Lake Junaluska, North Carolina. "Dissent is legitimate; we can disagree without being disagreeable."

John tells about a board discussion over whether to install air conditioning in the sanctuary, a $40,000 proposition. Some wanted it; others said, "Why don't we wait until we build a new sanctuary?" Someone else said, "In my reading of Scripture, I can't justify spending $40,000 to cool the sanctuary for only ten or twelve Sundays a year while just down the road there are people living in substandard housing."

"I and the rest of the board needed to hear that truth," says John. "We decided to postpone installing the air conditioner. Everybody must be committed to listening in a caring manner."

Where to start

For eighteen months, Jeff Spaulding and a bevy of laity at North Hills Church labored to draft a Vision 2000 statement. Fifteen months into the process, they began interpreting the data, and for the final three months, using discernment by consensus, they winnowed the results down to a twenty-four-page document. Not a single vote was taken.

The committee handled such explosive issues as staffing and capital improvements. Sure, they had their differences, and the process dragged on longer than if they had used RRO, but in the end, no one left the committee resentful. The plan submitted to the congregation was the plan that 100 percent of the committee members believed God had for the church.

Of course, none of this happened fortuitously. Several years earlier, Jeff had started a small group that discussed *Yearning to Know God's Will*, a workbook written by Danny Morris, which offers an entire section on how the church (not just individuals) can discern God's will. Over time several people began to catch Jeff's vision for a better way of making important decisions. "Wouldn't it be nice if our church operated like this?" they began to say.

Out of that group emerged leaders who ended up on the church board. A year later when a board issue about how to repair the parking lot erupted in a geyser of hurt and anger, several board members expressed their dismay at the division rending their fellowship. Because of prior study, they were ready to say, "Let's stop wounding each other and listen to hear what God wants for us."

"There will be a teachable moment," says John Boggs, "when a congregation goes head to head on an issue and realizes that ramming through that issue will only destroy the body of Christ."

John prepared his church by inviting his administrative council (church board) to study *Yearning to Know God's Will*. Not every board member accepted his invitation, but those who did met during the Sunday school hour, though John says now the setting didn't provide enough time. He eventually moved the group to an evening meeting.

Another way John prepared the way for discernment was by preaching frequently on the work of the Holy Spirit. "John is one of the youngest ministers we've had," says Frances Smith, chairperson of the administrative council at Long's Chapel. "One old-time member said to me, 'Do you realize John's been here for over a year and that for most of the time he's preached on the workings of the Holy Spirit?'

"John's preaching generated a feeling of togetherness where it became okay to say, 'I believe we'd better consider what the Holy Spirit would have us do in this situation.' "

Another important step is creating the mood in which discernment can take place. That's as simple as starting meetings, for any committee, with more than a token prayer. Douglas Steere wrote,

"When we meet for business, it is the same as if we're meeting together for worship."

John asked the nominating committee at Long's Chapel to be a prayer group. He said, "Our purpose will be to make nominations out of our prayer rather than just being a nominating committee that opens the meeting with prayer."

That raised a few eyebrows, John says. Some thought that meant more meetings, which it did. John requested that instead of scrambling to meet four times in late summer or early fall, the committee would meet monthly throughout the year. He wanted to make serving on the nominating committee more than just a seasonal job of slot-filling. No more arm-twisters. Just men and women who would seek God's will to match the right person with the right ministry position.

More than just a job

Spiritual discernment is not quantum physics, but it does require men and women committed to listening for God's voice. An important step is filling the church boards with active listeners.

Danny Morris recommends pastors start with the nominating committee. If that group becomes committed to discerning God's will, it is more likely to nominate for other boards people who seek God's best for the church. The one feeds the others.

One of the most important lessons for the nominating committee to learn is patience. If there's not a qualified candidate for a church board position, then the position should remain vacant. Morris calls this "stripping the church down to its fighting weight."

Things can get sticky, however, when someone yearns to serve on a board but isn't qualified. In one church, a woman wanted to be appointed chair of a high-level committee, and everyone knew it. The situation got more messy when instead of appointing this woman, the nominating committee stonewalled, and the position remained open for several months. They had discerned that she was not the best candidate. Angry, the woman eventually left the church.

Of course, there's the other side of the coin: qualified candidates who turn down the nomination. John Boggs remembers when the nominating committee applied the discernment process and came to a consensus about two names. They contacted both candidates, asked them to pray about it, and said, "Get back to us in a week or so."

Both rejected the nominations. One said, "I've been called to teach Sunday school, not serve on a board." So the committee returned to the drawing board and came up with another name. Thanks but no thanks, was the reply. Then it happened again. Six months later, the committee finally found the right person, someone excited to serve on that committee.

Each one who rejected the nomination, however, was a little taken back at how much time and effort the committee had invested. "I'm not your person," one of them said, "but I'm glad to know how seriously you take these nominations."

"We've stopped trying to get people to take jobs," says John. "We're trying to help people discover their call for ministry.

"We tell our candidates, 'If you can't take the job in the spirit of love and a sense of God's call, don't take it.' "

Full light

When a board uses spiritual discernment, it's as if the idea being discussed sits on a small rotating table in the center of a light-filled room. Instead of taking on each other, the people in the room take on the idea sitting on the table. Every time someone speaks, the idea rotates a degree or two, and then everyone views the idea a little differently than before.

Somebody else speaks; the idea shifts again. And again. Until like a light-refracting prism the idea is hit by the light of God's truth, and everyone can see it: God's will is discerned.

Spiritual discernment is no panacea, no three easy steps. It's not a technique; it's a way of life, a way of doing church that harnesses the wisdom of the laity to find God's will for the church. Yet it's not without a price.

"We must give up everything in order to find God's will," says Morris. "That means sublimating all of our wishes, our desires, our turfdoms. Only when our selfishness dies can God's will for the church be resurrected."

PART 3

Confrontation

14

When Not to Confront

Not all conflict has to go to trial.

—LeRoy Armstrong

Their wedding day approaching, a young couple I'd been counseling was stuck. They couldn't agree about anything—the order of the ceremony, the ring bearer, the reception. Feeling misunderstood, they couldn't look at each other without arguing.

My first instinct was to help them resolve their dispute. But in talking with the young man, I learned the real source of their conflict: his future mother-in-law.

She was terrorizing their relationship by second-guessing almost every wedding decision they made. This was more than just an enthusiastic mother of the bride. She ended up imposing her will on their wedding and their relationship. The bride felt torn between her mother and her husband-to-be.

I came to see their conflict on two fronts: the communication breakdown between the couple, and the interference by the future mother-in-law. The couple's conflict did not seem abnormal; engagement is always a time of high stress. The tension created by the mother-in-law, however, threatened their relationship.

But I chose *not* to confront their own tensions.

"Communication with your future wife will improve over time," I advised. "Your conflict is a normal part of learning to relate to each other.

"Your mother-in-law's meddling, however, is a different matter. Time will only make it worse. If you don't address the issue, it could potentially sabotage your marriage." I recommended confrontation.

I was right. After a particularly difficult face-to-face with the mother of the bride, both conflicts were resolved.

Two conflicts, two responses.

That experience taught me that some battles need to be fought, while others can be finessed. Church conflicts also require a variety of prescriptions. Conflict over critical doctrinal matters—how does one become a Christian, for example—demands immediate attention. The same is true with biblical lifestyle issues like immorality. Confrontation is the only option.

But drawing a line in the sand is not always necessary or helpful. Here are three ways confrontation can be avoided.

Friendly neglect

Our Sunday school had been dwindling for years. In a swing away from tradition, the church leadership decided to abandon the Sunday school ministry and pursue small groups. In addition to reaching a larger audience, small groups would provide the relational component so desperately needed in our large metropolitan community. Some of our members commuted from thirty miles away.

Conflict erupted immediately.

"Why are you messing with the Sunday school program?" grumbled an unhappy church member. Via the grapevine, she had learned we were thinking about changing our format.

To the few who attended, Sunday school was as biblical as David and Goliath. And changing the program was tantamount to abandoning the Christian faith.

The conflict wasn't shaking our church's foundation, but it wouldn't go away either. We had considered the feelings of the faithful few who attended week in and week out. Their concerns were important to us, but we still felt God's leading in launching our small-group ministry.

Instead of cutting out the Sunday school altogether (confronting the problem), then, we let it drift, treating it with benign neglect. The staff, instead of pouring its energies into what for us is a ministry of a bygone era, is implementing the small-group ministry.

Through neglect, the dying ministry has deteriorated even further. Now only one class meets regularly. But we're permitting the Sunday school, anemic though it may be, to exist. After we launch the Concord Center for Biblical Studies, we plan to have an official burial for our Sunday school.

Until then, appeasing the contingent who can't survive without a Sunday school is the most effective way to sidestep conflict.

Go the extra mile

When I first stepped in as singles pastor, the church had several choirs, one of which was a singles choir.

A conflict soon developed between the singles choir director and myself. Part of the problem was organizational: I reported directly to the senior pastor while he reported to the church's music director. But both ministries drew from the same pool of single adults.

The issue was his lack of cooperation. His only interest was the choir, not the overall singles ministry. Since I was the singles pastor, my concern was how to minister to all the single adults in the church.

"Bob," I said, "I'd like you to participate in our leadership planning meetings."

"I'm the director of the singles choir," he said repeatedly. "I don't need to be part of the singles ministry."

Aware of our impasses, the church leadership encouraged us to work together. But we couldn't; the tension only heightened. Repeatedly I invited him to our planning meetings. I wanted his input and direction to the ministry. But it seemed that unless the issue related directly to the singles choir, he wanted no part of what we were doing. After one tense meeting, he refused to attend any more.

Frustrated, I felt like confronting him. After all, wasn't I the singles pastor? I wanted to work through our differences and resolve the issues—quickly.

I restrained myself, however, and elected to go the extra mile—slowly. That turned out to be a wise move. The issue wouldn't have been resolved by banging our heads together. Though eager to clear up the heaviness this cast over the ministry, I patiently worked with, and around, him.

Eventually, due to a drop in participation, the singles choir disbanded.

I discovered later that our conflict was only a small part of the problems in his life. Looking back, extending grace to his hot-tempered leadership was the right decision. The situation called for grace, not confrontation.

Play your position

If every player on the Chicago Bulls tried to play Michael Jordan's position, the team would self-destruct. Jordan is the undisputed superstar and team leader. Even Scottie Pippen, an NBA all-star and Olympian, can't replace Jordan. Harmony—and championship performance—is the result of each person playing his own position.

Much of church conflict, I believe, can be avoided simply by playing our positions. Often conflict results when we're dabbling in someone else's area.

Recently, in a staff meeting, our lay evangelism director, who was new to the position, asked if the leadership could make an exception to their policy of not holding Friday night meetings. At our church, Friday evenings are sacred; people are encouraged to spend the night with their family.

"Friday evening is the only evening that all of my volunteers can make," he said. "The training will only run for six weeks. Can you make an exception this time?"

"Sure," I chimed in. "Your circumstances are unique. Go ahead."

What I thought, however, didn't matter. I wasn't the senior pastor. I had overstepped my bounds. A gentle discussion later with the senior pastor showed me my error.

"Your answer was correct," he said firmly, "but you should have deferred to me."

Overstepping our areas of authority can produce unnecessary conflict. Playing our positions—making sure that the decision at hand is our call—is often a simple way to bypass conflict.

In the Bible, God paints his trophies of grace with warts and all. Even among two of his choice servants, Paul and Barnabas, conflict erupted. Conflict, it seems, is a normal part of church life. But not all of it has to go to trial.

15

When You Need to Confront

Christians who are never reproved usually harbor some instability or unsoundness in their faith.

—Daniel Brown

H is wife was ready to leave him. He was a Christian, but he often lost his temper, saying terrible, hateful things. His conduct was breaking his wife in two and creating rebellious children. When his wife threatened to walk out, he finally consented to talk with me.

He was obviously uncomfortable speaking about his relationship with his wife and children. "What I do in my home is nobody's business," he said.

"That isn't true," I responded. "You may not like what I'm going to say, but I have to say it: You must find a way to change your behavior."

Transformation didn't come easily for him. "You're trying to turn me into an old mare," he groused. "I'm a stallion, not a mare." It took some time to convince him that his homelife was not merely his business, but that it affected the happiness of many others. But after three years, I have seen in his relationship with his family an incredible turnaround, and his children now demonstrate a genuine commitment to the Lord.

Why are such turnarounds so rare? Perhaps it is because they rarely occur without large doses of confrontation, a pastoral responsibility that is supremely difficult, scary, and often ineffective—because the response to it depends on the will of the one confronted.

One of the great challenges of leadership is learning to confront. As a pastor, I am to be "admonishing and teaching everyone with all wisdom, so that [I] may present everyone perfect in Christ" (Col. 1:28). As much as I'd like to, I can't confine that task to the pulpit, because my sermons cannot address each individual's attitudes, behaviors, and choices. From the pulpit, I can't say to one person, "I detect a bitterness in your soul. Do you think you truly have forgiven Ralph?"

People often need individualized help to apply Sunday's sermon to what they do Monday through Saturday. Though confronting will never be easy, here are some principles that have helped me approach this difficult but essential task.

Avoid avoidance

Often we think, *If I just ignore the problem, it might go away.* However, most problems that require confrontation do not go away. They are infections: if we ignore them, they get worse. Soon that nagging pain in one toe becomes blood poisoning. Why, then, do we avoid problems that need our attention?

One reason is that we fear the consequences. We may cause misunderstanding, we may create conflict, we may drive people away. While I was leading a Bible study at UCLA, a young man gave his life to Christ, and a few weeks later his live-in girlfriend made the same commitment. A couple of weeks after that, I learned they were still living together, but I didn't say anything. I knew it would be awkward.

Four months later, the young man figured out from his own Bible reading that he shouldn't be living with his girlfriend. He stopped me, looked me right in the eye, and said, "Daniel, why didn't you tell me about this?" I have never forgotten that. My fear of driving the young man away had caused me to fail in my role as a spiritual leader.

Another reason we may avoid confrontation is the prospect of being misinterpreted. Nobody wants to be known as a holier-than-thou meddler. People resistant to change can easily make us look like the bad guys. When confronted, some people have accused their pastors of abusing their authority. Yet there is a legitimate use of God-given spiritual authority, and we must bring it to bear upon each situation that demands it.

We must continue to confront—wisely, directly, humbly. I've been helped by realizing that Christians who are never reproved usually harbor some instability or unsoundness in their faith. Seen in that light, correction is not a bad thing. Loving confrontation helps people grow in Christ, and ultimately it spares them much pain.

Focus on prevention

I try to address problems before they become crises. "Minor" behaviors and attitudes, left to themselves, can take people far off the path; they usually betray a deeper problem that will worsen as time passes.

A man in our church has a great heart for God and will probably pastor a church someday. He is sharp, energetic, the sort of guy everyone wants on the team. I gradually became concerned, however, that he was in danger of overcommitting himself. He was taking on many church responsibilities before he had fully discovered his ideal place of ministry.

I could have let the situation unfold, but he might have become discouraged and burned out. So I decided to talk with him before a major problem began. My goal was to free him.

"You have many gifts and tremendous enthusiasm," I told him, "but you have to be careful. Other church workers will show you a ministry and try to involve you. But I sense that God hasn't shown you your true calling yet. He hasn't shown you the finished painting; he is simply showing you the possible composition of the colors. So now is not the time for you to take on every ministry opportunity."

He had been feeling guilty about saying no, even though people were requesting more than he could give. He needed his pastor to help him set some boundaries, something crucial to the process of finding his place in ministry.

Receive permission

I typically ask permission before I share my impressions with someone. For example, I may ask, "Do you want everything Jesus has in mind for you?" or, "Would you like to know what I see in your life right now?"

This sets the stage. The person better receives the correcting advice or admonition, since he or she has already agreed to hear it.

One couple had attended our church for six months when they

came to see me. As we discussed a problem they were facing, I said, "I don't know how well you know me, and I'm a little hesitant to say too much for fear I might be misunderstood."

"No, please, go right ahead," both said. "Tell us anything you see."

I broached a few concerns, and then, approaching a subject that was very sensitive for the woman, I said, "I don't want to be misunderstood, so please let me say what I'm thinking, and if it doesn't come out right, I'll try again. Okay?" When she nodded, I proceeded, "Perhaps part of what God is doing in your life is letting you know he accepts and loves you just as you are. Somewhere in your past the little girl and the woman got mixed up. When you were little, somebody made you be a woman, and now that you are older you feel like you have to be a little girl. No doubt God wants to sort that out for you."

She and her husband looked at each other, their eyes as big as saucers. During the preceding months, God had been conveying that identical message to them.

If I need to share several thoughts, I periodically repeat, "Is it okay if I tell you this?" Longtime members of our church know I usually request permission to confront people in just this way. Some occasionally take the initiative and say to me, "I want to tell you again—anything you see in my life, I want to hear it."

Build on people's strengths

If we tell people only where they're wrong, they'll become discouraged and stop listening. We need to show people where they're right, at the very least affirming them as unique, beloved creations of God.

When I talked with one man in our church, I affirmed that God had molded him as a true pioneer. I told him he was so resourceful that people gather around him, just as settlers gathered around the first building that went up in some frontier settlement. Because of that one cabin at the convergence of two rivers, a whole community would develop around it.

"God made you a strong, resourceful person," I said to him. "The downside of that quality is that you can become a loner. In a sense, you're so competent that you are self-sufficient. Part of your gifting is to be a leader, but perhaps because you feel you don't need others, you remain on the periphery. You think the issue is: 'Do I need them?' Could it be you haven't learned to consider: 'Do *others* need me?' "

That cut him to the quick, but my criticism was based on his positive strengths. I've already seen a change in him; he's started meeting with other men in the church. But that situation reminded me: If we can't think of something good to say about people, we have no business correcting them. It may mean we don't love them.

Tough, direct confrontation is always more effective when we start with what we know about the person we're confronting. If I can correct someone and at the same time tell him something true and positive about himself, he usually becomes excited about what I've discerned and can accept the pain of being corrected.

Instill hope

If we have a clear sense of the bright future Jesus Christ has for people, we'll have less trouble confronting them for their spiritual benefit. The Lord always corrects us in hope. As Jeremiah 29:11 says, God has plans for people, to give them hope and a future. As God's representatives, we ought to offer godly hope.

The Hebrew word for *hope* comes from the root word for *rope*, giving us the image of a cord attached far ahead in time that pulls us toward the future. God has a particular destiny in mind for each of his people, and the only way to arrive at that place is to hold on to this thing called hope.

We recently sent a man to pioneer a new church. For quite some time I had known he would be the pastor of this new congregation, so with his future ministry in mind I confronted him about several issues. First I talked with him about his marriage. He had been insensitive to his wife, loading her with numerous expectations regarding her looks, distressing her to the point that she had confided in my wife how hurt she was. I met with this pastor-to-be to discuss the issue.

"You're supposed to give people hope," I said. "How you treat your wife indicates how you will likely treat your congregation. If you don't change, you may become the kind of pastor who is always telling people they need to be more committed, need to do this, need to do that. Your people will feel they can't live up to your expectations . . . because that's how your wife feels right now." I went on, though, to talk of what a great leader he would be if he addressed these issues with God's help. I can't leave people with correction; I must leave them with hope.

Wrap truth in mercy

One of the greatest personal transformations in my ministry began a number of years ago when I came across the biblical proverb, "Let not mercy and truth forsake thee." I saw that I had been doing it backward, putting truth before mercy. Although I meant my confrontations to be helpful and good, I ended up hurting people more than helping. We correct people not because we're disgusted that they've gotten off the track, but because we see the good things that will happen if they get back on it.

My wife and I ate dinner with a couple who wanted to start an orphanage in Africa. Although they didn't yet know what country they were going to, or when, they had already started to raise money. I felt they were getting ahead of themselves. "If I were in business," I said, "and you came to me and said you wanted to raise money for an orphanage, I would want to know such things as where it would be located, who would be operating it, how many kids would be in it, and what organizational umbrella it would be under." I told them they couldn't do much in the long run if they didn't take a few practical planning steps first.

On the way home, my wife said I had deflated the couple. She was right. What I had said was true, but I should have communicated more emphatically that I was on their side and that I thought they had a great dream. I had gotten carried away; my spirit wasn't right. I later apologized to the couple.

Fruitful confrontation requires that I be genuinely humble and gentle. Confronting others will never be easy or pleasant. But if we want to see people change, we will have to develop the courage and skills to do it as well as we can.

16

Dealing With Deception

Any action to expose lying seems a foray into enemy-occupied territory.

—Kevin Miller

T he phone call couldn't have come at a better time.
Just that morning Ken McMahon had mustered the courage to fire his choir director. He needed to do it—he'd been putting it off for too long—but he hated to do it all the same. During his thirteen years at Levittown Community Church, people had often told Ken he was an encourager, a rescuer, the kind of person who could bring out the best in others. Maybe that's why it hurt so much to let Sharon go.

But the call took away the morning's bitter aftertaste. An old seminary friend who was now teaching at a college called out of the blue to say, "If you're ever looking for a music director, there's a sharp young guy who is coming to Philly for graduate work in music. He's one in a million."

Ken got the name and number and set up a breakfast appointment for the following Tuesday.

On Monday Ken called the guy's home pastor. The pastor was high on him. "Steve Borchard? Every time he was home from college, he jumped in with the choir. One summer he helped organize and lead a week-long ensemble tour. Another time he got our high school kids—can you believe it—to put together a cantata." Steve certainly sounded motivated.

The Tuesday interview confirmed everything Ken had heard. The first thing that struck Ken was Steve's rugged good looks—tall, about six-two, raven black hair with a slight wave to it. *Good looks never hurt*

Kennedy's popularity, Ken mused while they waited for their pancakes. *We won't have trouble recruiting sopranos.* Steve talked fast, and his hands were always moving, as if he were trying to direct Ken through a difficult aria. But Steve struck Ken as a mover and a shaker. "I'm excited," Ken told his wife, Jean, that evening. "You know how Sharon used to ask, three days before a cantata, what I thought should be on the program cover? Steve already has plans for two cantatas, including adult and youth choirs, complete with ideas for the program covers!"

On Thursday evening, Ken described Steve to the board. He admitted Steve was young, sort of a raw recruit. But the board was impressed by the work Steve had done at his home church, and most of them were happy just to find a choir director so soon, especially one who would work hard. They authorized sixteen to twenty hours a week for the position, and they were open to increasing hours if Steve proved himself.

Steve's first real assignment came in August, at the church's annual picnic in Washington Crossing State Park. Ken asked Steve to lead a short time of singing in the pavilion after dinner. That was always a tough situation, Ken knew, because everyone would rather be out playing volleyball or throwing Frisbees. But the visibility would be good for Steve, and Ken wanted to see how he'd handle himself.

When Ken introduced him, Steve walked to the front and strapped on his twelve-string Ovation guitar. "I'm really better on the piano," he smiled, "so you'll just have to imagine I have an eighty-eight-string guitar." People laughed, and from then on Steve had them right with him. He started with a couple of folk choruses to loosen everybody up. Steve moved around a lot, and his excitement was contagious. Ken looked around during one song and saw that even some of the high school kids were singing. Steve flowed smoothly from one song to the next—not talking too much, just enough to make you want to sing. He closed with "Fairest Lord Jesus," which Ken knew the older folks would appreciate. *I can't believe this guy is only twenty-four,* Ken thought. *I wish I'd had that kind of poise when I was starting out.*

Then Steve took off his guitar. "I appreciate the welcome you folks have given me so much that I decided to prepare a solo for today." He sang a beautiful arrangement of "At the Cross," and his rich, unaccompanied baritone voice fit in perfectly. Ken was moved.

Squeaky wheels

The fall breezed by quickly. Ken enjoyed having someone else to talk with in the office. And Steve was there a lot. Sometimes after finance committee meetings, Ken would leave the office after ten, and Steve would still be there, scribbling away on an arrangement for an upcoming anthem. Other mornings, Ken would come in at 7:30 to get a jump on the day, and Steve would already be at work. Ken felt vaguely guilty about it because he knew Steve had to be putting in more than twenty hours, but he figured Steve just ran on high-octane fuel.

"If I told him to cut back, he'd be hurt," he told Jean one time. "I think he not only *wants* to work hard, he *needs* to." Besides, Ken was enough of a mercenary not to look a gift horse in the mouth.

Steve's hard work paid off. During September, a couple of tenors—always the hardest section to recruit—joined the choir. And choir members actually smiled during the anthem. It wasn't long before people began saying to Ken, "Wonderful sermon today, Pastor, and wasn't the choir marvelous?"

So Ken was only a little surprised that winter when Clarence and Ruth Gillis called to make an appointment with him. "We want to talk to you about Steve Borchard" was all they would say. *I should have known*, Ken thought. *As soon as they can't call the shots, they yell.* Both in their sixties, Clarence and Ruth had been the choir's squeaky wheels for as long as anyone could remember. In fact, they had complained the loudest about Sharon. It was sort of understood that one had to let Clarence and Ruth speak their minds, and usually the choir followed along. Ken figured their noses were bent out of joint because Steve had taken charge and become so well-liked—without regularly consulting them.

Ken didn't know what they could possibly complain about. Steve's ministry ran like a well-oiled engine. The only vibration Ken had picked up was a couple of months ago when Steve had asked Ken if he could date somebody in the choir. Ken asked who and found out it was Gloria, a pretty nineteen-year-old alto.

"You have good taste," Ken said, "but I don't think it would be wise to date someone barely out of high school. It would be best for your ministry here to wait at least a year before dating anyone in the church." Plus, Ken was afraid Gloria might still be emotionally tender from her dad's death a few months ago. But Steve seemed to have accepted the counsel and hadn't raised the issue again.

Sure enough, when Clarence and Ruth came they fired a volley of petty complaints. "Steve never mails the line-ups for special music on time. He says they're in the mail, but they're sitting on his desk."

"How do you know?" Ken asked.

"We, uh, happened to be in the office one day, and noticed they were there."

"Wait a minute. It's one thing to tell someone, 'I don't believe you and I'm going to check on you.' But to snoop in his office!" Ken's voice rose a bit.

"We weren't sneaking," Ruth protested. "Just checking things . . ."

"But that's not all," Clarence added. "Steve never gives us a break during rehearsal."

Oh, give me a break, Ken thought.

On it went. Steve was unsafe when he drove the church van. Steve joked too much during rehearsal. Ken was about to politely end the meeting when Clarence said, "Steve borrowed $250 from me and never paid it back." That was worth checking.

"When?"

"A couple of months ago. He had a little fender-bender with the church van, and he said he didn't want it to go on his insurance. He was going to fix it himself. He borrowed from us for the repairs."

"When was he supposed to pay you back?"

"In just a couple weeks. But he hasn't paid us a penny yet."

So that's what's driving all these complaints, Ken thought. He promised Clarence and Ruth he'd check into the matter and thanked them for coming.

I can't believe Steve didn't tell me about the van, Ken thought, driving home after the meeting. *And if he doesn't pay that money back soon, Clarence and Ruth won't give him a moment's peace.*

The next day, before he saw Steve, one of the deacons, Bill Seifert, called. "Ken, I hate to bother you with this, but something's come up with Steve."

"What do you mean?"

"Well, Steve's been sharing an apartment with Guy Alben. A while back, Steve was short of cash, so Guy fronted the rent money for him. Steve hasn't paid him back yet. Guy doesn't mean to complain—you know what a good heart he has—but he really needs the money. He came to me because he didn't know what else to do."

Ken's stomach knotted. He didn't know what to do. Was Steve just immature, not too swift with finances? And why hadn't he told him about the accident?

Steve dropped by Ken's office that afternoon.

"Can I make a request?"

"What's up?" asked Ken.

Steve asked what the possibilities would be for him to work full-time at the church during the summer. "We'll both benefit," he said. "I need the money for fall classes, and things are starting to take off in the choir. If I could give it my full attention, we could have an outstanding summer program—maybe take a week-long tour. The possibilities are endless."

"That's worth considering," Ken hedged. He'd already thought of it, but then these money problems had popped up. "Let me check it out with the board." After Steve left, Ken called Irv Hadley, chairman of the board.

"Irv, Steve Borchard was just in here proposing that we take him on full-time this summer. But I think we need to work through something first."

"You mean the thing with the van?" Irv asked.

"Yeah, how'd you know?"

"Just talked with Clarence yesterday. He seems pretty upset."

So I wasn't moving fast enough for you, huh, Clarence? Ken was more than a little bugged. "Well, that, and another money thing. Maybe it would be best at this point to keep Steve part time through the summer, sort of a probationary period during which he can straighten things out. We can consider extending his hours a little in the fall."

"Do what you need to do," Irv said. "We don't have to have him full time yet."

Ken told some of the board members what he planned to do, and they also backed him. The next morning, he asked Steve to stop by his office.

"I've been thinking about your request to go full time this summer," Ken began. "The prospect certainly interests me, but first I wanted to talk with you about some signals I've been picking up."

"What do you mean?"

"I understand you borrowed $250 from the Gillises and haven't paid them back, and you borrowed several hundred from Guy Alben and haven't paid him back, either."

"I'm working on that," Steve said. "I promised them I'd pay them back, and I will."

"There's also an issue of integrity here," Ken replied. "I understand you had an accident with the church van and didn't tell me or anyone else about it. Is that right?"

Steve looked down. Ken continued, "There's no sense losing your honor and credibility over trivial matters like these."

"You're right." Steve put his forehead in both palms, and his voice quivered. "I . . . I've been struggling financially. . . ." Ken looked at him hunched over in the chair, and it occurred to him that Steve was only a few years older than his kids. But still, staff members needed to be above reproach. Ken outlined his proposal as gently as he could. Steve would continue through the summer on a part-time basis and get another job outside the church to supplement his income. This would allow him to get things in order. If everything went well during the summer, the church would consider extending his hours in the fall.

Steve was disappointed, but his acceptance of the decision was admirable. Within a day or two, Steve scaled back the summer schedule he'd planned for the choir and found a part-time job at a 7-Eleven. He even met with Clarence and Ruth—something of a stand-off, Ken heard, with the Gillises not being too forgiving. But Ken figured that was the best that could be expected.

Afterward, Steve wrote Ken a letter saying how sorry he was about the whole mess. Part of it read, *After our conversation, I spent a long time in prayer trying to figure out where I had failed both the choir and the church, and more important, how my relationship with Christ has slipped. How selfish and damaging my attitudes and actions have been! I want to restore what has been done. Thank you, Ken, for your strong yet compassionate handling of this problem.*

Ken felt relieved. He told Jean that night, "You know, it's not easy being a pastor, but it would be a lot easier if everyone responded like Steve."

Inquisition chair

Summer started smoothly. Steve directed a "Celebration of Joy" evening concert, one of the best-attended events the church had ever held. Ken met with Steve several times to discuss the summer choir trip. Two years before, the choir had taken a four-day trip through the Poconos and southern New York, performing four or five concerts at different churches and park band shells. Last summer's trip was washed out because of all the problems with Sharon. Now folks in the choir were begging for another trip.

Ken assured Steve he would go along, to greet the pastors—most of them were his contacts—and bring a short message at the Sunday concerts. "But I don't have time to make any of the arrangements," Ken told him. "It's your baby." Steve said OK. "You'll have to get those days off from your job, too," Ken reminded him.

"No problem," Steve said.

The Sunday before the trip, however, Steve came up after the morning service. "Bad news, Ken. They're not going to let me go."

"What do you mean they're not going to let you go? We can't take the trip without a director."

"The manager scheduled me to work."

"Didn't you tell him at the beginning of the summer that you'd be gone those days?"

"Yeah."

"Well, ask again," Ken said. "They gave you the days, and we need you."

Steve called Ken at home the next day, and he sounded glum. "They won't let me go, Ken. I begged them, but they insist they need me."

Ken didn't get mad very often, but he was hot. "We'll see about that," he said. He called the 7-Eleven manager.

"This is Pastor McMahon from Community Church," Ken said. "Steve Borchard, our choir director, is working for you this summer."

"Uh-huh."

"I really need Steve to lead the choir tour we're taking this week. Isn't there any way you can let him have Friday and Monday off?"

"Well, sure." She sounded puzzled. "Steve never told me about those days, but if he really needs them, we can work something out."

Ken was taken aback—and really angry now. *What's going on?* he wondered. He grabbed the phone again and punched in Steve's number.

"Steve, what's the deal?" Ken pressed. "I just called Fran, and she says you're welcome to go."

"Oh, well, I talked to her husband. She and Ralph run the store together. They don't communicate too well. Ralph says he really needs me. And since I've already committed myself to stay, I need to do that."

Steve's answer was so quick that Ken's anger vanished. *He can't be lying*, Ken thought. *That's too easy to check.* "Well, OK then," was all he could say. Ken thought about calling Ralph to verify Steve's story, but he felt like a louse even considering it. He couldn't see himself calling and saying, "This is the pastor of Community Church, and I'm calling to find out if my staff member is lying to me." *Steve knows he's on probation and that he's gotta keep his slate clean*, Ken reasoned. *Only a total nitwit would try to pull something like that.* He finally figured Ralph and Fran must not talk to each other.

Ken was the only one who'd had any experience directing, so he got the honors when the choir left on Thursday. The choir knew the music well enough, but Ken felt like an idiot. Once he forgot a piece was in three-quarter time and confused everyone by marking a four-four beat.

By the time the September board meeting rolled around, though, Ken had put the tour mix-up behind him. Steve said he'd paid his debts, and Ken supported the motion to increase Steve's hours to twenty-five per week. That was all Steve could handle anyway with his two graduate courses.

The next day he stopped by Steve's office and told him the good news. "By the way," Ken joshed, "how are things with Gloria?" Lately Ken had noticed them talking together after rehearsals. Since Steve had been there a year, he didn't feel too uptight about it.

"How did you know?" Steve's head jerked up like he'd heard a rifle shot.

"C'mon," Ken laughed. "I may have gray hair, but my eyes still work."

"Well, we just didn't want anyone to know until we announced it Sunday."

"Huh?" Now Ken was confused.

"Gloria and I are engaged. We're going to get married in February."

Ken stared for a second or two. Finally he collected his wits enough to say, "What a surprise!" He shook Steve's hand and left. Ken couldn't believe how fast they'd hit it off. *They must have been seeing each other all year*, he thought, but he didn't have any proof, so he let the idea go.

That fall Steve and Gloria began their premarital counseling with Jim, a church member with a master's degree in counseling who helped part time with the counseling load. One day Jim told Ken, "I'm concerned about Steve and Gloria."

"Because of their age difference?"

"Well, not so much that. Five or six years can pose some problems, of course, but lots of marriages make it with bigger gaps. It's their maturity level. I'm just not sure they're ready for the demands of marriage. There's also some friction with Gloria's mom. She'd always wanted her to go to college."

Ken's eyebrows raised. Gloria's mom was one of the most influential women in the congregation. *This had better be handled right.*

"If you're really concerned, you need to tell them. That's part of the role of the counselor. I'll be willing to sit in with you if you need me there," Ken suggested.

"I'll discuss it with them and see what happens," Jim promised.

After considerable discussion the next few weeks, Jim and Ken finally decided they could not play God. Steve and Gloria were determined to get married, and Ken couldn't see any good way to prevent it. If he refused to do the ceremony, Gloria's mom—the whole church—would be on his case.

In late January, Ruth Gillis made an appointment. Ken figured it was another semiannual barrage about choir matters.

"Reverend McMahon," Ruth said, once she and Clarence got settled, "we don't think Steve Borchard is really repentant."

"What makes you say that?"

"Because he hasn't paid us back a darn nickel," Clarence said, his face flushed.

"You mean he hasn't paid you anything? I thought he settled that last summer."

"He came and talked to us," Clarence said, "but he hasn't paid us back. Instead he goes out and spends his money on some tape player. And it's not just that. He's not in school like he claims."

The last comment hit Ken as outlandish. Steve had told him several times how hard his music theory class was. "What makes you think he's not in school?"

"We asked another student to check whether he's got a mailbox at the school, and he doesn't," Ruth said slowly, as if laying down a trump card.

"Not all students have mailboxes on campus."

"We also checked with the registrar, and Steve isn't enrolled."

"Are you sure?"

Clarence and Ruth nodded together.

"OK," Ken sighed, "I'll look into it."

The next morning, Ken asked Steve, "How's school going?"

"It's tough," said Steve. "But I'm learning a lot."

"You've got two classes this quarter?"

"Music theory and choral conducting. Why do you ask?"

"Just curious. Haven't had much chance to talk to you lately."

Ken went back to his office feeling dirty. *This can't keep going,* he told himself. *Clarence and Ruth are going to make me a bigger snoop than they are.* He called Ruth and told her that Steve was indeed in graduate school.

But a week later, Clarence and Ruth stopped by his office in the afternoon. "We've double-checked with the registrar, we've checked with the finance office, and Steve is *not* in school."

Ken had had enough. "Why are you two sneaking around checking on Steve?"

Ruth looked so hurt that Ken backpedaled a bit. "All right," he said. "We'll get this thing straight once and for all. I'll bring Steve in here, and you can talk to him yourself. Are you willing to do that?"

"Bring him in," Clarence said.

Now I'm chairing an inquisition! Ken thought. But it was too late. He'd promised.

Steve looked puzzled when he entered Ken's office and saw Clarence and Ruth sitting there. Ken tried to put him at rest. "Steve, there's a little confusion I'd like you to clear up for us. Clarence and Ruth feel they have good reason to believe you are not actually in graduate school. I've assured them you are."

"Of course I'm in school," Steve said, staring at Clarence and Ruth.

"Then maybe you should tell us why the registrar and finance officer don't have any record of you," Ruth shot back.

Ken didn't realize their relationship had deteriorated that far. "Uh, maybe it would be helpful if you clarified your association with the school, Steve."

"That's easy. I'm auditing two courses: music theory and choral conducting."

"Oh, you're *auditing*," Ken said quickly, before Ruth could say anything.

"Even so, wouldn't the registrar have some record of that?" asked Clarence.

"Yes, but you see, I made special arrangements with the professors since all I'm doing is sitting in. But I *am* in school." Then Steve got up and walked out. The meeting was obviously over.

But the assaults weren't. Four or five times over the next few weeks Clarence and Ruth called with new charges that Steve was guilty of some misdeed.

"That choir isn't big enough for the three of them," Ken told Jean one evening. "Clarence and Ruth would lynch Steve if I'd let them." Ken kept Jean up till 1:00 A.M. talking about the situation. He finally decided that, as painful as it was, for everyone's peace of mind he was going to have to ask Clarence and Ruth to leave the choir. "I hate to do it," he said, "but I can't have one of my staff members under constant attack."

With Steve and Gloria's wedding the next weekend, Ken didn't talk to Clarence and Ruth until the final week of February. He decided to drive to their home. "I came to talk about the problem with Steve," he said when Ruth opened the door.

"I'm glad," she said. "Clarence and I just can't quit stewing about it."

Ken sat in the recliner. "I've been very concerned about your relationship with Steve," he began, searching their faces. "The constant friction worries me. It's affecting the whole choir, and I'm worried about what it's doing to you two, to your peace of mind."

"We'd feel a whole lot better if Steve paid back our money," Clarence admitted.

"I know, and Steve assures me he's going to pay. But something has to be done. I've prayed and thought long and hard about this, and for the sake of the choir and peace of the church, I'd like you two to step down from the choir. At least for now."

Ruth gasped. "But Reverend, you can't mean it. Why, that choir is our whole life."

"I know, and it's painful for me to suggest it," Ken said. "This isn't an act of discipline, just something I'm asking you to do for the good of the church."

"What about *our* good?" Ruth asked. "Don't we count?" Ruth

looked him in the eye. "You don't believe us. You think we're lying about Steve."

"Of course not," Ken said quickly. But then he didn't know what to say. For what seemed like a long time they sat in silence. Finally Clarence spoke.

"Pastor, the reason I'm constantly harping on this lying thing is because I've been there. From the time I was thirteen until I was nineteen, I lived in my own world. I was a pathological liar, and my parents didn't trust me if I told them what time it was. I wouldn't have changed, but God brought a major disaster in my life and broke me. So I know lying when I see it. Steve is doing that to you. You're going to be very sorry if you don't check for yourself whether Steve's in school. We've checked it to our satisfaction. You need to do it."

Ken had never heard Clarence admit any mistake before, let alone something like this. *You don't just make up stories about being a pathological liar,* he thought. But to check on Steve? *All I need is people around town saying, "McMahon can't trust his own staff."* But there in front of him was Clarence, shaking as he spoke.

"OK," he said. "I'll check."

Passive-aggressive game

Ken waited until Steve got back from his honeymoon in the Poconos, just in case he needed to have him clarify something. Then on Tuesday Ken drove to downtown Philadelphia to the graduate school campus. His heart was pounding as he found Dr. Austin's office on the second floor of Old Main. "Dr. Austin," he said, once inside, "Steve Borchard is our choir director and a student here at the graduate school. Have you ever given him permission to sit in on your music theory class—not audit, just sit in?"

"I can't give that permission and I wouldn't," he said.

Ken pulled out a picture of Steve and held it across the desk. "Is this man in your classes?"

Dr. Austin shook his head. "Never seen him."

"Thank you," Ken said. "That's all I needed to know." Neither had the conducting prof seen Steve.

Once back at the church, Ken walked into Steve's office and remained standing.

"Hi, Ken," Steve smiled, "what's up?"

"About school," Ken said tensely. "Your profs don't know anything about your auditing arrangement. They don't even know who you are."

Steve blinked a few times but answered quickly. "Well, the classes are so large, and actually, I arranged the audit through the registrar's secretary. I never did talk to the profs themselves. But when I talked to the secretary, she said it would be OK."

"Thanks for clearing that up," Ken said, not convinced. Back in his study Ken called the registrar's office and talked with the secretary.

"I remember him asking last fall if he could sit in on classes," she said. "I told him I'd check, but he never came back. But we wouldn't grant that permission to anybody."

Ken hung up and called Irv Hadley. He explained the entire story: Clarence and Ruth's accusations, what the school had said.

"He talked to me for fifteen minutes one Sunday about his classes. And you mean to tell me he's not even in school?" Irv said.

"I can hardly believe it myself, but the registrar, the professors—nobody knows him."

"We can't have a staff member of this church lying like that," Irv said. "I don't care who he is. If he were one of my employees, I'd fire him in a minute. The rest of the board needs to know about this."

That Sunday night Ken recounted the story for the board. They decided that Irv and Ken should ask Steve to resign quietly.

On Tuesday morning the three of them met in Ken's office. Steve looked a little shaken with Irv in the same room.

"Steve," Ken began, "we called you in here today because it's come to our attention that you've been lying to us. Everything you've told us about your involvement in graduate school has been untrue. You're not going to classes, you're not auditing, you didn't get permission from the professors, and you lied about the secretary situation."

Ken thought Steve might deny it, but he didn't. He just looked down at his feet.

Irv jumped in. "I don't know why you've lied about all this, but you've made Ken almost destroy his relationship with Clarence and Ruth. You have compromised the integrity of this entire church. You have broken trust, and that's a precious commodity."

Steve started to cry.

"Steve, we love you and we want to help you," Ken added, really meaning it. "But for your sake and for the sake of the church, we're asking you to resign from leadership. You're our brother in Christ and we want you to stay in the church. But this pattern of lying is serious. You need to step down and work on it. We hope you'll cooperate in the process so you can be forgiven and restored."

No one spoke for almost five minutes. The only sound was Steve's sobs. Finally Ken said, "Steve, we know you'll need some time. Stay here as long as you need to, and when you're ready we'd like to meet with you again." Ken prayed briefly and then he and Irv left.

Steve stopped by Ken's office later that day. "I need to see you tonight, Ken. I can't go on like this."

Ken knew Irv would be busy that evening. He didn't really want to meet with Steve alone, but when he saw how upset Steve was, he felt he couldn't make him wait. "OK. I want you to tell Gloria what's happening and bring her with you tonight. It's very important that she know what's going on." Ken knew the fallout from Steve's resignation could wreck their young marriage unless they handled it together.

That night Ken was back in his office by 6:30. Just before 7:00 Steve walked in—alone.

"Where's Gloria?" Ken asked.

"I, uh, didn't tell her yet. Ken, I'm scared!"

"I would be, too," Ken said. "Let's talk."

They met until quarter of twelve. Steve cried much of the time. Ken read from 2 Corinthians 7 and encouraged Steve that godly sorrow would lead him to true repentance and restoration. He assured Steve that God would forgive him and the church would forgive him. Steve would have to bear some unavoidable consequences, but he could endure those knowing he was forgiven. Then they prayed together, and when they were done they stood and embraced. Ken was crying, too. Before they left, Ken urged Steve to come in with Gloria to talk things through. Steve said he would.

Ken was glad to see the bedroom light still on when he pulled into the driveway. He told Jean how good the meeting had been.

"Ken, he's got your number," Jean finally said.

"What do you mean?" Ken crossed his arms.

"All Steve has to do is hint that he needs your help and cry a little bit, and he's got you, because you're a rescuer."

"What's wrong with that? He does need help."

"It sure seems to me that Steve is playing the passive-aggressive game. He aggressively does his dirty work. Then when you confront him, he becomes passive and weak as a baby. You rush in to help, and suddenly he's in control because you can't confront him anymore."

Backlash

Ken couldn't sleep that night. He kept replaying what Jean had said. *Am I really that gullible? I don't know any other way to build a staff except to trust people.*

He wanted to be firm, but he couldn't shake the feeling that he wasn't worthy to issue ultimatums. *Everything I do is tainted, too. Am I really any better than he is? Maybe my sins are in different areas, but deep down we're the same. There, but for the grace of God, go I.*

On Friday Ken found a letter from Steve on his desk: *I thought I should straighten things out between you and me. Concerning my course work, I must confess I have not represented myself well. That error in judgment is mine. I apologize for the hardship this has placed on you. In a sense I have told only half the truth, but the real issue is that I have, by my omission of certain facts, been half honest.*

Nowhere did Steve admit he'd done anything wrong. He kept hiding behind "errors in judgment" and "omissions of facts."

Later in the day, Steve told Ken that he and Gloria needed to meet with him that night. Ken called Irv and found out he was sick and wouldn't be able to come. He didn't like the idea of meeting with them alone, because he was beginning to doubt his discernment. But he decided the issue couldn't wait.

Steve and Gloria arrived about 7:00. Ken had to give Gloria credit. For being such a young bride, she didn't look shaken at all.

"What can I do to get my job back?" Steve said. "I'm really sorry. I want to repent."

Be firm, McMahon, Ken thought. "It's too late for that, Steve. Your job is not the issue at this point. The issue is your integrity. We love you, but we don't feel it will be helpful to you or the church for you to remain in leadership."

Steve looked dumbfounded. *I don't think he realizes what his problem is,* Ken thought. Ken began to retell the grad school story so he would be able to understand how much damage he'd caused. But just as he was starting, Steve interrupted.

"Look, Ken, I don't want to argue with you. I just want you to know that we agree with the decision, and we want to be the ones to tell the choir."

"That's a good idea," Ken said, relieved that Steve was coming around. They decided Steve would tell the choir at next Thursday's rehearsal. Ken would also be there. "You don't need to tell all the details," Ken said. "But you need to confess that you've not been honest—and that it's been over a long period of time and with many people, not just a couple." Ken added this last part because by now the choir had split wide open, with Steve and Gloria and their supporters on one side and Clarence and Ruth and a smaller group of backers on the other. If Steve said he was resigning because of "a couple of people," everyone in the choir would immediately think "Clarence and Ruth."

"OK," Steve said. "Thursday." Then he and Gloria left.

Gloria hadn't said a word, but she had stayed calm. As Ken drove home, it suddenly hit him. *Gloria doesn't know what's going on. That's why Steve cut me off when I started retelling the details. He didn't want her to know.* Ken felt a twinge in his right side. *She must think we're just picking on Steve. Thursday night is going to be tough on her.*

All day Thursday Ken's mind kept racing ahead to the rehearsal. He struggled to concentrate on his 10:00 counseling appointment. Around one he gave up on a sermon outline and went out for a sandwich. He ran into Lucy Stanton, a long-time choir member, at the coffee shop. She said hi, but Ken could have sworn she gave him a dirty look. *I'm getting paranoid*, he thought.

Ken got to his office by 6:30 that evening to try to pray and clear his mind before the rehearsal started at 7:00. At 6:55, Doris, Gloria's mom, stormed into his office.

"You have no right to fire Steve!" Doris began.

"Wait a minute. Who told you we're firing Steve?"

"Steve did, this morning, after he told the choir."

"What? You mean he already told the choir?"

"Some of them. He called a few to explain things. They're just as upset as I am."

Ken was angry and scared all at once. "He was supposed to announce that tonight when we could discuss it. But tell me the story as you understand it." Whenever he got scared, Ken dropped into the pastor-as-listener mode.

"Naturally, Steve didn't feel free to share all the details, but you don't have to think too hard to realize it's because he doesn't get along with Clarence and Ruth."

That's not it! Ken was screaming inside, but he'd been a pastor long enough to contain himself. "What else have you heard?"

"Well, Lucy Stanton said Steve's being fired because he's not organized enough. Ken, he's still young. You can't fire him just because he's got some things to learn."

"Listen, Doris, neither of those things has anything to do with why we've asked Steve to resign. We're asking Steve to step down because he has lied to many members of this church about a variety of things for a long period of time."

"What do you mean?" Doris asked.

Ken proceeded to describe the whole web of lies about grad school.

"You have no proof," Doris said when Ken had finished.

"Doris, I can get the proof." Ken couldn't believe she wasn't convinced. "The point is that the lying hasn't been an isolated incident with Steve. It's been an ongoing pattern."

"I think he's being falsely accused," Doris said. They talked for another ten minutes, but nothing Ken said would shake Doris's belief that her son-in-law was an innocent victim. Doris finally left madder than when she'd come.

Ken looked at his watch: 7:50. *The rehearsal!* He jumped up from his chair and sprinted to the sanctuary. He rounded the corner, slowed, then stopped. The sanctuary was dark. Steve must have made the announcement and then let the choir go. *The most important meeting of my life and I miss it because Doris pins me in my office,* Ken thought. *If they've heard Steve's side of the story, they're never going to believe me. We've lost the war.*

When Ken walked in the door at home, he could hear Jean on the phone. "Yes, he should be home soon. I'll have him return your call." Jean hung up and turned to him. "Ken, that's the fourth call in the last ten minutes. They're all about Steve."

"I'll return them in the den."

"Ken, they sounded angry. What happened?"

"I don't know, dear. I don't know."

Ken emerged from the den around eleven, feeling like a weary infantryman crawling from a foxhole. Every time he'd hung up, another call had come in. He still had one call to make, but by now it was too late to call anyone. Each call had been sickeningly like his meeting with Doris, beginning with some sort of attack, like, "I can't believe you would fire Steve." Ken would ask, "What is the problem as it's been related to you?" and inevitably the person would say, "Steve's being fired because he's disorganized, but mostly because of Clarence and Ruth."

Ken would try to explain, but the caller either didn't really believe him or wanted to know what proof Ken had. After the second call, Ken began promising people he and Irv would come to the next choir rehearsal to clear up the matter.

What proof?

Sunday tested Ken's will. He had hardly slept since Thursday. He'd answered, at last count, thirty-five calls. The choir had been scheduled to sing, but obviously couldn't without a director, so they sat in the pews. Many of them glared at Ken throughout the service. And there was Steve, sitting near the back, surrounded by members of the choir, and smiling.

Monday morning Steve dropped by the church to finish clearing out his office. Ken asked him to come into his office and sit down.

"What happened last Thursday?" Ken asked, his voice edged with anger.

"I presented the whole situation to the choir as a positive and biblical decision," Steve said. "They took it about as well as could be expected."

"Then why do forty people have the wrong story?"

"Well, you see, an issue came up that I feel you should consider," Steve said. "The choir said to me, 'We forgive you, and God forgives you. Why can't we, as the people under your ministry, restore you?' So what could I say? There are a lot of people, Ken, who want me to stay. And not just in the choir, either."

So now the fighting gets dirty, huh? Ken thought. "Listen," he said, "ten words from you could save me a year of trouble, and I want those ten words. Thursday night you are going to come to choir rehearsal and tell those people the truth. Is that understood?"

Steve nodded. *Too quickly*, Ken thought.

When Ken and Irv walked into the sanctuary Thursday evening, the first thing they heard was crying. Most of the choir was standing in a big huddle, and the crying seemed to be coming from there. When Ken and Irv got closer, they saw it was Gloria. Steve had his arm around her, saying things like, "It's all right, honey. It's going to be all right." Everyone turned and stared at Ken and Irv. *They look like we've been beating her, and that's why she's crying,* Ken thought.

Once everyone had been seated, Ken said simply, "I know the last week has been very difficult for you. We'd like to straighten things out tonight. Steve has something he'd like to say."

Gloria was still crying, softly now.

Steve began rambling about misunderstandings and how things "hadn't worked out." He finished by saying, "I have not been as honest as I should have been with a couple of people."

Ken kept waiting for him to say something more, but he sat back down. So Ken stood up and said, "Steve, that's not the issue. You have repeatedly misrepresented yourself over a long period of time and with numbers of people. And you have used the reputation of the staff and the church to cover your tracks." Ken went on to briefly outline the situations with the grad school and church van. He wanted to mention the special music lists, the tour mix-up, and a host of other things, but he didn't have firm proof of those.

One of the tenors Steve had recruited raised his hand. "You're saying that Steve has lied."

"That's right. Repeatedly."

"But how can you prove that?"

"Let me give you an example," Irv said, and explained how Steve had told him about his classes while the professors said they had never seen him.

"But how do we know that what you're saying now is true?"

I can't believe this, Ken thought. *If this were about adultery, would anyone ask for videotapes and motel receipts?*

"Irv and I are not going to go into all the details," Ken said, "because it's not fair to Steve. We want Steve to stay in the church and work on this area, and he can't do that if his every action is for public consumption. This is a leadership issue. The board and I stand behind our assertion that Steve has repeatedly not told the truth."

The meeting ended soon after, which was just as well, Ken thought. No one was listening anyway because they were caught up by Gloria's crying.

Reconciliation rejection

"We lost that battle," Irv said in Ken's office afterward. "Steve's got that whole choir, except for Clarence and Ruth and a few others, on his side. And from what I can tell, he's got a good chunk of the rest of the congregation on his side, too." Irv leaned back in his chair and looked at the ceiling.

"They think *we're* lying," Ken added. "You can't minister to people if they think you're lying to them. And that hurts more than anything. If there's one thing I try to do, it's shoot straight."

"I know. But what are we going to do now?"

"I won't retreat, Irv. I can't."

The next morning Steve's mother-in-law called Ken at home before seven. "Steve told me about the meeting last night," she said. "What disturbs me is that it shows you don't have any proof of what you're saying. I can't believe this church has turned into a kangaroo court."

"We have proof, Doris," Ken said. "But it looks like the only way we're going to settle this thing is to get all the responsible parties together. You bring Steve and sit down with me and the board. We'll go over all the information together. But it's completely unfair to Steve for me to talk about him when he's not here to defend himself." Ken hoped Doris would accept the offer. It was the only way Ken could think of to keep the battle from raging underground, where Ken knew he couldn't win.

But the offer didn't slow Doris or her friends. Nearly every day for three weeks, one of them would call to accuse Ken of ousting Steve for personal, unjustifiable reasons. Ken stood firm: "You bring Steve, and we'll sit down with the board and go over the evidence."

Ken called Steve several times and told him what he'd told Doris. "They say you've never had a chance to defend yourself. Here's your chance. Come meet with us." Steve finally sent a letter saying, "I have strong feelings about the way this situation has been handled, the fairness of it" and saying he needed more time for his "emotions to lessen and healing to take place."

When Ken wasn't on the phone with Steve or Doris, he was talking with one of the choir members, what few were left. Over half the choir quit after Irv and Ken had met with them, and Ken was trying to keep up morale in the remaining members. "I'm not saying it's wrong to ask Steve to step down," one alto told him, "but do we have to kill the entire choir over it?" When he heard that, Ken wanted to cry.

One day Clarence and Ruth called. "Did you hear what Steve's doing?" they asked.

I'm afraid to ask, Ken thought. "No, what?"

"Ten or twelve people from the choir are meeting at his house every Thursday. We know because we saw their cars parked in front. One can only guess what they're doing."

Ken called Steve.

"Why, Ken, what a surprise," Steve crooned.

"Steve, I understand a group from the choir is meeting at your house every Thursday."

"Yes, that's right."

"Steve, you are not Community Church's choir director anymore. You should not have half the choir meeting with you every week."

"They wanted to. It's an informal thing. We get together to just, er, pray about things at church."

"I don't care what the reason is, those meetings have to stop. This is supposed to be a time of repentance for you." Ken paused, but Steve didn't say anything. "Steve, however incongruous it might seem, my heart is open to you. But this waiting game must end. I have made it clear we want you to come talk with the board. The ball's in your court. If you don't come talk with us in a month, by May 20, we will have to let everyone know that was your choice."

For Ken, the month felt like thirty days on the rack. Every day people would call: "What's happening to our choir?" "Ken, you don't have proof." "I have questions about the fairness of this whole thing." Ken stopped scheduling lunch appointments because he couldn't endure the hour-long assaults. He'd lie awake at night and think, *I'm helpless. Jean loves me, Irv supports me, but they can't protect me.*

Ken didn't do much that month but answer the phone and try to get his sermons together. Every Sunday, he'd look out and see Steve sitting there. "I know I want Steve to stay in the church and be restored," he told Jean after one Sunday, "but it feels like a divorcée attending the wedding of a former mate."

Ken did meet with Irv often. They'd pray, often on their knees, for strength and wisdom. They began to document their claims. Irv pored over all the church financial records dealing with Steve. He found several fishy items. The previous summer the board had authorized Steve to do miscellaneous maintenance projects around the church to supplement his income. The very days when the choir went on tour, when Steve had to work at the 7-Eleven, he had submitted a bill for thirty hours of caulking windows.

Ken called Steve's home pastor in Doylestown. He felt like a rat doing it, but recently he'd gotten a hunch regarding why Steve had lied about graduate school.

"This is Ken McMahon from Levittown Community Church," he began. "I want you to listen to me and gain my tone. You may not trust me, but please, listen to what I have to say."

"Go ahead," said the pastor.

"Did Steve ever tell you about the graduate music courses he was taking? Were you aware that he had not been taking any classes? Have you been giving him any financial aid?"

"Yes, we give $600 a semester to people studying for church-related careers. You're saying he hasn't been going to school?"

"I'm afraid not."

"I want to check on that."

A few days later the pastor called Ken to say he'd checked with the school, and the church was canceling the financial aid.

Steve arranged to meet with the board on Saturday morning, May 19, one day short of the deadline. He walked into the church lounge at five minutes after nine—alone. Ken was surprised that Doris and Gloria hadn't come with him. Ken and Irv and Bill Seifert stood up and shook his hand.

"Well, Steve, do you have something to say to us?" Ken asked when they were seated again. Ken felt like a racehorse in the chute—churning inside with adrenaline, anger, and fear, but still under control.

"Yeah, I'd like to apologize for our misunderstandings and for the hardship I've caused you."

"Does that mean you're admitting that what we've done is correct, and that the reason we disciplined you was properly stated?"

"No, I'm not saying that. I'm saying that I'm sorry we misunderstood each other and that I didn't help in that circumstance."

"That's not exactly what we had in mind, Steve," Ken said.

Irv was sitting next to Steve, and he leaned over, put his arm around him, and began talking in a quiet, steady voice. "Steve, we want you to understand that we love you and want to be reconciled. But the Bible makes it clear that first there needs to be confession of your sin and repentance, a change of mind about that sin. You see, we're not the ones you have offended. We're included, but you have offended the church. What we need to know today is whether you are confessing—not just admitting under duress—that you have sinned so that we can be reconciled to you. We're ready to do that, and we'd like to."

Steve shifted in his seat and looked out the window. Irv continued, "Let me tell you why that's necessary. One Sunday last September, you and I talked in the foyer for fifteen minutes about your graduate school experience. You went into great detail about how difficult your choral conducting class was, and how hard your music theory professor was, and about the papers you were writing. The bottom line is, every single one of those things was false, wasn't it?"

"Yeah, it was." Steve's eyes became moist.

Ken outlined the other lies about having to work the weekend of the choir tour, and not dating Gloria, about reporting hours that he hadn't really worked. Steve admitted to the situations where he could tell they had firm evidence, but he denied all the others. Finally Steve said, "What do you want me to do now?"

"We simply want you to confess your sin to us and the Lord so we can restore you. We would like you to write it out—not to be published, just to help you—and come meet with us again and read it. It would help you and the church if Gloria and her mother came also."

"All right," Steve said. "I'll set up a time, and I'll call you in two days."

Then he walked out of the lounge, and Ken never saw him again.

Epilogue

Steve's mother-in-law left the church shortly thereafter. The church hired a choir director on a temporary basis, then after a year hired a full-time replacement. The church has continued to grow, though the choir remained stagnant for years and only recently has begun turning around. Another church hired Steve, against Ken's recommendation, and dismissed him one year later. Steve is now serving another church.

Subterfuge safeguard

Deception assumes many guises. A church treasurer may skim funds. A board member may falsely recount what you said in a meeting. Regardless of its outward appearance, lying is a deadly weapon. It poisons relationships and trust.

How can we protect ourselves? What strategies can shield us from fleecers, flimflams, and frauds? Based on his own painful experience, Ken McMahon suggests the following:

Watch for repeated patterns of behavior. "Looking back, I can't believe we didn't pick up on Steve sooner," Ken says. "He seemed to leave a trail of debts and unresolved conflict." When a member of the church repeatedly mishandles money or kicks up dust, there's usually a character problem inside.

Of course, mistakes are often a sign not of malice but immaturity. How can you distinguish the two? As a general rule, the sincere admit their mistakes and learn from them. The swindler covers his "mistakes" and repeats them. Ken points out: "All Steve had to do was say, 'I'm sorry, I'm having trouble paying my bills and didn't tell the truth.' But he couldn't, because he feared looking bad. So when I hire somebody now, I look for a person who is not overprotective of his or her image, someone who can openly face detractors."

Do your homework. If you suspect a parishioner is conning you, gather proof. This step pains most pastors. "I hated checking up on Steve," Ken says. "First, snooping looks terrible to people outside the church. It gives the church a bad name. Second, playing detective goes against my grain. Maybe it's our weak spot, but we pastors believe the best of people. To doubt someone in my church, to double-check everything he says, tears me up."

But only such documentation will stand up "in court," whether that be a one-on-one confrontation or an all-church meeting. Deception, by its very nature, is the best camouflaged of all sins, the hardest to expose. And when someone is accused of it, everyone else in the church will demand to see the instant replay. Some inner urge makes people insist on seeing the evidence and deciding for themselves.

Never make a move alone. "Perhaps the biggest tactical error I made," Ken says, "is that I met with Steve alone several times. I shouldn't have allowed that. I needed someone like Jean or Irv, someone more discerning who could have firmly called Steve's bluff." Plus, when acting alone, no one can corroborate your story and prevent your-word-against-his situations.

Ken did, however, involve the board early on, and this proved wise. By acting in concert, each action taken against Steve became a board and church matter, rather than Ken's personal vendetta. And when the powder keg exploded, the board helped shield Ken from the flying fragments.

Another reason support is needed can be found in Jesus' description of Satan as "the father of lies." Any action to expose lying seems a foray into enemy-occupied territory. A pastor can expect to meet unusual spiritual resistance. "I found it almost impossible to pray during this," Ken says. "I relied on Irv and a woman in our congregation who prayed for me several times a day. When I felt confused, oppressed, and unsure of my ability as a pastor, I needed people who were 'true worshipers,' people who have been through deep waters and as a result know how to pray."

Hide inside the Mighty Fortress. As Ken discovered, even your best efforts may not prevent a considerable amount of damage.

"With a practiced deceiver, it's a no-win situation," he says. "You never come out unscathed. Only recently have I gotten to the point where I don't think about Steve every day. The choir is just now coming out of a prolonged drought. People are finally beginning to trust me again."

But Ken knew where to run for cover. "It's a truism, but the only thing that mattered in the middle of this was my relationship with the Lord. I finally realized no amount of self-effort could protect me. Yet I was not alone. God protected me."

17

Animal Instincts

We all develop survival responses in
threatening situations.

—Norman Shawchuck and Bob Moeller

T he women's ministries board was meeting, and you could cut the
tension with a spatula.

"If the church won't provide baby-sitters for the Friday Bible
study, I won't be coming back," Susan said, her voice trembling with
anger. "I don't need to spend my Friday mornings in a nursery,
changing diapers and holding crying babies, when I can do that at
home. I come here for a break, not more work. And I'm not the only
one who feels this way. Other young mothers besides me are planning to quit the Bible study unless the church begins providing paid
child care."

"Susan," said Helen, an older woman on the board, "I think I understand why some of the older women oppose paying baby-sitters.
They're concerned about the costs. When we were your age, we all
took turns in the nursery. None of us expected a free ride. While I
don't necessarily agree, some feel your generation isn't willing to
make sacrifices.

"But I have an idea. Why don't the mothers care for the nursery
one week, and the other week we'll pay for child care from the dues
gathered at Bible study?"

"That's not good enough," Susan said firmly. "It's fully-funded
child care every Friday, or we walk."

"I think we should drop the whole issue and plan our fall retreat,"
Denise said nervously, sitting at the other end of the table. "We're all

believers, and we shouldn't be arguing like this. Someone will get hurt."

The group paused for a moment, then went on with the debate.

"Excuse me," Denise whispered, "I just remembered my son forgot his lunch at home today." She stood and hurriedly exited the room, avoiding eye contact with anyone.

"I think this whole problem is my fault," Iola said. "When I was president last year, I should have started collecting money for babysitting. I'll be happy to serve in the nursery, and I've got a little nest egg at home that would pay sitters for the rest of the year."

The group knew Iola, an elderly woman, a "mother" to everyone in the church, lived on a fixed income and couldn't afford such an expense. Susan and Helen agreed that letting Iola pick up the tab wasn't the answer.

Eunice, the pastor's wife, was the last to speak. "There's a way to solve this problem, but it isn't by forcing a vote today. This isn't a battle to be won or lost; it's a problem to be solved. We need to re-examine the goals of the group and see if there are ways to accomplish them that will also strengthen our relationships. Resolving this may take time, but we'll be a stronger group for it."

Seated at the end of the linen-covered table was Alice, the current president of the women's ministries. What should she do?

Survival instincts

These women displayed a variety of conflict management styles—from aggressive confrontation to completely passive avoidance. Most likely these women follow the same style of handling conflict elsewhere, for we all develop survival responses in threatening situations.

Corporate psychologists have labeled these responses with animal names (for the solutions they seek): sharks ("I win; you lose"), foxes ("Everyone wins a little and loses a little"), turtles ("I withdraw"), teddy bears ("I'll lose so you can win"), and owls ("Let's find a way for everyone to win").

Fins in the baptistry: Sharks tend to be domineering, aggressive, and open to any solution as long as it's the one they want. Sharks use whatever it takes to prevail: persuasion, intimidation, power plays. Sharks don't always appear menacing and may even possess a quiet demeanor, but make no mistake—they play to win, even if others lose.

Susan probably learned early in life that sharklike aggressiveness helped her survive threatening situations, and she carried that into adulthood. Though she lacked gray skin and three rows of teeth, she still approached the baby-sitting issue in Jaws-like fashion.

Her threat to lead a walkout was a classic shark tactic. Either she and her friends would get their way, or they would fold their chairs and vacate the study.

There are dangers in always giving sharks their way. When I-must-win individuals are allowed to rule the church, anger builds in others, people feel coerced, and a precarious dependency on the strong-willed individual develops.

Foxes in the vineyard: Helen was not a competitor but a compromiser. Typical of the wily fox, she hoped to slice the pie so that everyone believed they got the biggest piece.

Helen's suggestion that they split the child care between the young mothers and paid sitters was her attempt to help everyone "win-a-little, lose-a-little." She sincerely wanted to keep the group from splitting over the child-care issue.

Unfortunately, in the church, compromise has gotten a bad name. In some circles it's a synonym for worldliness or moral laxity. But in organizational terms, a compromiser is defined as a person sincerely working through bargaining and conciliation to keep a group from breaking apart.

Foxes are flexible, and their primary interest is the common good. If people don't immediately respond to their bargain, they aren't above arm-twisting and manipulation to impose an agreement. Helen planned some behind-the-scenes negotiating to persuade both parties to accept her solution.

Sometimes a split-the-difference approach sensibly solves minor disputes. If one group likes dill pickles, and the other sweet, why not put out two dishes?

But compromise isn't always the answer. It can leave people half-satisfied and half-committed to the solution. In that case, the problem will emerge again later in a different form.

Helen believed she was pursuing both parties' interests. But her solution didn't address the underlying issues of ownership and control of the Bible study. Even if others accepted her compromise, these issues would eventually reemerge.

Avoidance in a half-shell: Denise grew up in an abusive home. She now was a young mother and favored the church subsidizing child care, but she was afraid to say so. She learned as a child that when others fight, she got hurt. And if she disagreed and said so, she got hurt even more. Her response to every threatening situation was to avoid the problem at all costs. Denise had become a turtle.

Turtles are so frightened by conflict that they pull into their shell. A world without conflict is the only one they can survive in, so they flee altercation. Some actually walk out, as Denise did, while others withdraw into emotional neutrality and numbness.

Because turtles abhor conflict, they are often mistaken for peacemakers. But avoiding thorny issues simply to preserve the peace unwittingly sets up the church for major problems.

At times, avoiding conflict makes sense. Proverbs reminds us it is the glory of a person to overlook an insult. We ought to choose carefully which hills we are willing to die on. Some battles aren't worth fighting.

But pulling into a shell as a long-term strategy for coping with serious conflict simply won't work.

Turtles, while appearing to be peaceable and gentle souls, often are hiding great reservoirs of anger and frustration. Denise appeared calm and sedate, but inside she struggled with unresolved rage and bitterness. She never felt the freedom or confidence to confront her abusive past and carried the resentment in her soul.

Denise couldn't accept even temporary tension to help the group reach a satisfying solution.

Cuddly and accommodating: Iola's willingness to provide the baby-sitting herself and to blame herself for the controversy is typical of the most lovable creature in the conflict management menagerie—the teddy bear.

In a threatening situation, teddy bears readily surrender their own interests to accommodate the disagreeing party. Iola never expressed her own opinion on the child-care issue but immediately attempted to placate Susan and the young mothers.

Teddy bears will maintain peace at almost any price. They attempt to steer others away from controversial issues. They show increased personal concern for others, working to create a relaxed, easygoing, loving atmosphere.

Who could fault Iola for trying to solve the dilemma herself? Her generosity was commendable. That's why teddy bears are often seen as super-spiritual. In sacrificial fashion, they attempt to atone for the problem in the group by bearing it themselves.

Such accommodation has an upside. Surrendering our selfish goals in pursuit of peace is often a sign of godliness and maturity. If someone wants roast beef rather than turkey served at the Christmas luncheon, though my diet won't allow it, it's not worth dividing the group over. I'll bring my own lunch and microwave it.

But there's a downside to the teddy-bear approach. Was it wrong for the young mothers to express their needs? Was it wrong for the older women to bring up their financial concerns? No. Both were expressing legitimate points of view. But Iola, like all teddy bears, believed relationships are more important than issues, and therefore any disagreement is bad.

Teddy bears unintentionally give sharks a false sense of rightness. On a personal level, though they appear cheerful and easy-going, accommodators can often struggle with inner anger over always giving in.

No one knew it, but Iola was tired of trying to keep the Friday Bible study together and planned to quit in the spring.

Spotting the collaborative owl: Eunice alone saw the babysitting controversy as a problem to be solved, rather than a battle to be won or lost. Her desire was to see everyone leave the table with a win-win solution.

Such collaborators "co-labor" with all parties until they arrive at a mutually satisfying solution. Their strength lies in their willingness to stay with a task or problem until it's solved.

Collaborators see disputes as an opportunity to strengthen a group, not destroy it. Eunice wasn't afraid of the child-care issue. She recognized it as a symptom of a generation gap in the group, an opportunity to address the larger issue of how the older and younger women would share control and ownership of the Bible study.

Eunice's goal was not to overcome or avoid adversaries but to help them understand and appreciate each other's needs.

Here's how she eventually helped the group solve the dilemma.

1. Generate as much useful information as possible. Eunice arranged for a meeting of young mothers and older women. She asked the young mothers why paid child care was so important to them. As they explained their busy schedules—many had part-time jobs to help make ends meet—the older women were surprised to learn how stressful their lives were. As Susan explained how her newborn seldom slept entire nights, they could see that exhaustion, not laziness, was behind her request to be relieved of baby-sitting duties.

As the younger women heard the older ladies, several of whom were widows, explain their difficulties in living on fixed incomes, they realized most couldn't afford higher dues on Fridays to pay for child care. They assumed it would be expensive.

Both groups learned the other brought different needs to the study. The younger women wanted a rest; the older women wanted companionship. That helped to filter misconceptions and wrong conclusions out of the discussion.

2. Help the group see where they agree. Eunice helped both sides see where they agreed and where they didn't. Everyone agreed they benefited from the participation of both older and younger women. They all believed that sharing their struggles and praying together helped them cope with their problems. And they all agreed they didn't want the group to split.

One major difference remained. While there was a consensus that the economic burden of child care should be distributed, the group still disagreed on how it should be done. Some continued to support the every-other-week plan, while others wanted weekly subsidized child care.

3. Bring everyone into the decision-making process and motivate them to personally commit to the final agreement. Eunice, the owl, knew that people tend to support solutions they help create, so she had the group brainstorm alternative ideas. One of the women suggested they hold a fund-raiser with the goal of raising enough money to pay for a year's worth of baby-sitting.

They decided on a holiday boutique sale. Several older women agreed to sew quilts, which typically sold for several hundred dollars in retail shops. The added benefit of the project was companionship; they could work on them together, filling up some of the empty time during the holiday seasons when loneliness was a problem.

As for the young women, several ran home-based computer businesses and agreed to generate mailing lists and publicity for the sale. Others had talent in watercolor and pottery and agreed to sell some of their work at the boutique and donate profits to the project.

As a result the women's ministries held the most successful fundraising event in the church's history, and they grew closer to one another in the process.

While the millennium didn't arrive, the shark, the fox, the turtle, the teddy bear, and the owl did learn to live with one another. The Wild Kingdom had been tamed.

18

Recovered Nightmare

In one short week, Kirk had been sucked into a quagmire involving the chairman of his board, a highly placed church leader, and two other members of the congregation. If the matter came before the board, it could polarize the church.

—David Goetz

K irk Thullin expected Rob to grunt his way through the hour of marital counseling. Last week's session had seemed futile.

But on this day, Rob, without his wife Jennifer, was eager to chat about his stormy marriage. The hour breezed by. As he stood up to leave, he said, "I probably shouldn't be telling you this, but Jennifer has been in sex therapy for the past year."

Pastor Kirk leaned back in his chair and swiveled a half-turn toward Rob. *I should never have agreed to see this couple*, Kirk thought. *I'm really not a marriage counselor.*

It was a favor to Ken Hutchenson, chairman of the church board. Ken had helped Kirk get his legs under him when he arrived at Harrison Flats Community Church ten years ago. Ken, a corporate lawyer close to retirement, was among his most trusted church allies. A month earlier, Ken had asked him to see his daughter and son-in-law, who had recently separated after six years of marriage and one son. Kirk didn't know them well.

Rob continued, "Her therapist says her sexual problems stem from sexual abuse as a child."

Kirk drew in his next breath sharply. *Lord, please don't let it be Ken*, he thought.

"It was Brian."

"Ken's brother?"

"You'd better talk to Jennifer yourself."

After Rob left, Kirk stared out the office window at a thundercloud forming in the reddening evening sky. *Not Brian*, he thought. Brian and his wife, Liz, also attended the church. An electrical contractor, Brian served on the church building committee and had just started a men's Bible study. He was Ken's younger and only brother.

Kirk tried to register what he'd just heard. *If the charges were true, there would have to be church discipline of a key leader, and the state might get involved*—Kirk stopped the train of thought before it crushed him. He would schedule an appointment with Jennifer in the morning.

Twenty-year-old memory

A week later Jennifer, slight with short, wedge-shaped hair, bounced into Kirk's office and greeted him by saying that Rob couldn't be trusted with any information. She patted her cheeks as if they were hot and said she felt embarrassed but that it was probably good that Kirk knew.

"It happened about twenty years ago," she began. "I must have been thirteen. My aunt and uncle often took care of me and my brother while my parents were away. Uncle Brian molested me repeatedly."

"Did you tell anyone at the time?" Kirk asked.

"I was too scared," Jennifer said, "and soon I buried it. My therapist said I've been repressing it all these years and that it's at the root of my problems."

Over the past few days, Kirk had mulled over what he wanted to say. He was the first to admit he wasn't highly trained in psychology. He was a pastor, not a therapist. But he had read a little about sexual abuse and knew enough to realize that Jennifer needed to be believed. One of his counselor friends once told him that over 50 percent of all women have been sexually abused.

"I believe you," Kirk said to Jennifer in his most affirming voice. Then he hesitated—but said it anyway: "I think Brian could have done this to you. Who else knows about this?"

"Everyone, now, I guess."

"You confronted Brian?"

Jennifer said she hadn't but that Brian's wife, Liz, had. After a therapy session in which she remembered Brian molesting her, Jennifer
stopped returning her aunt's phone calls. Liz had left several messages inviting Jennifer's son over for an afternoon of fishing at their
property pond. When Liz finally reached her, she asked, "What's
wrong? Have I done something to hurt you?" Jennifer tried to dodge
her question, but Liz persisted, so Jennifer blurted, "In my therapy
I've remembered that Uncle Brian molested me when I was thirteen."

That night, Jennifer said, Liz confronted her husband and threatened to leave if it were true, and he exploded in a rage.

"Brian denied it all," Jennifer said to Kirk. "So, I immediately told
Mom and Dad."

Kirk felt nauseated. He figured he'd heard just about everything.
This was a first. In one short week, he had been sucked into a quagmire involving the chairman of his board, a highly placed church
leader, and two other members of the congregation. Already it was
ripping two families apart, and if the matter came before the board,
it could polarize the church.

Seeds of doubt

Friday afternoon, two days after the session with Jennifer, Brian
strode into Kirk's office unannounced. He shuffled his stocky frame
up to Kirk's desk and cleared his throat. He mumbled a greeting and
then abruptly asked if Kirk had heard the news. Kirk nodded.

"Jennifer is lying," he blurted. "I did no such thing to her. Ken
knows I would never do anything to her." His face blushed with anger, the red darkening his tanned skin.

Kirk looked Brian in the eyes. "Jennifer told me what came out
in therapy," Kirk said. *Is he lying?* he thought. He groped for words.
"The charges are serious," Kirk said. "But I'll be there for you and Liz
through this."

Kirk felt as if he were telling a bold-faced lie. How could he support a felon? But then again, why would Brian be so open about it if
he were guilty? No, he must be guilty. A colleague of Kirk's had said
that denial is common in abusers.

Brian seemed satisfied with Kirk's reply. "That means a lot, Pastor," he said. As Brian left, Kirk let out a long breath. *What will dinner
be like at his home tonight?* he thought. He felt sorry for Liz and

thought about their son, away at Boston College—did he know about this?

The next Tuesday after the board meeting, Kirk asked Ken to stick around for a few minutes. Ken looked tired. When Kirk mentioned that he had talked with Jennifer, Ken hung his head.

"The less we talk about it, the better," he said. "The further this spreads, the worse it's going to be."

For a moment Kirk thought Ken might break into tears. A look of confusion crossed his face, but then his wiry frame stiffened. "I've been praying for you," Kirk said. He felt a little awkward putting his arm around Ken's shoulders but did it anyway. "I'll be there for you if you want to talk." Ken thanked him and left.

Kirk soon learned that when Jennifer broke the news to her father and mother, Ken and Beth paced their family-room floor the entire night. They picked up pictures of their daughter and grandson and held them to their chests and burst into loud sobs. The next morning Ken had angrily confronted Brian at a jobsite. The two almost came to blows when Brian called Jennifer a liar.

I'm in over my head, Kirk thought one day while driving home. *I've got to refer Jennifer immediately. . . . Pris would be perfect.* Dr. Priscilla Conrad also attended the church. She was a veteran Christian psychologist, and Kirk respected her judgment. But first he must see Jennifer one more time. He had to make sure she was positive about Brian.

When Kirk saw Jennifer again, she agreed to see the counselor. "I trust her instincts," Kirk said. "Pris has lots of experience. I refer to her often."

Then he pressed Jennifer. "Are you absolutely sure Brian was the one who abused you? Could it have been anyone else?"

Jennifer's face tightened, and she leaned forward. "I'm absolutely sure."

"The picture you have in your mind is Brian, right?"

With that Jennifer stood up, her voice rising. "Pastor Kirk, you know nothing about sexual abuse. You have no business questioning me."

"I believe you, I believe you," Kirk said. "These charges are serious—I just want to be sure."

Jennifer snatched Priscilla's business card out of Kirk's hand and walked stiffly out of the office. Kirk felt a twinge of guilt—and a little anger. He didn't mean to be insensitive. He wished he'd taken more counseling courses in seminary.

Fallout

After their emotions were spent, a deep hurt settled over the Hutchenson families. Jennifer started seeing Pris once a week for therapy and joined a support group for victims of sexual abuse. Within several months, though, she and Rob were divorced, and despite a fierce court battle, Jennifer got sole custody of their son.

Liz and Brian's marriage, however, seemed to have survived its knockdown. Liz had thrown her lot with Brian. But Kirk wondered how she could trust him. Wouldn't she always wonder? Kirk didn't talk to them a great deal.

Ken and Beth appeared together on the outside, though when Kirk saw them at church he often thought he saw their eyes well up. He never saw them speak to Liz and Brian. From time to time, Kirk stopped Ken in the church hallway and pulled him into his office to ask about his family. Ken never said much, but one time his lower lip began to quiver.

"Who am I to believe?" he said as his eyes filled up. "Things will never be the same." He sobbed so hard his body shook. At first Kirk thought he might be having a heart attack.

While some family members had quit talking to each other, no one left the church. On Sunday mornings Ken and Beth sat in their usual pew near the front of the sanctuary. Liz and Brian generally sat in the back, and Jennifer with her son on the opposite side. After the service, Liz and Brian usually scooted out before Kirk could shake their hands. They stopped having Sunday brunch with Ken and Beth at the Old Main Inn.

Kirk made a special point to hug Beth each Sunday. She had lost a son-in-law in the divorce and a brother-in-law through isolation. Maybe he could be like a son to her right now.

Numbing fears

A busy pastor, Kirk tried not to let the Hutchensons' problems consume his time. But he kept in touch with Jennifer's therapist, calling every few weeks. Pris would say Jennifer was healing but needed more time. Six months after the revelations, Pris asked to see Kirk.

On a Wednesday afternoon, she strode into Kirk's office. She asked how things were going at the church and mentioned how much she enjoyed Sunday's sermon. She was here to discuss the situation with Brian.

"What have you observed of Brian in church settings?" she asked. Kirk told her what he knew, which wasn't much, and near the end of the conversation said he also had a few questions.

"What is the memory Jennifer has of her abuse?"

"She is lying in the grass behind her uncle's house," Pris replied. "She feels numb all over, she hears Brian's footsteps, and then she is overcome with fear."

Kirk waited for Pris to continue, but she didn't.

"That's it?"

"What do you mean?"

"That's the only memory she has?"

"She has others," Pris said, "but that's her primary one."

"Is it possible she's mistaken?"

"Victims don't make mistakes," Pris said sharply. "Statistics show that repressed memories are most often true."

"But shouldn't Jennifer at least apologize for dumping this on the family? I mean, shouldn't she have waited until something more concrete came out?"

"You don't understand victims," Pris said. "You will hurt the process of healing if you push her to apologize. She had to speak out and expose the secret."

Pris then turned the conversation. "Why haven't you confronted Brian yet?" Kirk thought for a moment and was about to respond when Pris pressed her point. "Are you afraid of confrontation? You know he is lying. Perpetrators always deny their actions."

In fact, Pris continued, for full family healing Kirk also needed to confront Ken. Jennifer's problems had been made worse because Ken was an emotionally absent father and was never close to Jennifer.

"That's not fair," Kirk said. "What's he supposed to do? What does Jennifer want him to do?"

"Why are you protecting him?" Pris asked. "Why are you afraid to confront this situation head on? Are you protecting yourself from pain?"

Kirk could feel the heat crawl up his face. *I'm not on trial here,* he told himself. *I'll do the right things at the right time, but I'm a pastor, not a prosecuting attorney.*

After she left, Kirk felt the sting of her words. He wanted to do more, but what? Jennifer's memory wasn't much to go on, and he was beginning to have his doubts. Something didn't feel right.

Decidedly neutral

Pris continued to counsel Jennifer and brief Kirk about Jennifer's emotional health: She was growing stronger, and soon she would be ready to confront her abuser herself.

Pris also reminded Kirk that he was shirking his responsibility. Brian and Ken needed to be confronted, and since he hadn't done that, Kirk was now the "main obstacle to Jennifer's healing." His apparent skepticism about her abuse and his passive response were "revictimizing her."

Kirk countered by saying he wanted to help, but Jennifer's memory was too fuzzy for him to proceed with certainty. And if Jennifer felt her father wasn't supportive enough, she needed to talk with him herself. But Kirk wondered how that could be true. In the midst of this ordeal, Ken had paid for Jennifer's nasty divorce and given her the down payment to buy a house.

Still, over time Pris's comments began to seep into Kirk's spirit. He was angry at Jennifer for unloading her secret in a cavalier manner without thought of anyone else. He was angry at the suffering he saw in the eyes of Ken and Beth, and Liz and Brian. He had never seen such isolation among family members. He was angry at the sex therapist, who seemed to have concocted a nightmare out of a few abstract memories. And Pris? She seemed to be pouring gas on an open flame.

Still, Pris was doing her homework. She had contacted Dr. Bruce Swenson, one of the leading psychologists in the Christian recovery movement and author of several books. According to Pris, Swenson had repeated the axiom, "Victims don't lie," and said that well-intentioned but unskilled pastors often cause victims more harm than good.

Kirk had never before questioned his call and gifts so much. What good was his training in theology when what seemed to be needed was expert psychological care? He felt as if he were bucking the entire psychological establishment of Christendom. Then one Sunday a board member asked to speak to him between Sunday school and church. He mentioned that Pris had told him that something was going on in the Hutchenson family.

"I don't know any of the details," the board member said, "but I hear you're trying to protect Ken."

"You don't know any of the details," Kirk snapped, "and you're wrong."

Kirk went home with his head about to explode. The stress of the past year had chipped away at his confidence. He had carried most of his self-doubt alone—not even telling his wife. But that Sunday Kirk called a friend who pastored in Chicago and unloaded on him the events of the past year. Kirk's voice broke as he spoke of the indecision gripping his soul. He said he felt as if he were stumbling around in the dark.

"You need an outside opinion," his friend said. "I'm stopping through next week to see my father. I'd be happy to sit with you and Pris for a few minutes."

The next week Kirk's friend met with him and Pris. After the session, the pastor said, "I need to take a course on how to interpret memories. I haven't a clue how feeling numb and hearing footsteps translate into sexual abuse."

Kirk felt a little better, but nothing had really changed. What should he do? He was weary of Pris's psychoanalysis about his fear of conflict and why he avoided it. He knew himself better than that; he would do something if the situation were clearer. But he couldn't act unless he had something solid to act upon.

One day, while preparing a sermon, he read Deuteronomy 17:8: "If cases come before your courts that are too difficult for you to judge . . ." The words jumped off the page—even Old Testament judges found some cases too tough to decide. Kirk took comfort in that, and the wheels in his mind began to turn. He searched the Bible for other passages that could throw light on his uncertainty.

No one in Scripture, he discovered, was condemned without corroboration; by the mouth of "two or three witnesses" everything was established. He wanted to be as passionate about justice as God is. He felt for Jennifer, he really did, but accusing a man based on one person's twenty-year-old memory? This amounted to a lynching!

One fall morning while jogging, Kirk made up his mind. A year had passed since Jennifer had made her accusations. He decided with finality that he would remain absolutely neutral. He didn't have enough information, and he was no detective. He had to assume Brian's innocence until he admitted his guilt or more concrete evidence surfaced.

The other victims

A week later Kirk met with Jennifer, and her face darkened as he informed her of his decision.

"What you are doing," she sputtered, "will set me back years in therapy. You're just protecting yourself. I suspected you didn't have the guts to stand up."

Jennifer stormed out of the office. Kirk spent the afternoon flitting from one thing to the next; he dreaded the inevitable call from Pris, which came the following morning.

"Over 50 percent of women have been abused," she began. "Jennifer is not lying."

"Perhaps not intentionally," Kirk countered. "So are memories exempt from the influence of sin?"

"You are afraid to face up to the truth. Brian is guilty."

"You say if a man refuses to admit to sexual abuse," Kirk pressed, "he is in denial. That's a double bind. He's damned either way. Whatever happened to 'innocent until proven guilty?' "

Kirk explained the teaching of Scripture that no one could be justly convicted without the testimony of two or three witnesses. In this case, there was only one.

"You're hiding," Pris said, "and using Scripture as an excuse."

"It's not my role to judge who is telling the truth," Kirk replied. "I need to be a pastor to every family member, not just Jennifer."

Pris protested, but Kirk didn't budge. Near the conversation's end, she said she still wanted Kirk to be present when Jennifer confronted Brian. Kirk promised his support. One of his biggest frustrations was the way Jennifer had dumped her allegations on Liz. A tête-a-tête between Brian and Jennifer was long overdue.

After he hung up, he breathed a sigh of relief. For the first time in months, he felt confident about his handling of the situation. The Word of God had given him something solid to stand on.

The next evening Kirk visited Liz and Brian for only the second time since Jennifer's allegations. Before, he had taken for granted that Brian was guilty and felt awkward around him. Now he wished he'd been more of a pastor to him and Liz. His stomach churned as he rang their doorbell.

For the next three hours, Kirk listened to their heartache. Liz spoke of the agony of weeks of wondering if the man lying beside her in bed had molested her niece. Brian spoke of his humiliation and of his rage. "If she ever makes a public accusation," he snarled, "I'll sue her for custody of her son. She's an unfit mother." Brian's sudden anger startled Kirk, but then, just as suddenly, Brian's eyes filled with tears. He spoke of the weeks of silence between him and Liz and of his fear of losing everything that ever mattered to him.

It was dark when Kirk walked out to his car. His heart was heavy with their grief.

D-Day

A few months later, Pris called to say Jennifer was now strong enough to confront Brian. What Pris suggested seemed constructive, and when Liz and Brian agreed to it, Kirk called Ken to let him know. Ken said he'd be at Kirk's office in thirty minutes. He arrived with his lips pressed together and his face flushed. The veins in his neck looked as if they might rupture. He didn't sit down.

"If this pushes Jennifer over the edge," he fumed, "and she loses custody of her son, I will hold you responsible."

Kirk's face blanched.

"I'm sick and tired of this—mess," Ken continued. "This confrontation will only stir things up."

Kirk had never heard him swear before. Kirk didn't argue. He knew Ken wasn't mad at him. Ken was a competent lawyer, but this was a case without winners and losers. Everyone was a loser. After he left, Kirk put his head on his desk. Would this debacle destroy even his friendship with Ken? Would he leave the church? Kirk returned to preparing Sunday's message, but he should have just gone home.

The night before the confrontation, Kirk was still tossing and turning at 4:30 A.M., so he read his Bible and prayed and then tried to read a novel he'd been working on for three months. *Remember*, he kept reminding himself, *keep calm. Be objective. Be a presence for Christ to everyone.* He was counting on the confrontation to bring clarity to this conundrum.

Shortly before the confrontation with Brian, Jennifer met with Liz in Kirk's office. Jennifer had requested the meeting. It was their first conversation in more than a year and a half. Kirk simply watched.

"I never meant it to come out that way," Jennifer said, opening the conversation.

That's not much of an apology, Kirk thought, *after all the damage it caused.*

"But it's true. Uncle Brian assaulted me." Jennifer folded her arms and glanced over at Kirk.

"Here is my niece whom I've known since she was born," Liz said slowly, "accusing my husband of thirty-five years. Who am I supposed to believe?"

Liz told of her agony in deciding whether to believe Brian or to start a new life without him. She spoke softly. Kirk was surprised at how little emotion both women showed.

"Your uncle has never given me reason to doubt him in the past," Liz concluded. "I believe Brian, and I'll stick by my husband to the end."

Minutes later, Brian entered the office and sat beside his wife. Together they faced Jennifer.

Kirk opened in prayer, and then Jennifer spoke first. "What you did to me destroyed my life," she said. She then read a brief statement typed out on a half-sheet of paper. She concluded by saying she needed to hear Brian admit his guilt. Kirk kept eyeing Brian. Not a muscle moved.

"I'm sorry for whatever caused all this pain in your life," Brian replied, "but I didn't molest you. I have no recollection of sexually assaulting you."

"What I remember *happened*," Jennifer replied.

"I must have offended you deeply at some point," Brian said, "for you to accuse me of this."

The silence that followed was deafening. Jennifer kept her eyes locked on Kirk, and Brian reached for Liz's hand. *Somebody, please come clean,* Kirk thought. He glanced first at Jennifer and then at Brian, and then realized they had reached an impasse mortals could not resolve. "Why don't we put this entire matter into God's hands," he said. Kirk ended his prayer, "Lord, you know what happened, and we don't. And while this may not get fully resolved until Christ returns, I pray for your grace for each person here."

Silence hung heavy as everyone left. Kirk sat alone for a while and then went home and trimmed the bushes lining his driveway. It felt good to whack off a branch and have something to show for it.

Where chains never bind

Pris called early the next week. She wanted Kirk to set up another confrontation. "Brian must be made to confess," she said.

"There will be no more confrontations," Kirk replied, "unless we have something more to go on. For now, it's over, and there's nothing more I or anyone can do."

Pris made her case, but Kirk's mind was made up. A month later, Jennifer called Kirk to say she was leaving the church for good. She said it was undermining her healing and that she couldn't stomach listening to someone preach whom she didn't respect.

"I hope you don't get involved in a sexual abuse case again," she concluded. "Next time, you'd better stick to something you know."

Her words smarted, but Kirk replied simply, "I hope you find healing, and I'll continue to pray for that." When he hung up, he was surprised how calm he felt. Mostly he felt sad.

That afternoon, Kirk and his wife drove to Seattle to see the Broadway play *Les Miserables*, a date they'd planned for months. The play, set in France during the first half of the 1800s, is about a man named Jean Valjean, a thief. Kirk and his wife settled into their theater seats, and he put his arm around her. In the cool darkness he tried to put out of his mind the morning's events.

Kirk watched as Valjean, because he is shown mercy by a priest, makes a fresh start and eventually becomes a wealthy factory owner. In his new life, Valjean promises a dying woman named Fantine that he'll take care of her young daughter. Valjean makes good on his promise, even while being dogged mercilessly by his past. Near the play's end, Valjean lies dying. Fantine, now an angel, comes to him and sings, "Come with me / Where chains will never bind you / All your grief / At last, at last, behind you / Lord in heaven, / Look down on him in mercy."

Kirk covered his face with his hands. Something about those

words . . . In the auditorium's blackness, the sorrow of the Hutchenson families washed over him. Tears ran down between his fingers. In his mind, he saw each suffering face. It might never be over for them. But there was a place where chains never bind. Only heaven would heal their grief.

19

Hot-Potato Preaching

*The truth can be cutting, but the preacher
doesn't have to be.*

—Stuart Briscoe

I have twice passed out cards to my congregation with the following words: "I would like to hear a sermon no longer than ____ minutes on the subject: What the Bible has to say about _____." Self-appointed comics took advantage of this. One fellow said he'd like to hear a sermon no longer than five minutes on what the Bible says about God.

But many times people request the tough issues. People want to know if the Bible's message can stand up to modern pressures. I want to assure them it can.

It would be easier if we could preach a lifetime without ever touching on sin, morality, sexuality, lifestyle, or any number of other adrenalin inducers. Controversy makes preaching a more difficult proposition. But, as any pastor knows, a congregation needs the spicier issues if for no other reason than that God fills his Word with just such fare.

However, a crisis is not inevitable. We can preach controversial topics without picking a fight.

Turn the heat off and the light on

We need to credit people with enough maturity to handle the balanced presentation of an issue. Over the years I've addressed the role of women, eternal security, Spirit baptism, various issues of sexuality, and the church and politics. I've concluded that what's crucial is not so much the topic as the method.

When diving into an area of controversy, I don't expect total agreement. That's why there's a dispute in the first place. People's belief systems are complex. Much more is at stake than the particular issue at hand. I recognize from the start that I'm probably not going to change anyone's mind.

Thus, I try to broaden thinking rather than change it. Although people probably won't budge from their position, they may at least acknowledge other viewpoints. That's progress. Maybe, over the years, they will change. Maybe not. In any event, I agree with Oliver Wendell Holmes, who said, "Once a mind has been stretched by a new idea, it never returns to its original shape."

When I try to change people, however, I only add heat and dim the light. For instance, I have strong feelings about the way the talents of women have been wasted in the church. So I must be careful when I talk on the subject. People often say I feel this way because of the wife I have. I usually answer, "Has it ever occurred to you that I may have the wife I do because I feel this way?" That doesn't always go over too well!

Preaching out of anger may feel good at the time, especially when we've built up a good head of steam. But in the long run, it doesn't accomplish what we're after.

I also have to point out that I've been at the same church for nearly twenty-five years. That gives me a level of credibility that a fresh seminary graduate doesn't have. I would think carefully before I preached controversial themes in my first few years at a church. It's a matter of sensing the needs and maturity of the congregation. But I never provoke controversy just for the sake of controversy.

Drumming up a controversial topic is not hard. Currently American Christians are debating the relationship between church and state. Some Christians believe the state is working its way into church matters and trying to take away freedoms. Others insist believers must be more politically active. The issue of abortion is a prime example: the extent to which the church should be challenging the state on its laws concerning abortion is highly controversial. In many instances, people's spirituality is measured by their level of involvement on this issue.

Recently I addressed this in a message on the church and politics. I opened by saying that the politics of many Christians are often more determined by economics than theology. I pointed out that we live in a particular country in a particular socioeconomic group and that people living in other countries in widely differing socioeconomic groups may look at the Scripture differently.

I gave an example: If we live in a comfortable, upper-middle-class suburb in the Midwest, then we probably don't spend much time in the Old Testament where it talks about God's concern for the poor. But if we had grown up in an impoverished Asian or African country, we would. If we lived under a totalitarian regime or fascist dictatorship, then it's quite possible we would be interested in what the Bible says about liberty.

To further provide context, I mapped out the historical background, from the days of the early church when the state controlled the church to the modern period where the church and state live in a uneasy relationship.

I concluded that the church and the state should be separate but mutually respectful and influential. I also concluded that the church should encourage individual Christians to recognize the limitations of participatory democracy and to exercise their Christian citizenship responsibly in a less-than-ideal situation. I gave specific ways they could do this.

I could tell I had touched a nerve that Sunday by the debate stirred in our congregation. Our church is filled with thoughtful people unafraid to debate controversial topics. In fact, that's one way I gauge the impact of my sermons: Does it generate discussion? Discussion is an indicator that the lights have been turned on.

Do your homework

Few controversies in the church are new. Whenever I touch on eternal security, I remind folks that if Whitefield and Wesley struggled with this for a lifetime, I'm not likely to end the debate in a thirty-five-minute sermon. However, if I prepare well, I can at least give them an overview of the issues involved. A preacher who handles controversial subjects must do adequate research.

To prepare for a recent sermon on values, I read *A Question of Values*, a book that delineated three ways people arrive at a system of values. One is the individualistic approach—the it's-nobody's-business-what-I-do approach. The second is what society thinks—for example, the Supreme Court's debate over defining pornography. It finally decided that pornography is that which offends local community standards. The third way is based on the assumption that there is a sovereign Lord in whose character and nature reside absolute values.

In addition to *A Question of Values*, I also found helpful Robert Bellah's *Habits of the Heart*. Since in the last few years a tremendous amount of material on this subject has been published—in *Time*, *Newsweek*, and the *Atlantic Monthly*—there was no shortage of resources. Preaching effectively on controversial issues requires a lot of spadework.

Touch the funny bone

Humor is a tension-reliever, though one always runs the risk of offending someone. Still, I like the odds, so I occasionally weave lighter stories and quips into a controversial sermon.

I recently preached on a passage that preachers either harp on or avoid: " 'Therefore come out from them and be separate,' says the Lord" (2 Cor. 6:17). I spoke on the issue of separation.

"What Paul meant," I said, "is that identification is clearly wrong—but that isolation is totally counterproductive." I explained how Christians often develop subcultures that determine what is and isn't appropriate separation.

To illustrate, I told the story of the Dutch elders who sent representatives to check on the moral condition of the American church. The observers were horrified. They reported to the Dutch elders that American women wore makeup and wore expensive clothes. The Americans also drove big cars, had carpets in the sanctuaries, and had a piano as well as an organ. It was obvious to the Dutch the tremendous amount of money Americans were expending on themselves.

And as the old Dutch elders heard this report, some of them burst into tears—and the tears ran down their cigars into their beer.

One time that story backfired on me, however. Several people said, "Those Dutch elders couldn't be Christians because they smoked and drank. You're not suggesting they really were Christians, are you?"

Other times, though, humor has served me well. In the sermon I mentioned on church and politics, I ended it by saying, "The church playing politics is not unlike Michael Jordan playing baseball." That time, everyone laughed.

Give balanced treatment

When I preach on a disputed topic, I think it's only fair to present more than one side. I don't mean setting up a straw man only to knock him down, but rather trying to present all sides with honesty and empathy.

Often, after outlining different sides of the issue, I can present what I feel is a biblical point of view. Other times I can't. In that case I challenge people to come to their own conclusion. I have to remind myself that these people believe the Bible. If I present what it says, then Scripture remains the authority over us all, and we all have to wrestle with the implications. If I set up myself as the authority, then they wrestle with me.

I preached on Ephesians 5, with particular reference to the phrase, "Wives, submit to your husbands." I struggled to prepare for the message, because in some extreme instances men abuse their wives and rationalize it based on this verse. And many women find any talk of submission distasteful.

So to be balanced, I first pointed out that in Ephesians 5:22, the Greek word for *submit* is not there. Paul uses ellipses; the phrase is dependent on the previous verse, which says, "Submit to one another out of reverence for Christ." Literally, then, the passage reads, "Submit to one another out of reverence for Christ, wives to your husbands," which means it is appropriate to add submit in verse 22, but inappropriate to separate verse 22 from verse 21. Grammatically, you can't do that.

"Whatever it means that wives should submit to their husbands," I said, "it cannot be divorced from two other kinds of submission— both people submitted to the Lord, and both submitted to each other. Now that puts it into an entirely different context."

Careful exegesis helped me give what I believe is a more balanced view on the controversial issue of submission.

Consider pastoral needs

Whenever I preach on a controversial topic, I try to keep in mind that more than theory is at stake. Real people in my congregation are struggling with the implications. Some have had abortions. Some are confused about homosexual desires. Some are alcoholics. I can't just leave the issue "out there." I have to think through the situation well enough that I can suggest a sensible course of action.

When I spoke on God's plan for marriage, I took into consideration the couples in the congregation who were living together out of wedlock. I could have told them it's simply not God's will. But I realized some of these couples have overextended themselves financially. They can save several hundred dollars each month by doubling up. In that case, they need to hear that the church will help them locate inexpensive housing.

Sure, they should separate anyway. But if I can communicate to them that I understand their situation, they're more likely to change.

I also try to remember that behind topics such as abortion, divorce, or child abuse is an enormous amount of pain. I must be sensitive to people's experiences without blasting them with the truth. It took a while to learn this.

When I started addressing touchy subjects, the issue of abortion was causing a great deal of turmoil. It seemed everyone in the church was discussing it. Although our members were in basic agreement, some were confused about the details and proper biblical response. I decided it was time to confront the issue, however controversial it might be.

So I studied the appropriate passages, read the current literature, and delivered what I thought was an inspiring message on the sanctity of life. I felt fine about it until I heard the honest reservations of a good friend. "You know," he said, "by the law of averages, you probably spoke to three or four unmarried women who were contemplating abortion." Then he said, "I feel that what you said this morning would only add to their dilemma."

I had powerfully challenged them to make the right choice, but failed to show sensitivity to their painful situation and the shame they probably felt. I'd offered no help in dealing with the heavy responsibilities of carrying a baby full term. It was a vivid reminder of how easy it is to wound people with the truth. The truth can be cutting, but we don't have to be.

Seize the opportunity

I don't want to give the impression I announce controversial topics every month. If I did, I'd be guilty of sensationalism. I don't want
my sermons to be the ecclesiastical equivalent of supermarket tab-
loids. Most of the time, I deal with controversial issues while preaching on some other subject.

When I did a series on the Israelites' settling of Canaan, we came
to the passage in Deuteronomy that speaks of the sins of the fathers
being passed down to the children. I saw this as a beautiful opportunity to address the trend in some church circles where parents are
blamed for their children's faults, and where people fail to take responsibility for their sin. When I preached on that topic, no one came
expecting a controversial sermon, but they got one nonetheless.

I once preached a sermon based on Colossians 3:16 and Ephesians 5:19, which speaks of singing psalms and hymns and spiritual
songs. I had to address the controversy over musical styles in worship.

"In the sixteenth century," I said, "Zwingli would not allow any
music. Luther had to have music but said it must be simple. Calvin
said that only psalms should be sung but used modern music that was
disparagingly called 'The Geneva jingles.'

"In the seventeenth century, Pietists said that there ought to be
singing, but it needed to be unaccompanied. In the eighteenth century, Christians had orchestras, but no violins, because they were
called 'the devil's fiddle.' In the nineteenth century, the organ came
in and began to push the orchestra out.

"Then William Booth came along and said, 'Why should the devil
have all the best tunes?' so he started brass bands. The Scandinavians
came over to America and brought guitars. In the twentieth century,
the youth culture brought rock; from the South, we got folk music;
the charismatics began to emphasize praise songs; and from Britain
we got celebration marches.

"So what is your position on what is appropriate for worship music? Is it based on your theology or is it based on taste?"

Certainly preaching on controversial topics carries a risk. However, I've learned that if I ignore controversial issues, I also ignore a
timely opportunity to argue for the relevance of Christianity. And
that's an opportunity I don't want to miss.

20

And the Patriarch Fell

The church is no man's possession.

—Charles Wellington

The scene is burned into my mind forever. On a cold January day in Kansas, the fifty members of our church had gathered inside our toasty building for the annual business meeting.

What we had feared and tried to forestall for nearly a year suddenly exploded. The church patriarch, a heavyset redhead in his upper fifties, attacked me with angry words, plowing through the feelings of the congregation like a state truck clearing a lightly snow-covered highway.

One woman couldn't take it any longer, and she tearfully confronted him—"You shouldn't speak that way to our pastor."

The patriarch thundered out of the church. A stunned congregation sat praying, crying, shaking their heads in disbelief. But somehow we have stayed together to tell about it.

In the aftermath, my wife and I spent hours thinking back over the past twelve months to see how it had happened and if we could have handled it differently.

Clues from history

One year before—actually the Sunday I was voted in as pastor—my wife and I were sitting near the back of the 1950s-style, wood-paneled auditorium during the adult discipleship class. One person made a comment. Fred—loyal charter member, senior elder, the patriarch—rose slowly to his feet. Like bellows, Fred sucked a huge draft of air and announced, "You're rewriting Scripture! That's not what *my* Bible says. It's right here in red and white."

My wife and I were stunned. We were voted in that day. But it didn't take long for us to once again be taken aback by the patriarch. Fred and his wife, Martha, a meek woman, came to our house shortly after we moved. With a smile, Fred handed my wife an attractive clock as a housewarming gift.

"There will be more if all goes well," he said.

My wife wondered if she had heard correctly. She almost dismissed it but replied, "Thank you. This is a very nice housewarming present, but we won't be able to accept further gifts."

Fred was a generous man who had sacrificed often for his church. In one instance when the church giving was low, Fred paid the pastor's salary out of his own pocket. In the past, several pastors had become indebted to him.

Add to Fred's money, power. If he talked loud enough and pounded his fist often enough, he could get his way. In our first three board meetings, I saw Fred shut down—by emotional intimidation— every item of change brought up for discussion. Granted, I initiated several minor changes early in my pastorate and probably should have built more trust beforehand, but this angry behavior was not a new thing.

Confrontation

After a few months, the opportunity came for me to address the problem. In one board meeting, he once again shut down discussion on minor changes. After the meeting, Fred approached me and asked, "Why won't people talk about the issues? I keep telling them to say what's on their minds, but they just clam up."

"You are like the parent of this church," I replied. "You've been here longer and done more for this church than anyone here. When you come across loud and angry, people fear you. They don't want to oppose you because they don't want to receive what they perceive as a verbal whipping."

I then pointed to a few carefully chosen scriptures in First and Second Timothy and Titus about anger and quarreling, reasoning with Fred as with my own father. Fred listened, impatiently nodding his head as though he disagreed with everything I said, but at least he listened.

Fred eased up for a few weeks. We actually passed a couple of important changes, and the morale on the board improved. We had all been praying for Fred, and several members commented to me, "The Holy Spirit is really working in his life!"

Fred and Martha went on vacation for several weeks. We had one board meeting during this time, the smoothest to date. But the next was a disaster. Fred was outraged that we had proceeded with a particular item while he was gone, an item we had all thought rather minor—switching to a different adult Sunday school curriculum. I know now I should have kept Fred abreast of even the minor decisions we planned to discuss in his absence. I had done what was constitutional, not what was wise.

After listening for almost fifteen minutes to Fred's opinions on a variety of subjects, most of which weren't listed on our agenda, I interrupted, "Fred, I'm not concerned that we disagree about some issues, but I am concerned about the anger I'm hearing as we seek to express our differences."

"I'm not angry," Fred shouted, his ears red.

But his words convicted him, and he fell silent. Our time had almost run out, so we quickly heard some mumbled reports, and I offered a token prayer to close the meeting. Fred sat scowling. He looked *through* me as I offered a handshake and left the room.

Stripped of power

Weeks later, the committee on committees met to finalize nominations for leaders. A number of church members had asked the committee to move Fred to some responsibility with which he could do less damage. The committee agreed.

One member of the committee called out of courtesy to break the news to Fred. Fred didn't take it well. He claimed the constitution allowed him to stay in his place of service as long as he lived. "If these new people don't like the way our church is," he said, "why don't they just go somewhere else?"

When I heard about that comment, I realized what was driving Fred. He feared losing *his* church. Twenty-nine people had joined the church in twelve months, most of them new converts. God was work-

ing in a big way in our little church. Fred spoke with tears about the
need to reach people for Christ, but an inner battle raged within him.
He really didn't want the church to change; it would mean letting go
of something in which he had invested his life.

That's understandable, I thought, *but we can't allow the church
to be controlled by one person's feelings. A well-meaning man has
lost sight of who is the Head of the church.*

At this point, I toyed with backing down. But too many people
had pleaded for change. So we braced ourselves for the business
meeting and prayerfully prepared for what we knew could turn ugly.
Moments after the meeting began, Fred rose to his feet. He let loose
a string of accusations. Never using the term *pastor*, he said, "*That
man* over there is responsible for families leaving this church. *I've*
gone after them to find out why they are not coming back. It's because they're not getting fed."

Fred made other accusations. But one by one those in the sanctuary began bowing their heads, praying, crying. They weren't listening anymore. Then an older couple left, with the husband de-
claring, "I'm not going to stay and listen to this nonsense." A few
moments later, a young woman left in tears.

Finally, after I tried and failed to gain control of the floor, another
church member succeeded. She stood and poured out her heart.
Without attacking Fred personally, she said, "I've seen God working
in this church ever since the pastor and his wife came, but I've also
sensed that love is missing in parts of this body. It makes me sick to
my stomach to hear things like that said about our pastor. Where is
the love?"

Fred looked as though he had been slapped.

Then another member stood and asked Fred, "Who do you think
you are to run the church this way?"

Fred replied, "I'm a servant of this church!"

"You may think you're a servant of the church," the member replied, "but the way you're acting, you're certainly not serving God!"

Fred stomped out of the room.

All was still for a moment, as people tried to recover. Then some
began to sob loudly. Others sat with head in hands. After a while I
began reading scriptures about the body of Christ and love for one
another. As I read, I could feel anger and resentment ebbing away.

The sobbing ceased, and we began praying, for Fred and for the church.

After prayer, people started offering testimonies about how God had worked in their lives over the previous year. Some affirmed our call to the church, describing instances when my wife and I had ministered to them in crisis.

Finishing what we started

In the days following, my wife and I visited many people. Some told how powerless they felt as they had seen Fred control and then run off previous pastors.

"When you and your wife first came," said one woman, "I wondered how long it would take for this to happen. When I heard you weren't able to be bought, I knew God would do great things. I'm grateful he gave you the strength to stand up to him."

Another said, "We all love Fred, but none of us knew how to deal with his temper. Most of us knew this had to happen sooner or later, but we were too scared to do anything about it."

The following Sunday five people joined our church. Still, I sensed we were all waiting for the other shoe to drop.

One night, with the wind blowing so hard it nearly ripped off our coats, a deacon and I went to Fred's house, but he wasn't home. We left a carefully worded letter under the door, explaining that we needed to discuss the incident and work toward reconciliation. There was no response. We left messages on Fred's answering machine, but they were not returned.

We had tried to follow the guidelines in Matthew 18, but with Fred unwilling to meet, we reluctantly agreed that the entire body had to be brought into the matter of Fred's standing with the church.

We scheduled a discussion-only meeting. We thought this would give Fred a chance either to ask forgiveness and follow the will of the body or demonstrate his unwillingness and thereby determine our next course of action.

A few moments before the meeting was to begin, Fred walked in. He placed a glass of water on the pulpit and found a seat near the front by himself. Everything went well for the first hour. I gave rules of conduct for our discussion—such as, comments would be restricted to observations of fact—and people followed them. People shared their feelings without anger.

Then Fred strode to the front and took a long drink from the glass of water. Then he began to attack various members of the church. He was clearly out of bounds according to the rules of conduct, so I stood and said, "You will not be permitted to dishonor members of the body this way."

He turned and started to attack me. I turned to the congregation, declared, "I call this body to prayer," and dropped to my knees at the front pew.

In our tradition, never more than one person prays aloud at the same time; but when I began praying, almost everyone else in the room began praying out loud as well.

Soon one person's voice rose above the others. A quiet older woman began weeping, praying with mournful wails, asking the Lord to reclaim his church. For about fifteen seconds, Fred stood screaming and trumpeting at the front, trying to be heard above fifty praying people. Then he gave up and stomped out. Six others, supporters of his who had not been at the previous business meeting, left with him. The noise level quickly subsided, and a number of people prayed one by one for the church. In the terrible stillness that follows a crisis, we talked about the church's need to love Fred.

Several members said they believed God had finally reclaimed his church. My wife said, "I feel like we've just attended a funeral. We're terribly grieved, but tomorrow is another day."

Partial peace

The church still could have chosen some form of discipline with a view toward reconciliation, but Fred's wife, Martha, called within days and confirmed they would not be back. They now worship in a sister church where the pastor is aware of the events leading to their leaving us. God reclaimed his church that night, but there was no rejoicing as the patriarch fell. We were all humbled, awestruck at God's mercy and the sense of his presence when we needed it most.

Almost a year later Fred's father passed away. He had also been an active and beloved member of our congregation for many years. He left the church at the same time as his son.

I vacillated over how to respond. If I showed up at the funeral home, how would Fred react? Would he make another angry public scene and embarrass us all? I prayed a lot that weekend.

The evening of public visitation at the funeral home, a good friend and fellow pastor from a nearby church stopped by my house. "I'm going to drop in and sign the guest register," he said. "Do you want to ride along?"

That was just what I needed.

On our way into the small red-brick funeral home, we saw and visited with several church members. Then I saw Martha standing near the gray casket. When I approached, she welcomed me graciously. My blood pressure lowered significantly. We talked for several minutes. She said she was glad I had come and then suggested, "I don't know how Fred will respond, but you can try approaching him."

After Fred finished talking to a friend, I walked toward him. He saw me and walked in my direction. I smiled and put out my hand. He shook my hand, and then we bear-hugged each other. I don't know how he felt, but I was certainly glad that moment had come. We talked about his dad for about five minutes. He never brought up our church or the painful incident in our past. It felt good to stand there, looking each other in the eyes, talking again like Christians.

I honestly don't know if Fred will ever feel comfortable returning to our church, at least as long as I'm there. But we pass each other in town, wave, and greet each other. Now I'm praying and waiting for God to work out an even bigger reconciliation: for Fred to be restored to our church. (I admit I wasn't able to pray that for the first eight months after the blowup.)

If Fred does ask the church to accept him back, I don't know how we would manage it. I doubt we would allow Fred into a position of leadership, at least not without a long period of trust-building. God has reaffirmed to us that the church is no man's possession; Jesus Christ is the Head of the church. I'm beginning to feel genuinely thankful for all the lessons we've learned about forgiveness and confrontation. Our church is experiencing unity as it had not known for over two decades.

Still, we all hurt for Fred and Martha. In fact, the compassion people expressed for them after they left confirmed to me that God was in this. God was teaching us the meaning of love.

21

Wars You Can't Win

Sometimes church wars are winnable;
sometimes they're not.

—Andre Bustanoby

As a teen during World War II, I kept a scrapbook of newspaper clippings recounting the battles raging in Europe and the Pacific. Every evening at 6:00, I tuned in to Gabriel Heater on WWOR in New York, wondering whether he'd open his radio newscast with "Ah yes, there's good news tonight" or, "There's bad news tonight."

After World War II, we knew that wars could be just, and they were winnable.

I felt drawn to the military. I enlisted in the Air Force during the Korean conflict, and in 1965 I almost went to Vietnam. I seriously considered a commission as an army chaplain. A retired colonel in our church talked me out of it, though, arguing that the congregation needed me.

Vietnam, however, taught us all a bitter lesson: some wars are unwinnable.

During my years as a pastor, I experienced both kinds of wars within the church. Sometimes church wars are winnable; sometimes they aren't.

Winnable war

In 1950 my fiancée, Fay, accepted Christ as her Savior in response to my testimony. We married a year later and planned for me to go to college and seminary and then into pastoral ministry.

From the start we agreed on our roles. I would be husband, father, and pastor. She would be wife, mother, and ordinary church member. I didn't expect her to do any more in the church than any other Christian woman. And that's how she wanted it.

The arrangement worked well in my first pastorate. The people loved us, we loved them, and Fay felt like she fit in. She could be herself and still be the pastor's wife.

The church board was spiritually mature. They shared the responsibility of leading the church. They were the seasoned veterans, essential to the church's operational success.

And we were tested in battle. The congregation voted to relocate and build, but a faction fought it. The board and I stood our ground, letting them know the congregation had spoken. We expected them to cooperate with the program, to cease and desist from further factionalism. At the board's request, our district superintendent spoke at a church meeting, bluntly telling the faction to shape up or ship out.

The opposition had voiced its disapproval but followed the rules of engagement and refrained from further action.

This was my first experience with church discord, and the solution seemed so simple. From the battle-scarred district superintendent to the youngest member on the board, we moved as a team, quickly and decisively. The church grew, and though Fay hated conflict, she, like me, was encouraged by its outcome.

Unwinnable war

In 1967 a California church invited me to candidate. It was a larger church with multiple staff. Fay and I spent a week with them discussing their needs and ours.

I made it clear that I based my philosophy of ministry on Ephesians 4:11–13. I would bring God's people to maturity; they would do the work of the ministry. Both Fay and I told them she was not my pastoral associate but my wife and the mother of my children. They should expect her to do no more in the church than any other member. They accepted our terms, but I should have known something was wrong.

The board of deacons told me, "The previous pastor resigned largely because of the opposition from the director of Christian education. He couldn't work with her, didn't get rid of her, and couldn't do anything about the faction supporting her."

That's strange, I thought. *Baptist polity gives the congregation power to remove her. If this was what they wanted, all the deacons had to do was call a business meeting, vote, and fire her.* As I found out later, it was not that simple. Like Vietnam or Afghanistan, the elected leaders held office, but they weren't able to control the countryside.

The deacons had little power. This church, a split from another church, didn't want a strong board of deacons. They felt the deacons in the previous church had too much power, and they weren't going to let that happen again. Only after I was involved did I discover the real situation. On paper, the church's government was congregationally ruled and pastor/deacon led. In reality, the church countryside was controlled by a cadre of charter members who used their money and power of intimidation to thwart the elected leadership.

The victory in my first church still fresh in my mind, I assumed success was possible here.

I knew that if the church called me, we'd need to face the problem of the divisive director of Christian education (DCE). I told the deacons that the solution was simple. One of my terms of call would be the right to select my own pastoral staff. I would retain everyone except the DCE.

I was much like the naive Americans who thought they could do in Vietnam what the French couldn't. *I* would put this faction in its place.

Making war on civilians

The church called us by a sizable vote, and Fay and I and our four boys moved to California. The DCE did not submit her resignation prior to my arrival (though the other staff had submitted theirs). So in my first week at work, when I found her in her office doing business as usual, I went in and told her I was exercising the terms of my call and was letting her go.

She left in a huff. It didn't seem to matter that this was one of the terms of my call and that the church had voted to accept it. I tried to get on with my work. But the guerrilla war began.

I first realized the type of conflict we'd be facing when the woman asked Fay to speak at a church banquet and to become president of the women's group. Fay declined and offered to do work more suited to her gifts. One of the women (one of those appalled by how I handled the DCE) told Fay, "When Shirley (the former pastor's wife) was here, she was the president of the women's group. And she didn't turn down speaking engagements."

Shirley was a gifted, energetic woman, and she had endeared herself to the women's group. The exchange made Fay feel like a failure. These women pressed the attack.

Another time, one woman said to another, while looking at Fay, "If Shirley were here, she'd know what needs to be done."

The attacks began to feel like terrorist bombs. We never knew when the next would detonate. Once when the women's group was discussing the need for someone to lead a church delegation to a large meeting of church women, someone said, "What about Fay?"

In front of the whole group, another woman blurted, "Fay doesn't do things like that. Maybe we can get Shirley to come back and do it."

Fay came home in tears.

I was furious and personally spoke to the women involved.

"You agreed to the terms of my call, which in part said that Fay would find her own place of service in the church and would not be another Shirley," I said, gritting my teeth. "I expect you to honor that commitment."

Experienced guerrillas know how to handle this kind of confrontation. *My* behavior, rather than the rudeness of these women, became the issue. Not only was I to blame for removing the DCE, now I was "opposed to the women's group." The faction spread word throughout our community and denomination that I was an "abrasive person with a bad attitude, particularly toward women."

Like political terrorists, these guerrillas use noncombatants as pawns and justify it on the grounds they are an oppressed people.

In response, conventional strategy dictates that pastors must forbear, and when they act, be beyond reproach. I was not about to forbear attacks against my wife. They were right. I *did* have a bad attitude. I was angry. *They're not going to take advantage of my wife's gentle spirit.*

But like government troops, my efforts couldn't prevent the guerrilla strikes.

Fay attended a women's banquet, and several of the factious women sat at the next table.

"Well, did you hear about the pastor's latest stunt?" one of them said, loudly enough for Fay to hear. "He had the nerve to come to my home and tell me that I owed his wife an apology for the way I treated her. I told him that I owed no apology. What I said was the truth. The women's group needs Shirley."

"That man has serious problems," another chimed in. "I hear that his former church had problems with him, too—and now we're stuck with him."

Again, Fay came home in tears.

"It's bad enough that I'm no Shirley," she said. "But when they talk about my husband as though I'm not there, they're communicating that not only am I a failure as a pastor's wife but also that I'm a non-person! What did I do to deserve this?"

Her pain broke my heart. I had introduced her to Christ. But in so doing I had also introduced her to the hardships of ministry: the pain of being told your husband's a failure and, as his wife, you're a failure as well.

It was only a matter of time before they struck my children. My oldest son, in high school at the time, was dating a girl in the church. I was concerned that she was manipulating their relationship. He was afraid even to go out with the guys before checking in with her.

Not wanting his social development crippled, I relayed my concerns to him, reminding him that he wasn't married to this girl, that she had no right to constrict his social life.

"I'd like to see you date other girls," I said.

Soon a story was circulating around the church that my son was planning to run away from home. Another story had me angry and abusive toward the girl and her parents.

Then our youngest son, who attended school where a woman from the church volunteered as a playground supervisor, had a dispute with another child. This woman dragged the boys to the principal. Someone in the school office told me later that she had said to the principal, "Don't be hard on the boy. His father is the pastor of my church, and I can tell you he's a very troubled man."

In their gunsights

Though the terrorism against my family continued, I was the main target. They accused me of not being a caring pastor. This certainly was understandable given that the former pastor was a gentle spirit, patient with the people, and avoided challenging the power politics. Yes, by comparison, I was a bull in a china shop.

Another criticism was my preaching. I had made a deliberate attempt to avoid harping on topics by preaching through the books of the Bible. Unpopular subjects such as predestination and election, however, couldn't be avoided when preaching through Romans and Ephesians.

The faction also took issue with slang expressions I used in sermons, such as "hang loose," "gut feeling," and "wearing masks."

In one of their letters to the congregation, they said that I lacked "the confidence of a majority of the *responsible leaders,* as well as the *working, supporting* [emphasis theirs] members of the church. (Note—we are not necessarily referring to or implying a majority of the church membership as a whole.)"

Translation: The warlords in the church wanted me out, though they admitted the majority of the board of deacons and the congregation supported me!

Severed supply lines

In spite of the tensions, our attendance grew. We went to two Sunday morning services. The church had plans to build a new sanctuary, and now seemed to be the right time. We launched a bond program, with the trustees responsible for its execution.

The people of the church quickly raised the money, which was put in escrow. Though the trustees told us we had reached our goal, they never closed escrow. When we began to talk about actually building the church, we discovered three trustees had returned their bonds and withdrawn their money. This precipitated a raid on the escrow by the disaffected members of the church.

We never pursued the legality of the escrow raid. One church member was an officer of the bank holding the escrow, and I didn't want the church to get a black eye for suggesting legal action.

We also had a practical reason for not pursuing legal action. The unrest in the church didn't bode well for a building program. Enemies in the countryside was one thing, but having them within your own administration was another.

I felt the three trustees who had violated their trust needed to be confronted. I met with the deacons and suggested calling a meeting of the congregation to remove the trustees from office.

The meeting was a fiasco. The trustees justified their behavior by saying, "The pastor is demoralizing and ruining the church," and, "It is not a good time to build," and, "The pastor doesn't care about the people's feelings."

They were partly right. I *didn't* care about the feelings of those I considered saboteurs. If they couldn't cooperate with the board of deacons and the 80 percent who supported the church's direction, I felt they ought to leave.

Though the faction tried to make me the issue, the congregation voted to remove the three trustees from office. The three responded by leaving the church. I was sorry it had come to this, but I hoped that a public victory would demoralize the guerrillas and prevent further attacks. I should have known better.

Winning battles but not the war

After the church meeting, the stories, whispers, and undercurrents seemed to diminish. But it was only a lull before the next offensive. Within a few months, they began circulating a petition for my resignation.

One Sunday morning, as I walked into the sanctuary to prepare for the worship service, I saw several individuals welcoming the arriving congregation by handing out flyers, urging them to sign the petition.

I went out and said to one of them, "How can you do this to people who are coming here to worship and hear God's Word?"

"This is *our* church, not yours," one of them replied, "and it's about time you realized it!"

One of the deacons was making friendly small talk with those handing out flyers. I took him aside. "Do you expect me to lead worship and preach with this going on?"

The deacon, who loathed confrontation, replied, "Pastor, you have to understand these people. . . ."

I was devastated. The guerrillas were attacking our most sacred event, and one of my officers was telling me I needed to understand these people!

"You'll have to lead the service," I said, "because I'm going home."

I gathered my family, and we left town for the day.

Fay feared the future. "What are you going to do?" she asked. "We can't keep going on like this." My boys, in the backseat of the car, were silent. I'm sure they wondered what the future held for them, too.

That week I asked the deacons to call a congregational meeting to vote on my tenure. Though the constitution called for a two-thirds majority to remove the pastor, I told them I would resign if a simple majority wanted me out.

Previous church meetings had been about specific controversies, not my leadership per se. Perhaps by making my leadership the issue, we could finally settle the conflict. I still thought this was a winnable war.

The opposition beat the bushes and handed out absentee ballots to those who'd left the church but hadn't transferred their membership. Yet with all their effort, 80 percent voted in my favor.

After the vote, however, the war continued. I still didn't get it. It didn't matter what the congregation wanted. The opposition would have their way, even if it meant scorched earth.

While the deacons supported my leadership, many of the trustees did not. With their power over the purse strings, the trustees progressively demoralized the church by thwarting programs the congregation had voted into the budget. They would claim the bids for goods or services from outside vendors were unsatisfactory. As they waited for "satisfactory bids," enthusiasm for the programs died.

Another dodge was budget priority. Money budgeted for programs they didn't like wasn't available because, they said, other priorities (what they wanted to spend money on) came first.

One of the trustees made no secret about how he felt.

"I started this church and paid for it," he told me. "If you think I'm going to let you tell me what we're going to spend money on, you are mistaken!"

Is victory worth the price?

The deacons, realizing that nothing had changed since the vote on my tenure, tried to correct the situation by sending a letter to all the officers, committee members, teachers, and workers in the church. It said, in part: "When the church was given the opportunity to vote on the pastor's tenure, the board of directors announced 'that once the vote is taken, we expect all to cooperate with the majority vote and to seek the Lord's highest plane of outreach for this local assembly.' "

They attached to the letter a statement for all workers to sign. It was a pledge to support the leadership of the pastor and deacons, to attend church and Communion regularly, and to refrain from public and private criticism of the church, its pastor, and leadership.

But the faction fought back. When the deacons took their request for a pledge of allegiance to the congregation, the meeting quickly got ugly.

The moderator struggled to maintain control. He reminded the dissenters repeatedly, "You will address the moderator and stop your direct verbal attacks on other members."

Ignoring him, an angry member shouted at a deacon who had just spoken. "You don't deserve to be a deacon," he snarled. "You're just one of the pastor's pawns. You've forgotten your friends who've sacrificed to build this church. The pastor didn't build this church. We did."

Something happened inside of me. It had been coming for several months. As a result of marriage counseling, I had come to realize something important about myself. Sometimes I would fight for things, not because the cause was noble and just, but because I had to win.

I had often said to my wife, "It's a good thing that I was never a professional soldier because I would be either very decorated or very dead."

But now I had begun to change. I silently prayed, "Lord, I don't want people to be bloodied because I have to win." In my mind's eye, I saw God smile, and I knew what I had to do.

I asked the moderator for a recess to meet with the deacons. We went to my office, where I told them, "I don't want any more fighting, but I don't want you to feel I'm pulling the rug out from under you by resigning. I'm ready to leave the field of battle if you are."

We prayed, and to a man, they were ready, too.

After the recess I was given the floor, and I announced my resignation, stunning the congregation. My supporters knew that surrender was the only way out—for me and for them. Church history already had the Thirty Years' War. Two years was enough for me.

Prisoner of war

A few days later, a group of church members asked if I'd start a new church.

"I don't want any part of a church split," I replied. "The reason I resigned was to stop the fighting.

"Church split?" replied one of the delegation. "That's a joke. Whether you stay in town or leave, there's going to be a mass exodus. Many are disgusted and want nothing to do with this church. Others, like us, want to start again with you."

Given this argument and the practical reality that I needed a job, I stayed.

The new church blossomed, but I soon discovered that as long as I lived anywhere near my detractors, I would never be at peace.

One day a neighbor stopped me in the grocery store and said, "I'm sorry to hear about your son David" (who was away in the army).

"What do you mean?" I asked.

"His arrest for doing drugs and selling them."

"Where did you hear this?"

"A member of your old church told me."

I couldn't believe it. The war was continuing even though I'd surrendered. I didn't tell Fay because she had been battered enough.

But the stories continued. Another time I saw a friend as I walked in the park.

"It's good to see you're doing better," he said.

"What do you mean?"

"You were in the hospital under suicide watch, weren't you?"

Old friends and colleagues would see me in public and be surprised that I seemed to be functioning like a normal human being. Fay ran into old neighbors who expressed concern over something that was supposed to have happened to her—like her husband leaving her for another woman.

Fay often wept, saying, "Will we never get away from this?" After six months, I couldn't take it any longer. I finally resigned. I told the elders what was happening, and they understood. They gave us a lovely send-off.

Our plan was for me to take all of our household goods back to Washington, D.C., in a moving truck, and then to work a secular job while I built a counseling practice. When school was out, Fay would come with the kids. In the meantime, she functioned with "survival gear" (bedding, but no beds, a few cooking pots and dishes).

After I left, friends told us that the faction was saying that I had left my wife and children and that I was so mean I didn't even leave a stick of furniture behind for them. I remember crying all the way across the country, feeling such a terrible sense of failure. My seminary professors once thought of me as a promising pastor. What would they think of me now?

Signs of a no-win war

I wish my training had taught me how to avoid no-win wars and recognize when I was in one. What I didn't learn in seminary, however, I learned in jungle combat. Here are a few factors to consider when deciding whether you are in a no-win war.

Is there a history of factionalism? All pastors experience conflict. Some conflict is healthy; it can be a signal that the church is moving ahead. But a church that has a history of driving pastors away is probably a political quagmire, unlikely to turn in your direction once they've decided you are the enemy. Tragically, too many pastors, like myself, discover the church's sordid history only after they've accepted the position.

Are peace initiatives having no effect? In a winnable war, when you make repeated constructive efforts at peacemaking, there is some positive response. When peace overtures are rejected outright, however, you may be in an Afghanistan-like conflict. Peace is unlikely; the only question is whether or not you and your family will get out alive.

Are the leaders willing to pay the price to win the war? Look at the battle-readiness of your leaders (the elders, deacons, or "official board"). Leaders who've never been through conflict may be disillusioned and devastated by it. They may be unwilling or unable to take the heat.

When trouble breaks out, veteran non-coms and lieutenants are priceless. Without them, you can't survive. By the time my board of deacons became seasoned veterans, the war was out of control.

Your leaders must be willing to make decisions that will result in casualties. They must have the resolve to continue despite losses and discouragement. They must have the ability to prevail. Above all, they must be able to maintain their humble dependence upon the Lord amid a hostile climate.

Is there enough popular support to continue the war? There will always be some who advocate "peace at any price" and refuse to stand up to opposition. But you need a critical mass of congregational support. Without that, you're in a no-win war.

Is the opposition willing to negotiate, or do they demand unconditional surrender? A determined faction is all but impossible to defeat. Guerrillas can commit atrocities, while the actions of legitimate government must be beyond reproach. If the opposition is willing to sit down and work on the issues, the war can be settled. But if they refuse to settle for anything less than unconditional surrender (or your resignation), the chances of winning are remote.

Are you unable to protect your own family? You may be willing to endure a no-win church war, but what about your family? I thought my wife and children were safe because they were non-combatants. But they weren't. Not only can family members be wounded in battle, but they can carry scars for life. Having a spouse become bitter toward the church or a child reject the faith because of a church conflict is a price I'm not willing to pay.

Do you know why you're fighting? Are the objectives clear? Are the reasons becoming more personal? Do you have a need to win? Because militaristic themes enamored me, and because I had a personality that needed to win, I saw things through the lenses of scriptural phrases, such as "fight the good fight."

What is more, my first experience with conflict, which resulted in the growth of the church, gave me a false sense of competence. I didn't know how vicious a church war could be. In my first church, the conflict was different. The opposition did not act like terrorists. They followed the Geneva convention.

I have come to believe that there are times when we should turn over scorched earth to determined terrorists. Yes, you will feel a sense of defeat. I did. In those dark days, ironically, the reality of God's sovereignty sustained me. The sermons I preached from Romans came back home, and I was able to pray, "God, I don't know what you're doing, but I believe you do, and that's good enough for me."

As I look back on this some twenty years later, I recognize that God did not abandon me. He has blessed me beyond anything I could have imagined. I have a solid marriage and a satisfying counseling practice.

Though this episode of my life was painful, if I could write the finale, it would read as Job's: "The LORD blessed the latter part of [his] life more than the first" (Job 42:12).

22

Surviving a Power Play

Nothing is bloodier than a religious war.

—Marshall Shelley

C harles Westerman was surprised when Jack Kenton was picked by the nominating committee for the position of board chairman. Only six months earlier, Charles had heard via the grapevine that Jack was thinking of leaving Morningside Chapel. Charles remembered several occasions when Jack had mentioned, "Pastor, the church isn't as friendly as it used to be; we're growing too fast to keep up with everyone."

That wasn't an unusual observation, and Charles agreed but said he guessed it was a nice problem to have. The church, just outside Harrisburg, Pennsylvania, had grown in the last two years—lots of people drifting in and staying, others drifting off, blaming the church's size for an impersonal feel. Charles was doing what he could to foster intimacy through Sunday school classes and small groups, but he also knew larger churches would naturally "feel" different than small ones.

One of Jack Kenton's closest friends, Clarence Porter, was chairman of the nominating committee, and Judy Kenton, Jack's wife, was also on the committee. The Porters and Kentons were among the "old guard," charter members of the church. They'd apparently convinced a majority of the twelve-member committee that Jack would make a good board chairman.

When he first heard about the nomination, Charles spoke with Clarence Porter. "I've worked with two board chairmen in the five years I've been here," he said. "And I had a close relationship with both of them. I've had lunch once or twice with Jack, and we're not particularly close. We don't always see eye to eye. I'd prefer another candidate."

"Jack's a good man, Pastor," Clarence said. "He's a spiritual leader in his home, a student of Scripture, and he's memorized more verses than most people have read. He knows our church and its needs. I think he'll work well with the board. Besides, he's already accepted the nomination. If we take his name out, he'll know someone objected, and he'll probably leave the church."

Charles suspected Clarence would tell Jack who "someone" was. In fact, he suspected a bit of a power play by the old guard to limit his leadership, to put the brakes on the church's growth, to move the attention away from new people and back to the core group.

He didn't want to alienate the charter members of the church. They were an important part of the flock and deserved to be heard. And yet, Charles felt part of the church's mission was to continually reach out. Jack would undoubtedly resist that.

Nor did Charles want to veto the twelve members of the nominating committee. He honestly didn't want to stack the board, and he didn't want to be accused of running a dictatorship. After all, he was pleased with the rest of the slate. Why be picky over one nomination?

So he committed himself to serving with Jack and making him a successful board chairman. From the pulpit, Charles thanked the nominating committee for the "strong choices" and watched as the entire slate was unanimously voted in.

A breakfast meeting with Jack seemed to go well, both men agreeing to work together and Jack quoting his verse of the week, Psalm 26:8 (KJV)—"Lord, I have loved the habitation of thy house, and the place where thine honour dwelleth"—but Charles was slightly uncomfortable with Jack's tone.

"He said he hoped he could help bring more depth to our ministry," Charles confided to his wife. "He said he'd be praying for revival in my life and the lives of our staff. You can't argue with that, but he definitely puts you on the defensive. It feels like spiritual one-upmanship."

Despite their promise to work together, Charles and Jack were butting heads from the first board meeting, the air thick with tension and distrust. Jack had a way of questioning motives and intentions, especially regarding growth.

"Are you sure you're not just trying to build an empire?" he asked Charles more than once. Charles didn't know how to respond. "No, I don't want an empire, Jack," he said. "Neither do I want to limit what the Spirit can do."

Jack continued to voice his suspicions. Anything that suggested enlargement—renting space for new Sunday school classes, re-arranging the Christian education offices, hiring a part-time secretary—Jack was against.

"Why should we try to attract more people when we're not doing that great a job with those we've already got?" he asked.

He vehemently opposed a plan to relocate so the church could build a larger building, and he persuaded a majority of the board, defeating the plan. He refused to help select an architect to draw up plans for enlarging the existing facility, but this time the board out-voted him 11–1.

That was the first of many 11–1 votes. Even though he was out-numbered, Jack's Luddite assaults often caused the board to delay votes, hoping to reach consensus. It rarely did. But action was bogged down for weeks.

Charles continued to meet with Jack once a month for breakfast. Jack complained, "I don't like the way you make unilateral decisions. I hear you're going to California in July to speak at Mount Hermon for a week. You never cleared that with me."

"I don't work for you," Charles said. "I don't even work *for* Morningside Chapel. I work *with* Morningside Chapel. I'm self-em-ployed—look at my IRS form! I submit myself to the board of elders and the church, but I'm not an employee. I'm an ordained minister, charged with shepherding this flock. Some of these personal ministry decisions are mine."

Jack wouldn't buy it. "I think you have a spiritual problem, Charles. I don't think you're the man for this church. If you had the gift of discernment, you could see that this church needs more depth, needs revival. Have you been praying for revival in your own life?"

"Yes I have been . . . daily." *Actually*, Charles thought, *I should have said nightly.* Most nights he had been waking up at two A.M.—tossing and turning till four or five—praying and worrying about the direction of the church, asking God to show him any ways to resolve the tensions, trying to think of any angles he hadn't seen yet. Was there really a growing dissatisfaction, or was he just more aware of it because of Jack's constant harping? Was the church growing too fast? If people kept coming, what other alternative was there than trying to minister to them all? *Is Jack right about my motives?* Charles asked himself night after night. *I don't think so, but how can anyone know for sure? Of course, my ego feels better when the church is growing, but I can honestly say my greatest desire is that God be honored by what we do here.*

Charles continued to lose sleep, but he didn't know how to work with Jack. The monthly breakfasts were becoming an ordeal. Jack's persistent charge was that Charles wasn't spiritual enough to lead a church the size of Morningside. Bickering about spirituality, Charles concluded, is the most perverse kind of bickering.

Eventually, Charles told two of the elders about his deteriorating relationship with Jack. "We're like a husband and wife who bicker not only over the way the house is kept but whether the other partner is fit company," he said. "There's no way a marriage can last if that keeps up. We've been stymied as a church, the spirit is gone from our board meetings, and we aren't acting with one accord. Eleven-to-one votes are becoming a Monday night liturgy. We're spinning our wheels. Am I the cause? Maybe if I resigned, the church would be more united."

The two elders said no, they didn't see the situation as serious. "Eleven to one doesn't bother us, Pastor. And I'm sure you and Jack will eventually work things out. You just see things differently." Charles realized none of the board had heard Jack's private philippics. While he laid into Charles at the breakfasts, Jack's board meeting criticisms were more general, less pointed, and only Charles felt their full impact, because only he knew what was behind them.

Charles could not tell how many others in the congregation Jack represented. At the breakfasts, Jack kept bringing up names of people he'd been talking to, and to hear him tell it, half the church was disgruntled.

The tensions not only cost Charles sleep, but they also led to some errors of judgment.

"One Sunday I preached from First Corinthians 1:10 about 'them,' those people in our lives who cause confusion and discord, especially in the church," Charles remembers. "I could tell by people's expressions that I'd completely lost them. Afterward my wife said, 'I think I know what you were saying, but I'm sure no one else did.'

She was right. It was an oblique sermon, preached out of my own frustration, and the congregation wondered, *What in the world is he talking about?* They thought everything in the church was going fine."

In September, just after school started, the sanctuary was packed for both services, and people were sitting in folding chairs in the aisles. Charles asked all the members of Morningside to stand up. "Look around; see how crowded we are," he instructed. "Now you know why we're thinking of enlarging our sanctuary." With nervous laughter, people sat back down.

"It was tasteless," Charles now admits. "It was not something someone from Princeton would do. It was driving a thumbtack home with a sledgehammer. I did it out of frustration, knowing we had to grow but very aware of the people opposed to growth."

In November, six months after Jack had taken office, the hostilities escalated. Early one Thursday morning, Charles was sitting in the restaurant, waiting for Jack to arrive. He was sipping coffee over the sports page, when Jack tapped him on the shoulder. "Can I see you outside?" he asked.

Strange request, Charles thought as he followed Jack outside. *He's a busy man, but if he can't stay for breakfast today, why didn't he call or just say so at the table?*

Once outside, however, Jack angrily turned on the pastor. "I've lost all respect for you, Charles. You're no spiritual leader, and I don't think I can even talk with you anymore. It's a waste of time for us to keep meeting for breakfast. We don't get anything accomplished because you don't understand what the people need."

Charles was stunned but managed to say, "Maybe you're right, Jack. I've thought for some time now that we needed to take this matter of my leadership to the board and let them decide."

"If you do that, I'll resign, and the whole church will know you forced me out." Jack turned, got into his car, and drove off. Charles was left standing alone. *This is ridiculous,* he thought. *We're arguing about who's more spiritual, and we can't act like Christians and share a meal together.*

Should he take this to the board? If he forced the board to decide between him and Jack, Charles was confident the board would back him, but that could also split the church. Who could tell how many of the old guard would follow Jack out the door? He didn't want to call Jack's bluff. Without any better ideas, he finally decided to do nothing and pray for a miracle of reconciliation.

At the next board meeting, in a rare unanimous vote, the board made the difficult but necessary decision of asking for the youth pastor's resignation. Charles agreed: Milt Runyon simply wasn't a youth pastor. The high schoolers were not attracted to him—with 150 names on the roll, Sunday school attendance had dwindled from 75 to 40, and Wednesday night youth group attracted 30. Milt's wife resented his being out evenings or off on weekend retreats, and he was discovering youth ministry can't be done nine to five. Even Jack said, "We need to confront the young man that he's really chosen the wrong career."

As distasteful as any firing is, Charles was relieved that at least he and Jack finally agreed on something. The Christian education board approved the action, Charles received Milt's resignation, the situation was explained to the staff, and Charles was confident that all the proper procedures had been followed.

But how to announce it to the congregation? The board felt a brief announcement from the pulpit wasn't adequate. By consensus, the board decided a meeting after the Sunday evening service should be held with those most affected—the high schoolers and their parents—to explain the situation. Charles was designated to make the explanation.

That night two hundred teens and parents packed the chapel. Milt hadn't been able to attract many high schoolers, but when he was let go, several had been grumbling about the abruptness of it all. Charles hoped to calm the waters.

After explaining that Milt's gifts were in other areas, that the church wished him well as he sought the Lord's direction for his life, and that he would be paid for the rest of the school year, Charles asked if there were any questions or comments.

Immediately Jack stood up. "Yes, I'd like to ask a question."

Charles wondered what he didn't already know about the situation.

"I think you presented only part of the truth about Milt's situation," Jack began. Charles felt anger begin to smolder. Was Jack calling him a liar?

"Isn't it true that Milt was let go because he wasn't attracting enough kids? It seems to me he was trying to run a quality program for the few. He was at my house last week and we had a small group over to pray for him, and he told me the goals he'd had for the group. He had a core of thirty on Wednesday nights. You can't develop a huge following in just a year and a half, nor perhaps should you. Isn't it better to build solid ministry with thirty kids rather than chase after a hundred on the fringe?"

While Jack was making his speech, Charles was feeling his temperature rise. *Why is Jack pretending he wasn't in on the decision to let Milt go? What's he trying to do? Embarrass me? Start a mutiny? He's publicly contradicting me.* The hostility that had been building up for six months suddenly exploded.

"All right, Jack, you win. Farewell, friend," Charles said bitterly and walked from the room, slamming the door and leaving the teens and parents speechless. As far as he was concerned, he had quit Morningside Chapel. He was fed up, tired of the battle. Let someone else knock himself silly against this brick wall.

No sooner had he gotten home than Dan Moran, his associate pastor, and two of the board members knocked on the door wanting to know what was going on. They were confused. They had talked with Jack after the meeting, and he was calling for the pastor's resignation. "If the pastor doesn't exercise any more self-control than that, he doesn't have the spiritual qualifications necessary to lead us," he had said. The elders said they were having an emergency meeting the next night to discuss the situation, and they wanted to have all the facts.

Charles explained the whole story, beginning with the discomfort at the nomination, the early tensions, the blowup at breakfast, everything.

"I guess we made a mistake agreeing to the meeting with the parents tonight. You don't explain a firing publicly; you make the decision, take the heat, and let it pass," he concluded. "But tonight isn't the real issue. The real issue is the direction of this church—are we going to reach out and continue to grow, or are we going to shut down our growth to concentrate on those we've already got?"

The whole board, minus Jack, met with Charles on Tuesday night. On Thursday night, minus Charles, they met with Jack. On Friday night, the board met with both of them. Jack raised the issue of his authority as board chairman: "The pastor isn't in submission to me." They discussed what it meant to be in subjection to one another. The authority of the chairman, the board, and the pastor were argued, and delineations were made. After two hours, Charles agreed to submit to the board's authority, and Jack agreed that the chairman was "first among equals" on the board and that he, too, would submit to the authority of the board as a whole.

But Saturday morning, Jack changed his mind. He called Charles, said the situation was intolerable, and that he was resigning. Charles said, "I'm sorry you feel that way," but didn't try to change his mind. A congregational meeting was announced for Sunday night.

"I did not appear in the pulpit on Sunday morning," Charles says. "I had really blown my cool the previous Sunday night, so I went to the high school class and apologized. I did not use the name of our chairman, but I explained that frustrations in the ministry had been building up and that night they boiled over. I let them know I had acted badly and I was sorry."

Sunday night, the church was packed for the congregational meeting. Rumors and questions had been circulating: Was the pastor resigning? Had the elders fired him? What was happening?

When the chairman's resignation was read, the crowd was silent, but the more perceptive ones knew a power play had been attempted and failed. The vote to accept the resignation was overwhelming: 498–12.

The Kentons and the Porters both stopped attending the church, but almost none of the rest of the old guard did. In the months following, congregational votes on expansion issues passed 80–20, but the 20 percent, while complaining, did not leave the church. Today, people continue to debate ways to make such a large church personal, but the ministry continues to grow. The old guard no longer threatens to leave.

"I was fortunate," Charles concludes. "I made some tactical errors and bad judgments, but I survived because our staff was well-liked and our vision for the church was generally accepted. But if Jack Kenton had been able to gain more of a following, he could have split the church."

War-room analysis

When two groups differ over the direction of the church, tensions naturally rise as each tries to gain the upper hand. If the issues are significant, both sides know the consequences of losing—the church won't be the same again. All the ingredients are there for a firefight . . . with all the resulting casualties.

Even the New Testament church knew the pain of living as a house divided until some key issues were settled.

In Galatians 2, Paul described his power struggle with some "false brothers" over the expectations laid on Gentiles who were converting to Christianity.

It was theological, emotional, and ecclesiastical hardball. When the clash was over, the church was split, the winners—Paul, Peter, Barnabas, and Silas—going on to take the lead, write the New Testament, and turn an empire upside down. The losers faded into history, nameless characters known only as Judaizers.

The power struggle ended, we all agree, with the right side on top. The essence of the gospel was at stake. Wouldn't it have been different, and tragic, if the wrong group had won? Yes, some wars have to be fought—and won.

Churches today have power struggles just as brutal. Most of them deal with matters of practice, not belief, but the hostilities aroused are as heated as if the essence of the gospel were at stake. One church nearly split over whether to accept a wealthy member's designated gift of a new organ or to sell it and give the money to the poor.

A significant issue. But worth fighting for? Worth splitting a church for?

How much firepower is appropriate in a church fight? No "Geneva convention" has established any rules.

A healthy congregation doesn't allow one or two members to set the church's direction or change its mission. Neither is the solution open warfare.

What can we learn from the power struggle at Morningside Chapel and the multiplied thousands of others that could be told? Pastors who have won, and those who have lost, agree on several key principles.

Face into the wind. Boat captains in a storm know that running before the gale can force them onto the rocks. When faced with political typhoons, the best chance for survival is facing them directly.

Charles Westerman let himself be tossed by the wind, and his frustration built to the point of losing emotional control, almost landing him on the rocks.

"I think it was Napoleon who said, 'Never let your enemy choose the battlefield,' " he reflects. "I don't consider Jack Kenton an enemy, but I certainly let him choose the battlefield. I lost control. If necessary, I should have offered my resignation before the board, not before two hundred people already upset over the youth pastor.

"I should have taken our disagreement to the board from the beginning, certainly at the point when he refused to have breakfast with me," he says. "They could have helped me gauge the strength of the opposition, instead of my losing sleep wondering. If I was out of line, they could have corrected me. If he was wrong, they could have stepped in sooner."

Prevent church fights from becoming holy wars. Nothing is bloodier than a religious war. Issues aren't just human squabbles; everything is elevated to eternal importance. How easy to forget that it was the devil whose tactic in Genesis 3 was getting two people to believe, "You will be like God, knowing good and evil." How tempting even today to mistake our will for God's; how devilish to believe that disagreeing with me is disagreeing with God.

Despite the pop spirituality that says, "Every problem is a spiritual problem," not every disagreement is a clash between good and evil, between the divine and the demonic.

"I wish my church members could recognize that they're just having a barroom scrap," says a Bible church pastor. "Some people enjoy going out on Friday night and getting in a fight with the good ol' boys. You mix it up awhile, but nobody holds it against anybody. But in the church, people have to justify their scraps, so they're determined to cast them as the spiritual versus the unspiritual."

Not all problems are spiritual problems. Some are just a dogged desire to disagree. If people can be given permission to disagree without having their sanctification called into question, church fights won't be so bloody.

One Massachusetts pastor had just seen his church break ground for a new sanctuary, but the battle to get the congregation's approval had been costly, and the funding would be a continuing struggle. The next day he was in the hospital having X-rays for severe stomach pain. His youth pastor came to his bedside.

"I know what's bothering your stomach," the associate said, pausing and looking out the window. "You know, Pastor, this building isn't the greatest thing that's going to happen for the kingdom of God in Massachusetts this week."

"I needed that," the pastor said after his release. "The X-rays didn't show a thing, but Mike touched the problem directly. I realized our million-dollar building wouldn't bring God's kingdom one inch closer. He might choose to honor it, but the fact is he doesn't need it, nor does he need any of our self-important efforts."

The pastor's stomach pain disappeared and has not returned.

Learn what you can from the opposition. Power struggles make you do your homework, forcing you to cover every angle, anticipate every criticism, and go by the book.

During a tussle over remodeling the Sunday school department, one pastor learned more about preschoolers' developmental characteristics and square-footage requirements than he ever wanted to know because he knew the opposition would bring those things up at the board meeting. Now he is glad he had to learn those things, since his own children are preschoolers.

General Dwight Eisenhower reportedly would not make a tactical decision until he found someone who strongly opposed it. He wanted to see any weaknesses before proceeding. Some pastors have discovered that policy works in the church, too.

"I'm a better administrator because of the difficult people in my church," says a Congregational pastor. "In one case they prevented me from hiring a staff member I really wanted. I eventually discovered they had been right about his weaknesses. In another case, their criticism of our building plans prepared me for the town council's questions. They made me do my homework, which kept me from looking like an idiot before the community.

Finally, remember that failure is not fatal. Even if the worst happens—a power play succeeds, and a pastor is compelled to resign, whether out of frustration or the efforts of the opposition— it doesn't mean the ministry is over. Just as one dissident isn't the whole church (though at times the angry voice is deafening), so one pastorate is not an entire ministry. Winston Churchill once said, "Success is never final; failure is never fatal; it is the courage to continue that counts."

Pastors who survive church wars unscathed are a small minority; those who have left a pulpit under less than happy circumstances are legion.

"When I was about to be forced out of my church," says a Kansas pastor, "I was feeling sorry for myself until I talked with an old veteran missionary who was visiting our church. I told him my troubles and he said, 'Phil, better men than you have been kicked out of a church. It's not the end of the world.' That was just what I needed."

That pastor, at fifty-eight years old, is now happily ministering in another, though smaller, congregation.

"It's doubtful that God can use any man greatly until he's hurt him deeply," said A. W. Tozer. In weakness, God's strength can be revealed. Joseph was jailed, David driven into hiding, Paul imprisoned, and Christ crucified, but even in defeat, God's servants are not destroyed. Part of the miracle of grace is that broken vessels can be made whole, with even more capacity than before.

PART 4

Redemption

23

The Spirit of Church Discipline

*I want to treat others the way I'd want to be treated
when needing reproof.*

—Donald Bubna

D ebbie was a young woman in our congregation who had a knack
for touching lives. One day she told me something that was troubling her in the life of a mutual friend, a fellow believer in our church.

Reviewing biblical principles together, we agreed certain logical steps of confrontation should be followed. Debbie hesitated, then said reluctantly, "I know biblically that's right, but it seems so hard."

Debbie's orthodoxy is sound and so is her heart, but her response to church discipline is typical of many in the church.

The exercise of discipline in the body of Christ is too often unpracticed. More often than not the exceptions are legalistic groups where discipline is applied rigidly to codes of dress and other externals. These surface problems are not of great or lasting concern.

But what should the church do with a person indulging in delinquent behavior? Or when we are faced with violations of honesty, morality, or integrity—issues to which the Bible clearly speaks? What about the person who is showing an unusual amount of interest in someone other than a spouse? Or one whose business ethics are frequently questioned? Or the person who is flirtatious? Or one who stretches the truth? Or the young couple who seem to have no control over their child, or their finances? How do we help these people?

Rather than caring enough to confront, we tend to allow much error to go on and on. Only if a scandal breaks out or pressure breaks up a marriage do we begin to express concern. Usually, this is too late.

God calls us to a better way. I was convicted to think hard about discipline when a parishioner asked me about my views on the subject. My response was immediate: "I don't think we deal with 50 percent of the discipline cases we should deal with in this church."

"But that's 50 percent more than what anybody else we know is doing," he replied.

Although this answer was probably an overstatement, it was an indicator of a severe deficiency.

These, then, are the principles of discipline I share with fellow Christian workers. My convictions are not meant to imply expertise. Rather, as a pilgrim and a learner who deeply cares for the church, I am calling us to loving action.

Why discipline?

Paul told the Galatians that if a person is caught in any trespass or sin, those who are spiritual ought to restore him (6:1). Discipline in the church is always to be redemptive in nature. Its aim is not to show that we are right and others are wrong. A child is corrected to save her from delinquency and to help her grow into maturity. The Galatians text sees the person caught in sin as the victim of a trap of the evil one. The call for the church is to "rescue the perishing."

Take, for example, the case Debbie discussed with me. Her friends had a teenage daughter, Ann, who worked in a store after school. Several times she had to work into the evening and was brought home by the store's owner, who was also in our fellowship. An open note sent to Ann by this man thanked her for listening to his long tales of mistreatment as a child and lack of appreciation as an adult. He emphasized the significance of Ann's sympathetic ear, since no one else, even his wife, seemed to understand. Ann's alarmed parents shared this with Debbie, who brought it to me.

It worked out naturally for me to visit with the parents. The father told me his first reaction was "to paste the guy good!"—not an abnormal response for a protective father, but hardly a redemptive act.

Since Ann's parents were acquainted with the store owner and were mature Christians, we decided they should confront him directly. After the father's initial reaction, I felt he took a balanced view of the situation and realized his intention was to be redemptive rather than vindictive. We agreed the store owner was probably caught in an emotional trap, or at least did not have perspective. Such an encounter might well keep him from going off the deep end.

Neglecting a confrontation, on the other hand, might contribute to our brother's downfall and even indirectly cause serious injury to another less fortunate "Ann" in his future.

Relationship web

The church is a family; we are brothers and sisters. We cannot choose our siblings, for it is the Spirit's work to bring them to new birth and into the family. As family, we belong to one another.

"Family" implies responsibility and accountability. I sometimes do things or take risks for my two earthly brothers only because they are my brothers.

A church family is equally responsible and accountable to one another. Effective discipline takes place in the context of these relationships. "Faithful are the wounds of a friend" (Prov. 27:6).

Our church was involved in a building program, never an easy time in the life of a local congregation. One day the moderator of our board requested that the two of us go to lunch, and that I stop by this office before we ate. Richard, a capable executive and good friend, came right to the point: "I know you have a mind for details, Don, and this building program is not the easiest thing we have ever done. But you're driving our building chairman up the wall with your ceaseless probing of every detail."

That hurt. I thought my questions were necessary. I'd thought I caught several mistakes just in time to prevent serious building errors. Richard kept boring in: "Don, you have to back off and give this man room." He was right, of course.

As I left, I felt much chastised. But I also felt something else. Richard had taken a great risk in confronting me, and therefore I knew he cared about me deeply. I felt that love. Our close friendship gave him credibility.

If a parent or sibling in the family communicates with another family member only to correct, little positive response is guaranteed. The church elder as well, seen only from a distance serving communion or interviewing for membership, has built little basis to give reproof when it is needed. If he never visits or invites others into his home, he will not be heard as clearly as the elder who has become a true brother.

Disciplers of men and women are tuned in to the web of relationships in their fellowship. A weakening of this web produces a distress signal in the caring church and should initiate action. If we reach out early, our later efforts in times of serious trouble will be more meaningful. If, however, we allow someone to grow distant from our fellowship without trying to find out why, there is no platform for later confrontation or healing.

Bible procedures

"When all else fails, read the directions," we often say. The words of Jesus (Matt. 18:15–17) give us clear directions on the procedure of church discipline. Too often, leadership within the local body, charged with the responsibility of discipline in the church, is either unfamiliar with these instructions or treats them as irrelevant.

"If your brother sins against you, go and show him his fault, just between the two of you." This calls for an open fellowship where people can honestly talk to one another about differences, shortcomings, sins. When I sense there is sin, to take action is a loving act. Every marriage counselor knows that where wrongs have taken place and no communication follows, that marriage is on the road to failure.

But the reproval should be private. The person who feels offended may have misunderstood. This is the time to gather information and to learn. It is not the time to gossip, an act that brings injury to the church family. In a healthy church, private reproval will be common practice.

Let's say, for example, John is irritated by Roger's habitual absences from board meetings and seeming laxness in corporate prayer ministries. It's time for John to take the matter to the Father in prayer. Then, if a valid concern persists (not borne solely out of irritation), to face Roger gently. He may learn that Roger's time and energy have been drained by family or business pressures. The confrontation will enhance John's understanding of Roger; it also should enlarge Roger's sense of accountability and bring into focus the need to balance his priorities. If both of their attitudes are correct, brotherhood will thrive.

When approached by a fellow member of the body of Christ about any matter, the Matthew passage says we have a responsibility to listen: "If he listens, you have won your brother."

When confronted, my first tendency is to think, *Here we go again!* This is quickly followed by a raising of my defense mechanisms. I immediately want to justify my actions. Learning to listen, however, stretches me. One way I try to listen is by summarizing to the person what he or she has said. I ask the person to correct my summary; I want him or her to know I have really listened.

My attempts to listen to reproof have been good for my character, an aid in my development, and a bridge-builder in our church's web of relationships.

Once in a staff gathering I felt pressed and harried. A matter arose that irritated me. Wishing to dispose of it in a hurry, I responded quickly and firmly.

Later, a fellow staff member said, "Don, I'm not sure you understood how you handled that." He then role-played my actions. I immediately saw my overreaction. His reproof brought direction to me, strengthened my relationship with the staff member who cared enough to confront, and allowed me to mend the fence with the person I offended.

"If he will not listen, take one or two others along." If the first step does not bring the needed response in private, it is time to involve three or four people.

The new people are not there to substantiate our prejudices but to bring new objectivity as God gives them spiritual insights. Again, the emphasis is on listening. God wants us to make an effort to understand what is being communicated. The risk is greater now, and it always must be remembered that the motivation is redemption. Although moving into the group process is scary, it does improve the attention level.

The winning of a brother or sister is not apt to be a simple, one-time contact; it will most likely be a series of contacts. Restoration takes a lot of nurture.

Some years ago, a close friend of mine and leader in our church became involved in a relationship that seemed unhealthy. Mary was an empathetic person whose official church responsibility brought her into frequent contact with Tom. It appeared Tom and Mary were seeing each other outside their official responsibilities.

When I approached Mary, she admitted it, defending the friendship as a needed ministry to Tom, who was struggling physically and emotionally.

The first confrontation brought no changes, so I went again. Mary kindly informed me that I was misjudging the situation. She would be cautious, but I should not be concerned. I felt she was not listening. At this point, I found it necessary to involve other church leaders. This time, both Mary and Tom listened, and both families were helped.

"If he refuses to listen to them, tell it to the church." In Jesus' time, there was not a structured local church. The organism did not yet have the form it would take in the book of Acts and in the Epistles. This aids us in understanding the importance of the *principle* of communicating a situation requiring discipline to the larger body.

I am not certain that there is one way to "tell it to the church." Scripture seems ambiguous about this; when this happens, I lean toward cultural flexibility in carrying out principles.

Thus, in our church, we use our full elder board. Two or three cases reach this level each year. In such instances, the elders report it in our bulletin along with other agenda items. Names are used only in the extreme cases involving excommunication.

Several years ago our church was hit with an epidemic of divorces. Several were among leaders or prominent families. All of us were concerned, and some of our older members were upset at "what our church was coming to." After consultation, several elders and I decided to make a statement to the church regarding our position toward the discipline process.

Near the close of a Sunday morning service, I asked the people to listen prayerfully to a statement of concern. I placed the statement in the context of the troubled marriages we were experiencing in society. I regretfully informed them of what we all already knew: that our church was not untouched by these tragedies, and that some of our families were in crucial struggles.

I said that the elders were concerned and were working with two hands extended: one of mercy and grace toward healing, and the other of the unchanging standard of God's Word, which stood for the sanctity and permanency of the home. I reminded them that marriage vows were for life.

I then called the church to love these people, to pray for them, and to abstain from judgment; and to pray for the elders who were making difficult decisions. I committed us as a church to teach more effectively the scriptural admonitions for husbands and wives.

"If he refuses to listen even to the church, treat him as you would a pagan or a tax collector." An outcast. We treat the person as a nonbeliever, because he or she is not walking as a believer. It means to keep loving the person as Jesus loved the publicans and sinners. It means to reach out to her in witness, but not to relate to her as a member of the body of Christ. Like all evangelistic outreach, the goal is to bring a soul to Christ and back into the functioning body.

In twenty-five years as a pastor, I have participated in the step of excommunication only three times. This is an extremely heavy responsibility. But Jesus says in this passage, "Where two or three come together in my name, there I am with them," and this action—loving discipline—is agreed upon in heaven (Matt. 18:20).

Some years ago Dick and his wife started attending our church about the time we were developing a newly-married couples group. Dick, a student at a nearby Christian college, announced to the church that God had called him to preach the gospel. People admired his dedication. His sincerity seemed evident to many by his frequent testimonies. Some folks concluded that this exceptionally spiritual young man should be groomed for leadership within the young marrieds' group.

Fortunately, Dick never rose to leadership, for God provided sufficient checks in the hearts of more mature people not to place him in a leadership position.

Shortly, a relationship developed between Dick and his wife and another couple, and they began to spend time together. Their lessening involvement in our fellowship should have been a warning to us. A few months later, Dick announced he was divorcing his wife to marry the woman from the other couple.

One of our pastors continued to reach out to Dick but wasn't heard. Finally, several went to confront Dick. He refused to listen to these men, stating flatly, "God told me my first wife would never be compatible in the ministry, and that I needed this kind of wife. God told me to do this."

The matter was now brought to the entire board of elders. They decided prayerfully to remove Dick from fellowship and then communicate it to the whole church by way of a bulletin announcement.

A letter was written to Dick expressing our concern, our understanding of what he had done (based on Scripture), our love, and the responsibility we accepted in dismissing him from our fellowship.

Within a few months, Dick, now remarried, moved to a distant state where he thought he could start a church in a small community. We felt it our obligation to write the ministers of that community about the action we had taken. This was done in hope of restoring Dick to fellowship.

Young couples in our church watched us to see what the church would do about Dick. They were not "out to get" him. Their question was: "Does the church really believe what is preached from the pulpit about the permanency of the home, about purity, about the sanctity of marriage?"

Our courage to act was well received; it strengthened our people's confidence in the church.

Five years later, Dick visited Salem, and he left word that he now felt our church had done the right thing. He had finally recognized his error.

Tough kind of love

The New Testament makes clear that the exercise of church discipline is for those "who are spiritual" (Gal. 6:1), and that discipline is to be carried out in a spirit of "meekness." Every incident of serious discipline is an awesome reminder of my own weakness.

I want to treat others the way I'd want to be treated when needing reproof: I would desire the absence of harshness or condemnation, and a preeminence of the spirit of Christ, who, as our living high priest, would put his arm around us, saying, "I know, I understand, I also once lived as a man."

Where this is true, there will always be the extending of forgiveness up to "seventy times seven."

Debbie is right. Church discipline is hard. It requires courage—a tough kind of love. It is biblical; it is right. Do we believe this truth enough to act?

24

The Exacting Price of Ministry

How do you answer a charge that you aren't godly?

—Kevin Miller

The service had ended an hour ago, and Pastor Brian Wells had long since said goodbye to the last departing worshiper, but here he was, still lingering in the cool of the narthex. He didn't know why, really; he'd already sent Carol and the boys home while he closed up, and he knew they'd be impatiently waiting to start Sunday dinner. He leaned forward against the tall panes of glass separating the sanctuary from the narthex and gazed over the empty pews one more time.

The message had been strong that morning. At times his energies had been so focused that he seemed to enter what athletes call *the zone*, a feeling of effortlessness and euphoria experienced when one's concentration is most intense. He was tired now, but it was a "good tired," and he wanted to savor it, like a basketball player after a big win.

As he looked across the sanctuary, Brian found it hard to believe he'd been at Community Church of Madison only eight months. He and Carol had fit right in. They'd been asked to dinner more evenings than not. Brian's eyes followed the smooth oak beams up and across the ceiling of the darkened sanctuary, and they seemed like great arms embracing him.

Well, Carol's waiting, he thought, and he started toward the door. He noticed a morning bulletin left on the floor near the coat rack. He leaned over and in one smooth swoop picked it up. It wasn't a bulletin after all, he realized as he looked at it, but some sort of leaflet.

Restore Community Church to Its History of Biblical Integrity! it said in flaming red. *Remove Pastor Wells. . . .*

"Unh." Brian groaned reflexively, as if he'd been punched in the stomach.

Brian Wells is bent on imposing his liberal views on our church. His utter disregard for the inspiration of Scripture will tear Community Church from its cherished biblical moorings—unless we act now. . . .

Brian scanned down, looking for something identifying who wrote it, but the paper ended with only the words ACT NOW! He stared at the leaflet. It was his name all right, but he wasn't sure they were talking about the same person. If anybody was committed to the trustworthiness of Scripture, it was he. He'd even gone to an inerrancy conference last year.

Who would write something like this? His mind quick-filed through people he'd met since coming, but nobody seemed capable of it. *Do a lot of people feel this way, or is it just one or two? Why didn't anyone say something to me?*

Normally, Brian prided himself on his sensitive pastoral antennae. When there was discontent in the congregation, he quickly knew it. But this came without warning. *Why didn't I sense anything?* Brian crumpled the paper in his fist.

Stand up

When Brian walked into the kitchen at home, everyone stopped eating and looked up. "Your dinner's getting cold," Carol said.

Brian didn't feel like talking, much less eating. He unrumpled the ball of paper and handed it to her. Carol read the leaflet silently and then looked up with wide eyes. "Brian, who would write that?"

"I don't know, but I'm going to find out," he said, sounding braver than he felt. He walked down the hall into the bedroom and picked up the phone. Then he put it down again. He wasn't sure whom to call. From his predecessor, J. Walter Landis, he had inherited one associate pastor and a youth pastor. They were cordial but still tentative about him. Brian had to admit that was fair; he was tentative about them, too. Still, right now he needed solid support. He finally punched the number for Henry Meyers, chairman of the elder board and part of the search committee that selected him.

"Henry, have you seen the leaflet about me?" Brian asked.

"What leaflet?"

Brian explained what it said.

"That's crazy," Henry said.

"Henry, who in the world would write something like that?"

"I don't know for sure. But I guess you should know something that happened just before we extended you a call. Landis heard about our intentions and called me long-distance from his new church. He said, 'I hear you're going to extend a call to Brian Wells. Let me tell you, Brian's not your man.' "

"But Landis doesn't even know me!"

"No, but he knows you went to Stanton Seminary, and in his mind that brands you. He used to talk against Stanton from the pulpit."

"C'mon. I'm as orthodox as they come."

"I know. I'm just telling you what he used to say."

"How did you respond when he called?" Brian asked.

"I told him, 'Thanks for calling and sharing your opinion, Walter, but the committee feels good about Brian, and we believe he's the person God has led us to call.' That was the end of the conversation. But my guess is some people are against you because of Stanton."

"How many people?"

"Who knows? Probably just a handful."

As Brian hung up the phone, he finally understood why Landis had preached so often on doctrinal dangers. He must have been utterly devoted to purity. But he'd left the people—some of them, at least—ready to shoot anything that moved.

The next ten days were quiet but unnerving. Brian couldn't shake the feeling he was being watched. Writing his sermon was excruciating. No matter how many times he scrutinized each line, he still feared it could be misinterpreted. In the pulpit he knew he was holding back, yet he felt powerless to do anything about it. As he shook each hand following the service, he wondered, *Are you for me or against me?* When everyone was gone, he searched the narthex floor for something he hoped he wouldn't find.

The one reprieve was when Larry stopped by. Larry's wife was a committed Christian and for years had been trying to persuade her husband to come to church. Larry, an insurance executive, was frank about his distaste for religion, but he had finally consented to try church again. They ended up at Community a month after Brian arrived and had attended regularly ever since.

Larry walked into Brian's office and sat down. He was a big man in his early forties, though he looked older. He leaned forward and looked at Brian. "Pastor," he said, "I want to tell you something. I'm not a Christian yet but I'm just about there, and it's because of you. You're doing a great job."

When Larry said that, Brian had to smile. *If only you knew how others felt.* But something in the words released the tension.

"Larry, I . . . you don't know how much those words mean to me," Brian managed. "I'm glad you're close to becoming a Christian. You know, there's no time like the present to make that decision, if you're willing."

Brian and Larry talked for fifteen or twenty minutes, and then Larry said he'd made up his mind. He knew it might be hard following Christ, but he was ready to start. They bowed their heads, and Brian led Larry in prayer. When Brian looked up at Larry afterward, he didn't know which of them was happier. He threw his arms around Larry and gave him a hug even a man his size would remember.

On Friday Brian was sorting through the morning mail and came to a letter with no return address. *Dear Pastor Wells*, it began, *You will have to answer to God for your perverted teaching that there is a Mr. and Mrs. God. We can no longer sit back and watch you lead Community Church into error. . . .*

Brian quickly read to the bottom: unsigned. Brian read the letter again, but there was no clue, either from the paper or typewriter used, as to who sent it. The line about a "Mr. and Mrs. God" galled him. And perplexed him. He could understand, perhaps, some people's misconceptions of Stanton Seminary, but this charge was utterly disconnected from reality. It made him sound like a cultist.

Then it hit Brian: *George Mason!* George, a devotional teacher with a national reputation, had spoken at the Wednesday evening service. He had said something like, "We need to be careful in our devotional life that we do not view God as the traditional father, if by that we mean one who is aloof, distant, and uncaring. He's the perfect parent, who also like a loving mother takes a child to his breast." Brian admitted it was a new thought for some people in Community Church, but it certainly squared with Scripture.

The more he thought about the letter, the madder he got. He hadn't even asked Mason to come; Landis had made all the arrangements before he left! And to construe from what George Mason had said that Brian believed in a Mr. and Mrs. God was absurd.

What am I supposed to do, anyway, Brian thought, *rip the microphone out of the hands of any guest speaker who has a fresh idea?*

"Cheap shot," Brian muttered under his breath.

Brian had been preaching through the book of James and had planned to cover James 4:1–12 on Sunday. But now, no way. He'd had enough of being the sitting duck, the passive minister who lets people fire away and keeps on smiling. He might not know who sent the letter or who wrote that leaflet, but they were going to hear about it Sunday, whoever they were. It was time to take a stand.

Truth triumphant?

By three o'clock Brian had an outline and a rough draft. The thoughts had flowed. Brian was surprised at how productive he could be when he was fired up. Titled "Honor and Honesty," the sermon was going to call to account members of the congregation who had been disregarding both.

Brian was about to head home when the phone rang. It was Vern, an old friend who pastored a large church near Denver. Vern had been through it all during his years of ministry, and even though they didn't see each other often, they made it a habit to check on each other periodically. Brian had even thought about giving him a call a few days ago.

Brian told Vern about the leaflet and the unsigned letter. "But this Sunday I'm going to set things straight," Brian said. "I can't let this kind of thing keep happening.

"I can appreciate how you feel," Vern said. "But I'd think twice before I blasted anybody from the pulpit. When I was an associate at Third Street, Sawyer started being attacked by people, and he took the battle into the pulpit. All that did was make people defensive and angry. The people who hadn't done anything wrong felt, *Hey, I like him. What's he after me for?*"

"So what am I supposed to do?" Brian asked. "Just let these people continue their guerrilla warfare?"

"Truth will triumph. Where you're wrong, admit it. Where they're wrong, don't defend yourself. But just focus on what God has for you to say. As hard as it is, if you don't take your fighting into the pulpit, truth will win out."

Brian lay awake in bed that night. The leaflet and letter hurt so much he didn't want to think about them, but he couldn't stop. They were so unfair, so one-sided, so insane. But Vern was usually right. If he dropped the bomb on Sunday, he'd wound not only the guilty but countless innocents. Part of the passage in James he'd studied earlier in the week began to come back to him: "Humble yourselves before the Lord, and he will lift you up." Then Brian drifted asleep.

When Brian walked into the pulpit Sunday, he slipped out of his pocket a card on which he'd handlettered TRUTH WILL TRIUMPH. He laid it in front of him and took a deep breath. He'd never been angry and afraid yet calm all at once. But somehow he was. He launched into James 4:1—ironically, "What causes fights and quarrels among you?"—and when he finished preaching eleven verses later, he walked back to his seat with his head up. He'd had the chance to lash out, but he hadn't used it.

Confidence vote

After the service, Henry Meyers pulled him aside. "Pastor, I think we've found our man."

"Oh, yeah?"

"I got a call late last night from Ed Anderson. He said that, under your teaching, Community Church was falling into error, and that we as elders were responsible to do something about it."

"What did you say?"

"I said yes, that was our responsibility and asked him what sort of problems he was having with your teaching. He said that you did not believe in the inerrancy of the Bible and as a result had fallen into deception, including that there is a Mr. and Mrs. God." Henry stopped and looked at Brian, and Brian nodded for him to keep going.

" 'Well, Ed, to be honest,' I said, 'the other elders and I feel Brian does believe in the inerrancy, and I doubt very seriously whether he believes there's some sort of husband-and-wife God.' "

"What did he say then?"

"He got really mad. He said he wasn't the only one who felt this way, that a lot of other people were also concerned, and that if we didn't care about the Bible, they'd find a pastor and elders who did."

"What did you say?"

"At that point, I knew we had to give him a chance to air his grievances. I asked him if he'd be willing to talk to the elders about his
concerns, but told him that in such a case you would be present to
defend yourself."

"Did he take you up on it?"

"We set a meeting for this Saturday, provided you and all the elders can make it."

On Saturday morning, Brian was in the church lounge at 8:30.
They weren't scheduled to meet until 9:00, but he wanted to pray for
a few moments. He had bags under his eyes from waking up at night.
But every time he woke up, he'd think through what he could say to
defend himself, and he was feeling confident about his projected responses.

Brian didn't know much about Ed except what Henry had told
him: in his fifties, a fairly wealthy attorney, and a natural leader used
to running his own show. He had wanted to be on the board, but
Landis had twice nixed the idea, and he was probably still smarting
from that.

When Ed arrived, shortly after nine, he chose a chair directly
across the room from Brian. He grunted a general "Good morning"
to the others in the room and sat in silence until one more elder
showed up a few minutes later.

Henry wasted no time beginning the meeting. "Ed, we're here to
listen to whatever you have to say to us. We've asked Brian to be here
to answer questions that come up and to clarify what he believes and
teaches. So why don't you start."

Ed glanced down at a legal pad in his lap and then looked across
at Brian. "Pastor," he said, "how many epistles are there in the New
Testament?"

Brian panicked. He didn't know what Ed was driving at, and he
wasn't prepared for that question. "I don't know the exact number
offhand," Brian said, "but let's see . . . there's Romans, two to the Corinthians . . ." At that point, Brian's mind went blank. He couldn't
even think of the next book in the New Testament. "Uh, I don't know,
but I'd say about twenty or so."

"Twenty-one," Ed informed him. "What I want to know," he said,
looking around at the elders, "is why you wrote in the last church
newsletter that there were twenty-eight."

"I, uh . . ." Brian stalled, and then it came to him. "I said in that article I was also counting the letters to the seven churches in the Book of Revelation. And besides, the point of the article was not the exact number but that each of us is an epistle, known and read by all. People read our actions to see if our faith means anything."

"That's a nice, allegorical way to avoid the fact that you don't know the Bible very well."

"Regardless of who's right, Ed," Henry broke in, "that's a minor issue. Let's get to the heart of the matter."

"All right," Ed said. "You don't believe the Bible is inerrant, do you?" He leaned forward and looked at Brian.

"That's not true. I believe the Scriptures are without error."

"But you never preach on it."

"Well, not all the time, but since I've been here I've preached one sermon on the reliability of Scripture, and *all* my sermons show the Bible as our sole authority."

"But would you be willing to sign a public statement saying that you believe in inerrancy?"

"I already have. When I accepted the call to Community Church, I signed a statement saying I was in complete agreement with the church's constitution and statement of faith, and that includes inerrancy."

Gordon, one of the elders, joined the attack. "You went to Stanton Seminary. Would you say they teach inerrancy?"

Brian was stunned that Gordon was supporting Ed's cause. "I can't vouch for all the professors there, but I know I believe in inerrancy."

"Gentlemen," Ed said, looking away from Brian, "what you have here is a man who says he believes in inerrancy, who will even sign a statement saying he believes it, but who in his heart of hearts really doesn't believe it. How can a man like that be our pastor?"

Brian didn't know whether to laugh or to cry. Was he supposed to sign in blood? But he doubted that would convince them either.

The rest of the meeting was a stalemate. Ed refused to accept Brian's professions of belief. Henry finally tried to close the meeting. "Ed, thank you for being willing to share your concerns with us. I don't know what to say. Pastor Brian says that he believes in inerrancy and has even signed a statement to that effect. To us, that's enough proof. If it's not to you, we're sorry."

"You mean you're not going to take a vote?" Ed demanded.

"A vote on what?"

"A vote on whether we ought to remove this man as our pastor."

"I don't see why that's necessary, but yes, if you want us to go on record, we can take a vote. All those in favor of removing Brian Wells as pastor of Community Church, say aye."

"Aye," said Gordon loudly—with Ed, who couldn't even vote.

"All those opposed?"

"Nay," said the rest of the room.

"I want to warn you," said Ed as he stood up. "Gordon and I aren't the only ones who are concerned about the pastor. His own staff doesn't support him. I love this church. It kills me to leave it. But if you men are too weak to remove a pastor who's subverting it, we'll find a church that does preach the Word." Then he left, with Gordon close behind.

As Brian drove home, he felt sick. What had Ed meant by "his own staff doesn't support him"? Was that another one of his outrageous claims, or was there some truth to it? And how did Ed know? Had he and the staff been meeting behind Brian's back? It hurt, too, that Gordon, who ought to know better, had turned against him. He'd been so supportive on the elder retreat, and now, in the middle of a meeting, he decides he can't trust his own pastor.

Brian was proud of the rest of the elders, though. They'd been pure gold, tested and refined. They and Brian had "won," though strangely, Brian almost didn't care. Maybe that's what bothered him most about this whole thing. No matter how wrong Ed and Gordon might be, the whole affair had inflicted such a severe emotional beating that Brian hadn't felt good for anything. *What kind of ministry can you have when you're constantly under siege?* he wondered.

Ungodly mess

Three weeks later Brian found out that Ed and Gordon and about seventy-five other people had started meeting on the other side of town. He called Henry Meyers to let him know.

"So they carried through on their threat," Henry said.

"Yeah. They're renting the Seventh-Day Adventist church building on Sunday mornings, and they're talking about calling a pastor soon."

"There's not much we can do about Ed, but it sure hurts to see so many people go with him."

"It hurts me, too," Brian said, "but in a way I'm almost relieved. Maybe this is natural fallout when a new pastor comes. Maybe now things will calm down and we can get back to ministry."

"Brian, I hate to tell you this since you just said that, but remember in our meeting with Ed how he said even the staff doesn't support you? I've been puzzling over that statement ever since."

"Me, too," Brian said. "I couldn't tell whether he was bluffing or whether he knew something we didn't. And I couldn't exactly confront Doug and Tim with 'Are you loyal to me?' or, 'Have you been meeting with Ed?' "

"Well, my wife was talking with Tim's wife, and she said that the month before that leaflet came out, Ed invited Tim and Doug over to his house. He wanted to know what they thought about how things were going in the church. Apparently Tim supported you, but Doug was pretty negative. It upset Tim and his wife, but they didn't feel right saying anything about it earlier."

Brian hung up, leaned back in his chair, and looked at the ceiling. *So it's not all over.* Now the problem was within his own staff. But what could he do, fire a person because he criticized the pastor? During his own days as an associate, he hadn't always agreed with his senior pastor. Still, this was different, and Brian didn't know what to do.

Several Sundays later, just before his sermon, Brian looked out and saw Larry sitting near the back. Suddenly all the anger and frustration he had felt over the past months came bubbling up. *Here's this new believer*, he thought, *looking for a warm and safe place to grow in Christ, and we can't give it to him. My faith is hardly strong enough to stand all this backbiting and gossip, and we're subjecting him to it. He's never going to make it.*

Complicating the whole matter was that Larry and Doug lived near each other, and their kids had become good friends. Brian wasn't sure how close they were themselves, but if Doug was making comments critical of him or the church, Larry would probably hear them. And if Brian and Doug had to part ways, Larry would witness the whole mess. Brian didn't know if Larry's tender faith could withstand any more church dissension.

In the spring, Brian asked Christian scholar and writer R. T. Bradfield to come speak at Community Church. Following the church's usual policy, he had his secretary send Bradfield a copy of the church's doctrinal statement to sign. Bradfield called him the next week and said he deeply wanted to come to Community, but he couldn't in good conscience endorse some of the fine points of eschatology that were part of the statement. Brian said he didn't think that would pose any problem, but he wanted to get the board's approval. He was still tender from the blowup over George Mason's comments.

At the elder board meeting the following Thursday, Brian explained what Bradfield had said.

"I've read two of Bradfield's books," said Henry. "Heavy stuff, but good! And didn't he write the book on biblical inerrancy? To refuse to allow him to speak because of a minor point of eschatology is ridiculous."

The other elders agreed wholeheartedly. "Of course we're going to have him," said one. "Besides, nothing in the constitution says a speaker has to sign the statement or he can't preach."

Brian thought Doug looked disgruntled. But he wasn't sure.

At the next weekly staff meeting, Brian was going over the preaching and worship calendar for the coming quarter. "How's it look to you?" Brian asked.

"I've been meaning to say something about this, and now seems like the time," said Doug. "A lot of people have said to me, 'We need more meat, more depth in our messages.' So I was thinking it might be good if you preached on Sunday morning and let me feed the people on Sunday nights."

Brian consciously tried to keep his expression steady. He could handle criticism, but if "more meat" meant a preaching style like Doug's, he had grave reservations. One time Doug was preaching and asked all the men in the congregation to stand. Then he said, "Women, look at these men. If one-third of these men became as spiritual as they ought to be, this church would be a different place."

"Let me think about that for a while, Doug," Brian said. He wanted to make sure he handled this right, and he was afraid if they got into it now, the quiet exchange might escalate into verbal war.

The following week Brian decided on his strategy. He was going to be on a badly needed vacation the following month, so he asked Doug to take the Sunday evening service while he was gone, and at least one Sunday night each month from then on. As much as Brian disagreed with some of Doug's preaching tactics, he wanted to support him; Doug was a capable discipleship leader and had given six years to Community Church.

When he presented the idea, Doug seemed happy for the opportunities, and that helped blunt the news that Brian didn't think it was time for him to take every Sunday evening just yet.

On the first Sunday evening of their trip, Brian and Carol stayed in a Holiday Inn outside Indianapolis. Brian was sitting up reading *USA Today* when the phone rang. *Who would be calling me?* he wondered as he walked over to the phone. *No one even knows I'm here.*

"Pastor, I'm really sorry to bother you," the voice began, "especially it being so late." It was Henry Meyers.

"Henry! What's going on?"

"It's Doug. You know he preached tonight."

"Yes?"

"Brian, he really blasted the elders. He said we were weak, not being completely truthful with the congregation. And since we don't measure up to the biblical standards, we shouldn't be followed until we return to complete truthfulness."

"Oh my."

"I feel bad calling you like this, but the congregation is in an uproar. I've had five phone calls about it in the last hour. I hate to suggest this, but I think if you could be here, you could calm things down."

The next morning, Brian headed their Reliant wagon north on I–65 back toward Madison. Carol sat in silence, and the kids, knowing something was wrong, were mostly quiet. Brian didn't know what to say to Carol. She understood—she really did—but he felt like Scrooge tearing her away from this vacation. She'd been waiting for it for months, and all the promises that they'd get away again soon sounded cheap.

As they drove past the fields of knee-high corn, Brian formulated what he would say to Doug. And every now and then his thoughts would wander to Larry. *I was afraid this was going to happen,* he thought. *How's he supposed to understand that Christ is great and it's just us Christians that are the problem? Larry, friend, if you give it all up, you have no one to blame but us.*

That evening, Brian and the elders met with Doug in an emergency meeting.

"Doug, you have publicly charged the elders of this church with not being truthful," Brian began. "That's a serious charge. Explain what you mean."

"I've been in this church six years," he said, "and I've always been able to support and work with its leaders. But it deeply disturbs me when I see elders who don't have integrity on fiscal matters, and who hide the fact they let any speaker, no matter how off-base, into the pulpit."

"Which speakers, for example?"

"R. T. Bradfield. Anyone who can't sign this church's statement of faith ought not to be allowed to speak in its pulpit."

"We discussed that at the elders' meeting," Henry snapped. "If you had a problem with it, why didn't you say something then, rather than immaturely blasting us in a public worship service? There's nothing wrong with Bradfield, anyway. He's as orthodox as anyone here."

The meeting lasted over an hour. Doug never did produce any evidence of financial wrongdoing, and Brian knew he couldn't, because there wasn't any. The issue at heart was Doug's objection to the church's "weak leadership." Near the end, Doug said, "I'm stunned. Community Church has been my home, my family. But since it's clear that you men are not willing to lead this church in a godly direction, I can no longer be part of it. I resign."

Brian hurt inside, but he didn't try to stop Doug. In truth, he didn't know any other way to resolve the problem. How do you answer a charge that you aren't godly?

"Doug," Henry said, "we accept your resignation, though we want you to know we're sorry you feel this way. And I personally want to ask your forgiveness for snapping at you earlier this meeting. Please forgive me."

The room was silent. Then Doug nodded at Henry, stood, and walked out.

Open epistle

On Sunday the church held a farewell reception for Doug following the service. Brian saw Larry say goodbye to Doug. Larry's kids were crying. Larry had to know all the dirt behind the resignation.

Brian wanted to run over and say something to him, but what could he say?

For five weeks Brian didn't hear anything about Doug. Then the leader of an adult Sunday school class told Brian that half his class had stopped coming; they were meeting with Doug on Sunday mornings now. When Brian checked into it, he found that in just the two weeks Doug's group had met, attendance had swelled to over one hundred.

The news sent Brian into an emotional tailspin. When Ed and all his people left, he'd almost felt relieved, but to have the same thing happen again so soon was too much. *I must be setting some sort of ecclesiastical record*, Brian thought. He could see the headlines in the Stanton alumni magazine: WELLS'S CHURCH HAS RECORD SECOND SPLIT IN HIS FIRST TWO YEARS.

What am I doing wrong? Brian thought, spinning a pencil in circles on his desk. *Oh, God, I'm tired.*

Brian looked down at his desk calendar, hoping his afternoon would magically be open, but two appointments stared at him. The first was with Larry. His secretary must have set it up. *That's the crowning blow*, he thought. *Larry's going to come in here and say, "Pastor Wells, I've given this Christianity thing a fair shake, but it's just not all it's cracked up to be."*

Lord, Brian prayed, *I thought that where you guided, you provided. But you have not given me the emotional makeup to be a pastor. I just don't have it.*

Larry came five minutes late, and when he walked in, Brian thought he looked troubled. He sat down in the brown chair across from Brian's desk, then leaned forward. Brian braced himself.

"Pastor," he said, "this last year has been hell for me."

"That sounds rough. Tell me about it," Brian said mechanically.

"My boss is the most abrasive person I've ever known," he said. "He never has a kind word about anyone or anything. For three years I've sweated under that, and then I came to Community Church . . ."

. . . *and you found we Christians aren't any better,* Brian mentally completed his sentence.

"And I watched you," Larry went on. "I watched the slander, the accusations, all the gruff. You had every right to retaliate. And you didn't."

Brian was silent.

"I figured if God could enable you not to retaliate, with all you went through, then he could enable me not to retaliate with what I went through. So I went back to my boss and I did something I've never done before in my life. It had to be God, because I couldn't do it. I apologized to my boss, and I asked his forgiveness for the way I've bucked him and for the bad attitudes I've had."

Brian opened his mouth to say something, but he couldn't get anything out.

"So that's why I came in here today. I wanted you to know that in the last year you not only helped me meet the Lord, but you proved to me that God is real in the middle of hard times."

Brian's eyes started to well with tears.

"If you didn't come to Madison for anybody else, Pastor, you came for me."

It's worth it, Brian thought. *It's all worth it. We really are epistles read by all.* Then he started to cry. He knew he must have looked like a fool in front of Larry, but he didn't care. He let the tears come.

25

The Care and Feeding of Critics

Every leader has to develop a plan for handling criticism,
because criticism will come in any dynamic organization.

—Fred Smith

H aving been the head of several organizations, I've had my share
of critics. So when LEADERSHIP asked me to write about the care
and feeding of critics, one word came to mind: arsenic.

Then I remembered three occasions when friends cared enough
to confront me. At the moment, their criticism stung, but it has been
a blessing for a lifetime. Criticism properly given and properly received accounts for much of the progress in a person or an organization.

Every leader has to develop a plan for handling criticism, because
criticism will come in any dynamic organization. Capable people
bring out friction and difference of opinion. In fact, if an organization
is completely placid, I have found it's generally not very productive.

Expect criticism whenever one or more of the following is true
(unless, of course, the church is made up exclusively of other saints):

The change costs money.

The change causes inconvenience.

There is a shift in power or recognition.

You can also count on criticism when you have an "inspirational
program"—one that comes suddenly, that sends you into an emotional high. Criticism will likely come from those who have not had
that thrill.

Therefore, the leader must expect criticism much as an Olympian
would expect and plan for pain. I listened to Bob Richards, the Olym-

pic gold medalist, interview younger Olympic winners of the gold. He asked them, "What did you do when you began to hurt?"

None of these Olympians was surprised by the question; all had a specific way of handling the pain—some even prayed.

After the interviews, I asked Bob why he had asked about handling pain, and he said matter-of-factly, "You never win the gold without hurting."

A leader must accept the challenge of criticism rather than let it become a threat. When criticism is a threat, a leader becomes defensive, but when it is viewed as a challenge, he or she can handle it constructively.

Let me share some of the positive approaches I have learned in handling criticism.

Classify your critics

Critics come in many shapes and sizes. Some are overt, and some are covert. Some hit you in the nose, and others stab you in the back. I have found classifying my critics helpful; it helps me anticipate what a person may say.

I'm sure you'll have no trouble putting people's names with these types (but be sure to classify according to people's performance, not your personal feelings for them).

1. People who resent authority per se. These critics have never outgrown their disrespect for any authority but their own. As children they rebelled against their parents, as employees against their bosses, and as adults against leaders in whatever groups they joined. They adhere to the bumper-sticker slogan, "QUESTION all authority."

Such critics can be worked only in a loose harness. They must be given permission to rebel, which is almost an oxymoron . . . but practical.

2. People with natural leadership qualities who are not part of the majority. As a result, they become leaders of the minority, and they feel they have to be in opposition to serve their function. The more capable they are, the more difficult they are for a leader to deal with.

In my place of work, I looked for this type of critic. We even kept a list of the young, unofficial leaders—those whom other people listened to. Unless we utilized their natural leadership qualities constructively, these critics would become destructive. So I tried to move many of them into management, often with good results.

3. People who criticize to show their superior knowledge. Those who consider themselves good in a particular area will criticize others not so good. For example, a great dresser will criticize others' clothes. Sometimes these critics can be turned into coaches if they genuinely have an area of expertise. (More on how to do that later.)

4. "Natural howlers." Most organizations have people who are like the hound dog lying on a cockleburr: he would rather howl than move. Every new idea becomes another cockleburr.

5. People who use criticism to exorcise internal conflicts. As a friend says of these critics, "They are a fight going somewhere to happen." Generally their criticism is perpetual and petulant. In fact, most bitter criticism is personal, not organizational; it's not over doctrine but ego.

I've found I can use such criticism as a way of identifying those who are hurting. A person dissatisfied with himself or herself will generally show that in some way, and as a pastor, knowing who is hurting goes with the job. Criticism might be an invitation to meet someone at a place of deep need.

6. Genuine, honest, interested critics. Finally, there are some who feel responsible for the welfare of the organization. I must treat these critics with respect, attention, and courtesy. They are not my enemies but, ultimately, my friends. Good critics are like buoys in the river: they keep you in the channel.

Sorting through your critics is not always easy. Sometimes we have to take the approach Solomon did: recommend cutting the baby to find out who is cause-oriented and who is vindictiveness-oriented.

Turn critics into coaches

A good critic and a good coach both see what is wrong. They see for different reasons, however. The critic sees the problem to point it out and establish his authority or expertise, while the coach sees the problem in order to work on it and improve it. I believe that with proper care most critics can be turned into coaches. What we normally think of as liabilities then become assets.

A few months after I became an executive with Genesco, I grew concerned about all the things that were wrong with the organization. I felt it my undiluted responsibility to talk about these to Maxey

Jarman, the president, for fear the company might go out of business (regardless of the fact it had risen from a tiny start to become the fifth largest firm in the apparel industry). Fortified with my list, I went to see the president, even without an appointment.

Maxey was gracious and asked me to sit down and recite the list, which I started to do. About halfway through, he commented that I was right on target with several of my observations (immediately he became one of the smartest executives I'd ever met). When I finished the list, he asked me what I was doing for the next three weeks. He wanted me to take on, in addition to my regular job, writing a better way of doing everything I had criticized. As I walked toward the door, he gave me a faint smile and asked my permission to continue operating in the way we were, since it was the best he knew. I gave him my permission and headed for my office.

Three weeks later, I didn't call Maxey—he called me. He wanted to see my write-up of better ways. I had to face him and say, "I've been here only a short time, and I don't know a better way of doing everything I criticized."

With unusual firmness for this Christian gentleman, he said, "Fred, we're glad to have you with this company. We want your suggestions, even your criticisms. But don't ever criticize another thing in this outfit until you've got a better way of doing it worked out on paper—and you're willing to risk your reputation as an executive on its workability."

In Tennessee we say, "He learnt me that," and as far as I know, I did not make that mistake again. Maxey taught me an invaluable lesson: always to be positive when looking for the negative. I had been a critic; Maxey taught me how much better it is to be a coach.

The first step in turning a critic into a coach is to define his or her area of responsibility. I don't believe in saying, "If you see something wrong, tell me about it." That's too general. That fails to define his or her area of responsibility.

I'm careful to use people at their point of strength, so they will be good coaches. For example, if someone has been critical about matters of finance, and I believe he or she genuinely knows about finance, I will invite that person to coach me in that area. Or I might invite someone to coach me in the areas of personal relationships or theology.

For many years I was alternate teacher of a large Sunday school class. I chose three people to be my coaches.

My wife, Mary Alice, was responsible to be sure that when we got in the car I had my notes and my glasses and that I had the right attitude. If I was negative or judgmental, my attitude soured the milk of the Word.

I also recruited an executive and a doctor, both of whom I respect intellectually and spiritually, to be responsible for telling me if the lesson hung together well, if it was practical and clear. I also wanted to know if there was "too much me and not enough He."

These three coaches kept me on course.

When turning a critic into a coach, it's important not to argue with the person's honest opinion or to try to make him or her defend it. The only thing coaches are responsible for is to give me their considered opinion in a designated area. I'm not obligated to agree, but I must listen with appreciation.

Sometimes if a person is naturally critical, you can make him a constructive coach by letting him know. "I expect you to criticize in this particular area, but you are responsible for giving *high-quality* criticisms as an outgrowth of your talent." That tells the person to refine their numerous criticisms into the best few and pass along only those.

When a coach criticizes you, after listening, get the person to repeat it and write down the specific criticisms.

If it's a weak criticism, the more the person repeats it, the weaker it will get.

But if it's a valid criticism, it will grow stronger, and you will have a record of it to act on.

Anticipate specific criticisms

A naval officer told me that one time the brass in Washington wanted to find a submarine captain who would volunteer for a dangerous experiment under the ice cap. They talked to one particularly capable captain, but he asked for permission to talk to his crew before he volunteered their services. He wanted to take on the mission, but he knew it was dangerous.

The captain took the offensive. He called the crew together and started listing on a sheet why they should tell the brass the mission was too dangerous. He put up the first criticism, and immediately a

crew member spoke up, "That's true, but not in every case." Then
the crew suggested how that objection could be overcome.

By the time the captain got through the list of negatives, his crew
had convinced each other that the negatives could be overcome. The
captain concluded, "I take it, then, that you want to attempt this mission." They agreed, and they did the mission, successfully. The captain won their support because he anticipated their criticisms and de-
fused them.

Some leaders bring a program into a group without proper planning, hoping to get an approving vote. They may get the vote, but
criticism is likely to follow. People don't like to be surprised: surprises give the impression of a manipulated agenda.

Every capable leader knows the "thought leaders" in a group and
often talks to them ahead of time, enlisting their support or listening
to their criticisms before a meeting. You can't go into a meeting without knowing how the voting will go.

Assume criticism is logical

It's usually best to assume that a person's criticism is sincere.
Given the base from which the person is working, the criticism will
be entirely logical. The key is to understand where the person is coming from.

For example, my wife criticizes my sports-car style of driving, because her premise is, "Anybody who drives like that will eventually
have a wreck." With that base, her criticism of my driving is entirely
logical. My perspective is different, but to me just as logical: "The
more I drive like this, the more experience I get, and the less likely
I am to have a wreck."

In church votes on finances, for example, a business executive
may feel that the economy is going down and that church debt is a
dangerous thing. Another business leader in the church may have an
entirely different base: inflation is on the way, and therefore, church
debt is sensible. Another person may hold a theological opinion that
churches should never go into debt.

Thus, to work with people's criticisms, we must know their deep
beliefs, biases, experiences, theological positions, and especially
their ego levels. There's generally a majority and minority group on
any board (just as there is in the legislature), and someone in the

minority will generally be an obstructionist simply by virtue of his or her position.

When you understand the person's internal logic, you can show respect for the criticism without being namby-pamby.

Limit the criticism you'll accept

A leader must know how to limit the criticism he or she accepts. I learned this from a day laborer who wanted to be a success in life. Many years ago he spent the day with me in Chicago and went over a simple plan he had written out, and he gave me a copy.

Recently I read in the newspaper that this man had contributed $6 million to higher education. I immediately went back over the points of his program and saw how he had followed them so successfully. One of his points was, "I will accept criticism only from someone who has something to gain from my success." To him, those people were his family, his superiors, and his friends. By limiting his acceptable criticism, he no doubt missed some that might have been helpful, but he missed a great deal that would have been harmful. As he told me, "People think you ought to keep an open mind, but if you keep it too open, people throw garbage in."

Many times I have let one critical person keep me from recognizing the strength of the hundred who are in agreement. When I'm speaking, for example, if I sense a critical person, he or she can distract me.

I've learned not to over-credit criticism. It's possible to turn a cold into a cancer. Some criticisms sting more than they damage, and every bee sting is not a snake bite. Remember the old philosophical adage, "This, too, shall pass."

Those of us who have known Billy Graham for many years have admired the way he has not answered his critics. Sometimes if a racehorse pays too much attention to a horsefly, it makes the fly too important. Some people's only taste of success is the bite they take out of someone whom they perceive is doing more than they are.

It's helpful to have a friend or two who can help you sort the minor criticisms from the major ones. Then you can treat minor criticisms in a minor way—such as ignore them. But you can also take seriously major criticisms that will grow and can't be ignored. Honest people with a fresh perspective can help you recognize what is a deep and powerful current and what is just a surface wave.

One way I limit the criticism I accept is to refuse any that distracts from the organization's main purpose.

Bill Waugh, owner of a restaurant chain, was asked to become chairman of The Salvation Army. He chose as his theme "Keep the main thing the main thing." By that he meant, "Keep the purpose of the organization clearly in mind and do not get diverted from it."

Make constructive criticism part of the culture

Since criticism is going to come, it pays to make constructive criticism a part of the church culture. Every well-led organization needs to have an established, stated, understood, and agreed-upon culture. Why not make it part of the ongoing definition of the organization that criticism, when offered constructively, is welcomed.

For this to happen, the people must hear you as leader—over and over and in different ways—say you value it.

The statement can come in the form of a sermon, for example. David's life would not have turned around if it had not been for Nathan. That's an excellent passage to point out the value of a loyal opposition. Lift up the responsibility of people to keep leaders from serious mistakes, to make sure we look at alternative solutions, and to keep us conscious of our responsibilities rather than our rights.

Often I've heard a capable speaker say on a sensitive point, "Now here's something that I haven't always believed—in fact, I used to oppose it vehemently. But some people have helped me rethink this position." Such a speaker is making constructive criticism acceptable.

List the times that critics have been helpful to you. After all, even the mule was helpful to the prophet. Then, if you preach about criticism, you can illustrate from your list the type of criticism that is appreciated.

Give strokes for good criticism. In a meeting, you might say, "You are the lighthouse that will keep us off the rocks." Or point out that a constructive critic is the tail to the kite: the kite may feel it's a tremendous drag, but the kite would dart all over without it.

My mentor, Maxey Jarman, felt that every organization needed a perceptive and persistent cockleburr. Lou was a great one. Once we were developing a golf course for employees. As usual, he saw the other side and said we should be developing fishing facilities because so many more employees fished than played golf. As a side remark, I told him, "I don't like to fish, because I never seem to catch any."

He replied, "I can understand that, because in order to catch anything you have to be smarter than it."

Lou was a valuable member of the team, though at times irritating. He kept us from "slumber in Zion." Maxey didn't squelch that quality but instead encouraged Lou to use it responsibly for the common good.

If we make constructive criticism an accepted part of the culture, we won't increase the amount of criticism; instead, we will channel the existing criticism so that it accomplishes something valuable.

Don't turn criticism into a personal contest

Some leaders have gotten sidetracked into depending on their popularity for agreement. This can later develop into a contest between those who are for the leader and those who are against the leader. Making your popularity the issue gives the opposition a firm base from which to work. So often we make criticism into a personal contest, when, if left alone, it will die of its own lack of meaning.

My dear late father was constantly in fights: first, because he thought he was right, and then, because he thought that right was always in a fight. Every opposition was an attack of the devil. Too often, the purification of the faith is much more an ego matter than a spiritual one.

Recently, I led a leadership retreat with a successful retiring pastor. I asked him about the early days of his ministry, and he told me that as a seminary student he offered $100 to several leading pastors to simply let him sit and ask them some questions. (I don't think a single one refused the interview, though I don't think they took the money.)

One of his questions was, "How do you handle critics?"

Each one had a plan that varied greatly according to the individual. One had the spirit of inquisition: "Get them out." That is one way, but I doubt it's the Christian way. Critics are not heretics, and we can't take the position that wrong has no rights.

In one church that was having difficulty, for example, the pastor determined he was not going to take sides on the theological question at hand. He told the people he had been called to be their pastor, not to dictate their policies. The lay people worked out the matter amicably, and the pastor ended up with little criticism.

Learn to lose a battle in order to win a war

When Charlton Heston was asked how he enjoyed such a long marriage, he gave credit to "those three little words"—not the ones we think of, but "I was wrong."

I have found I can sometimes make a friend of a critic by adding three more words as a preface: "You are right . . . I was wrong."

I try to look on every reasonable criticism as a chance to review my position. It just might be that I am wrong. While the Scripture might be inerrant, those of us who lead are not infallible. I had a friend who often confessed that he had been wrong in the past, but I could never get him to admit to being wrong in the present.

It helps me a little bit, when I'm being criticized, just to realize that I, too, have done some criticizing in the past that was dead wrong. Through the years I have developed a "humility list" of criticisms I made of situations, programs, investments, and people that turned out to be totally wrong.

I still blush when I think how cocksure I was that the "Tiger in the Tank" advertising program wouldn't work. I couldn't believe people would hang miniature tiger tails out of their gas tanks. Yet that program went down as one of the longest and most successful advertising campaigns ever.

In the give-and-take of criticism, it's a warning sign when we fail to see humor in the situation. In the longest study of successful executives done by Harvard, one of the four qualities they identified in these leaders was a sense of humor. There are many times in leadership when we can either laugh or develop high blood pressure, and the laughing keeps us human.

Once I was coming out of the factory during a snowstorm, and several of the employees were standing at the door waiting for their rides. As I passed them and started down the steps I said, "God put skis on me," referring to my size-fifteen shoes. After I had gone down a couple of steps, I heard one of the employees say, "And from where I'm standing, he gave you a pillow to fall on, too."

All I could do was turn around, smile, and say, "You're so right, my friend."

Don't take revenge

It's difficult to stay objective about critics. Sometimes we feel they're a needle in a balloon factory. Still, leaders must take a firm stand without a vindictive spirit.

If someone criticizes you publicly, you can use your critic to show that you're a reasonable person. "I know that some people here whom I admire the most will be the first to be against this idea. If I didn't think they were fair-minded enough to consider the things that I have considered and to realize that I have thought long and hard about this, then I would have been skeptical about proposing the idea myself."

It's so important to personify tolerance and avoid all retribution. " 'Vengeance is mine,' says the Lord." That means, for example, not using the pulpit to answer your critics; in doing so, you are riding a horse and hitting somebody who's walking.

We must also be careful to avoid answering critics in our public prayers. Prayers are directed to God, not to the board.

Gerry-rigging a meeting to have certain questions asked—to me—is unethical. So is promising answers and then not giving any in hopes the issue will die.

Effectual prayer is one of the appropriate armaments against criticism. A dear friend was being emotionally crucified by his critics. These people had profited from him and owed him gratitude rather than criticism, but still they bitterly fought him.

When he died, I found a prayer list in his Bible. At the top of his list were these simple yet powerful words: "Pray for those who are lying about me."

26

Quailing Before the Critics

When forced to accept the reality of my preaching,
I managed to find some good in it.

—Doug Jackson

A *nd you have never heard a worse preacher!*—2 Corinthians 10:10 (TLB)

Those caustic Corinthians found preachers they preferred to Paul, and they let Paul know it.

We pastors often deal with similar attacks but without Paul's track record to bolster us. How do we respond when people turn sour and assault our preaching? Two recent experiences taught me that such an onslaught brings pain but also benefits.

Our church property backs up to the Fort McDowell Indian Reservation. One morning, as I took a stroll through the desert, the issue of criticism crystallized.

Two Gambel's quail, a male and his mate, skittered among the scrubby bushes before me, picking their way through the appaloosa sunlight of early morning. I studied the male especially. Larger than his partner, he strutted out front by half a length. His James Dean crest flopped over a Lou Costello face, an absurd specimen of gray-feathered aristocracy.

"Do you know how silly you look?" I snorted to him. He didn't.

I scrutinized his mate a moment, a modest thing in hausfrau gray and brown. Unliberated, she kept demurely tailfeatherward of her companion.

"He probably tells you he stays out front to protect you," I mused.

"Fact is, he only means to get to the chow first. Why not deflate the clown?"

Then something spooked the pair. As predicted, Sir Quail made no move to tilt a lance for this lady. Both exploded in fury, pounding skyward. The female fluttered easily, while her mate tried to shatter the hold of gravity in short, shuddering strokes. But what grace he stole as he hit airspeed! He swept the wind on outstretched wings to land softly among the neon thorns of a paloverde tree.

I returned to my study and squared off against a dry pile of books and notes that were refusing to become a sermon. The image of Sir Quail lingered in my mind. He was a picture of my preaching.

How my self-image had changed! Only a few months earlier, I would hungrily enter my study, convinced I had found the preacher's motherlode that eluded Spurgeon. Confident of my abilities, I found myself strutting along, self-important in my stuffy calling. Come Sundays, I flew on word-wings, barnstorming truth to the awed congregation, then settling gently at the back door to receive their coos of admiration.

But now I was awkwardly walking through a wasteland of facts, awaiting the terror of Sunday morning to give me wings—wings that no longer seemed able to get past the shuddering strokes to the graceful flight.

What had happened?

Church sociologists say that most honeymoons last about three years. I had been in my present pulpit just shy of thirty-six months when two of my most faithful members came to see me. They respectfully addressed me as "Pastor." They never raised their voices, but these two men came to tell me, in essence, "You look ridiculous."

One talked about "too much secondary application." I had to ask what that meant. He said I should deal with "just what the text said" without so many digressions into what people should do about it. He offered me an out, noting that it must be hard for a preacher not to want to tell people, "Now get with it!" a phrase that to him, I suppose, summed up my applications.

I responded as best I could, saying it sounded like what he wanted was a lecture, not a sermon. (I remembered my preaching professor at seminary had said that dispensing textual background was "exegeting in public," and although it wasn't illegal, it should be.) If I wanted to lecture, I said, I would get a college teaching position. That during most of my sermon preparation I thought about the text from the practical side. He seemed unimpressed.

Another criticism focused on my illustrations. One of the men had been keeping score and had noted that the bulk of my illustrations were not from the Bible but from "secular sources," his term for the newspaper articles, personal anecdotes, and literary quotes I used. He unsheathed the Reformation phrase "comparing Scripture with Scripture" and aimed its point at me.

I parried by saying that illustrating a Bible verse with a Bible verse was like using a red crayon on red paper. I pointed out that many people, especially the large number of new converts in our congregation, had told me how much they appreciated the stories, which provided a contact point between the Bible and daily life. However, I did admit I probably focused too much on the sermon text, ignoring parallel references.

Then I heard that I was not "fiery" enough. As near as I could tell, this was a call for more volume and insults. I responded that I had to preach as I felt led and in keeping with my own personality. I pointed to some instances of fairly stern exhortation in recent messages.

Finally, they left, and I crawled away to lick my wounds.

What were these men really saying? From the vantage point of time, I see that both came to our church from large congregations with sharply chiseled preaching traditions. "Good" preaching was the kind they were used to, but each used different criteria for "good." They did agree, however, that *my* preaching was way off the beam.

In the words of Anne Limburgh, hours of gold turned to hours of lead. The elastic texture of my preaching went wooden. Texts that had glittered like gemstones faded into dull Hebrew roots. I began to do more visiting, holding at bay sermon preparation until as late in the week as possible.

What to do? I wanted to flee to another congregation, but no invitation materialized. I would have quit outright, but the call of God tyrannized my cowardice.

I thought of the quail. Covered with dust, I again tried to fly. Though my solution often leaves me somewhere between the fuss and the feathers, it has kept me preaching, and I offer my reflections as encouragement for the sick at heart.

Crash-landing

Until my encounter with the critics, I had blissfully assumed that my preaching was fine. My fall from this illusion brought a crash-landing into reality. In many ways, I wish I could have continued living in fantasy.

Our illusions serve a purpose. When I was four years old, a realtor told me a hippopotamus lived in the attic of our new home. He shared a graphic account of the missing digits of naughty boys who ventured beyond the trapdoor in the storage room ceiling.

I bought the whole thing. A couple of years later, I learned that the salesman's story was a ruse designed to keep me out of a dangerous part of the house. I was not happy. Staying out of the attic just to be good was no fun compared to staying out to avoid a chomping hippopotamus.

Life runs more smoothly and with more zest when greased with illusion. For that reason, I never assume the superiority of reality over daydreams. As David Morrison of the Menninger Clinic says, "Fantasy, not reality, will determine what you and I do." I may have preached better—or at least with more zest and energy—before my pulpit bubble burst. I enthusiastically gave myself to creative study and application, and entered the pulpit with confidence.

Still, reality blesses us with objectivity, even longevity. When forced to accept reality, I managed to find some good in it. For me, reality brought humility, better relationships, and a renewed appreciation for people in the pews.

Humility's gift. One Sunday I thundered forth in power, my blue pinstripe suit looking remarkably like camel hair. Every eye focused on me. I had them this time, and not a single Philistine would escape with his paganism intact. Another instant showed me the reality behind their absorption. From the front pew, my wife held aloft a rapidly lettered sign reading, ZIPPER. The words of Isaiah took on a new meaning as I lamented, "Woe is me, for I am undone."

It helps (though it hurts) to hear the truth about the fly in the ointment, even when that fly is unzipped.

After the interview with my critical church members, I realized I had cherished the proud and false idea that people came each week with a burning desire to hear my sermon. I now saw that their motives were mixed. Some came to church *in spite* of my preaching; many preferred the style of previous pastors or famous television and radio ministers. Some came out of religious duty and did not care about preaching one way or another.

If this was the case, better that I know so. Worse than being washed up is being washed up and not knowing it. Tolstoy, in *Anna Karenina*, sculpts the image of obliviousness:

> At almost the same time that his wife left Alexei Alexandrovich, there had come to him that bitterest moment in the life of an official—the moment when his upward career comes to a full stop. This full stop had been arrived at and everyone perceived it, but Alexei Alexandrovich himself was not yet aware that his career was over.

Then comes the most chilling moment:

> Alexei Alexandrovich did not merely fail to observe his hopeless position in the official world, he was not merely free from anxiety on this head—he was positively more satisfied than ever with his own activity.

Better Relationships. I also ended up with a better relationship with my members. When the Shekinah draped my pulpit, I had excused my social reticence as devotion to a noble calling. Since my preaching was to lift people to exalted heights, I had good reason for being absent when they needed to chat. In short, in the name of eloquence, I had withdrawn.

When my tower of oratory caved in, I tumbled down smack into their living rooms and offices and backyards. Fearing that I was losing touch with them as a preacher, I decided to reach them as a person.

Yet these new relationships resulted in better preaching. Topics for sermons bombarded me, and application became as easy as taking inventory on the week's conversations.

Renewed appreciation. I had pouted that no one celebrated my efforts, until one blunt friend reminded me that most people are never celebrated. The people in the pews toil daily. Come quitting time, they get a paycheck and maybe a handshake, but no brass band plays for them.

My bout with discontent also introduced me to what Calvin Miller calls the "back door" of life. Everyone has a back door, where all the unfinished and imperfect work of our life piles up. The occasional Sunday visitor sees only the front parlor and may even compliment us on it. Real friends, however, are those who have entered our lives through the clutter of the back door. Those who kindly ignore the negative reality may prove more genuine friends than those who praise positive illusion.

I learned to appreciate even more those real friends who saw me for what I was and didn't mention it.

Redemptive criticism

After my painful interview I realized that some people wanted different preaching. I knew I couldn't satisfy everyone, but as I reviewed my previous months of preaching, I had to admit I had become a formula expositor.

Not long ago, a TV commercial for a particular brand of clothing portrayed a fashion show behind the old Iron Curtain. The announcer drones, "Swimwear," as a cruiser-weight model appears in a green smock and carries a beach ball. Ham-faced men in gray suits respond with Pavlovian applause. The announcer says, "Next, eveningwear," as the same Medusa returns, draped in the same green smock, now carrying a flashlight.

I shuddered to admit that my pulpit ministry had the same lack of variety, and that the congregation's response, even when positive, was perfunctory, Politburo-like applause.

I opened each sermon with some sort of story or object lesson and plugged in one illustration for each point. I also closed with one story or example, no matter how much I had to shoe-horn it to fit the message.

My weekly study began, always, with a translation of the text from the original language, followed by word studies, followed by commentary work. Bang, bang, bang, and I could be through with the examination without ever truly engaging in the text.

I blushed when I reviewed my applications. I exhorted them to be faithful in church attendance, to avoid my denomination's cardinal sins (drinking, fornication, failure to vote Republican), and to be earnest in daily Bible reading. I realized any Pharisee in Jesus' day could have passed one of my sermons with an A+.

I thought of a veterinarian who once described to me his disappointment when, after months of studying diagrams of the insides of a cat, it came his turn to operate. The textbook kitty presented clear lines and labeled organs set off in various colors. The animal stayed still, there was no blood, and the whole thing was shaped by symmetry. When he performed his first actual surgery, the real cat behaved quite badly. It was full of bits of life that wriggled and bulged. It bled and squirmed. He could not objectively study the situation because the subject's mortality made time a factor. Still, he knew no one wanted a vet who could operate only on a picture of a cat.

I had to admit I had been preaching pictures of sermons rather than sermons, reducing my efforts to energetic but lifeless diagrams. Thanks to the criticism, I had to open up the slipper inside of a living craft.

"Except a man's reach exceed his grasp," asks Browning, "what's a heaven for?" My preaching had spoken of heaven, but my attitude had left little need for it. The loss of my illusions forced me once again to take up the preacher's burden of improved technique.

I varied my study habits by varying my genres. A straight expositional style allowed me to choose small portions of Scripture and study them in the same in-depth manner. When I began choosing longer passages, I had trouble outlining and studying them. That forced me to think about what I was doing. I ventured into topical sermons, which required an array of cross-references. I took a shot at my personal nemesis, the overhead-projector sermon, complete with a printed study sheet for the listeners. Some of it did not work, but some of it did.

I tried to use more personal anecdotes and fewer literary quotes. I swore off *Barlett's Quotations* for a short while. If I had two brief word-pictures that fit a given point, I used them both. If I had none, I used none. I tested each illustration by a simple criterion: Did it illustrate? If not, I left it out.

As I stated above, application improved as relationships improved. I would simply take a few moments at the end of my study time to think of certain members of my congregation. What were their needs? What did this passage say to them?

My pastor father once told me, "The only bad kind of preaching is the kind we do all the time." His wise counsel launched me into new methods.

Vexing value

In our church, we have three weekly preaching services: Sunday morning, and Sunday and Wednesday nights. I played it safe with the larger Sunday morning crowd, but I began to experiment with the evening services, when smaller crowds made the risks less formidable. These changes may have appeared subtle, perhaps unnoticeable. To me, however, they seemed daring. They demanded of me a new attention that worked toward curing my staleness and helped me regain the challenge of preaching.

Some of my flock disliked even the small changes I made. One man fondly remembers my first sermon at the church, which set the standard for him: a standard which should never be violated, world without end.

Others felt the changes had not gone far enough. I soon noticed, however, that those in this class simply hoped I would adopt their favorite style as "the" style. They had no clear use for variety, but preferred the tyranny of their form of monotony.

Dick Vermeil, when head coach of the Philadelphia Eagles, once told the rowdy sports writers' establishment that he had no intention of letting the press pick his starting quarterback. I learned that I could not let the pews control the pulpit, and that most people respond well to variations of style, so long as doctrine remains uncompromised.

Discipline's flair

A boy lost an arm-wrestling match to the neighbor's daughter. His dad reproached him for this breach of "machismo," wanting to know how he could lose to a mere girl.

"But Dad," the boy protested, "girls aren't as 'mere' as they used to be!" Forced to realize that some of my sermons were more mere than majestic, I found liberation in the thought that "mere" preaching may not be so mere after all.

Style, elan, panache, flair—whatever the name, most of us covet it and feel apologetic if our preaching lacks it. Still, preaching, when it cannot soar, should at least walk, or even crawl.

Real preaching gets somewhere, or at least heads toward somewhere. Even preaching that is pedestrian still holds value. Content is ever the key. Prosaic preaching, as only as it remains biblical, at least gets its message out.

Spurgeon deals wisdom when he advises,

> Better far to give the people masses of unprepared truth
> in the rough, like pieces of meat from the butcher's block,
> chopped off anyhow, bone and all, and even dropped down
> in the sawdust, than ostentatiously and delicately hand them
> out upon a china dish a delicious slice of nothing at all.

Prosaic preaching also liberates the preacher from his heavy ser-
vitude to the goddess of inspired preparation. We all like to prepare
under the Spirit's inspiration, for study is not fun without it.

Author Stephen King takes exception to the common conception
of "the Muse" as some ethereal fairy who dusts writers with a magic
wand. His own sprite, he says, is a little guy in overalls and a crewcut
who smacks him on the side of the head each morning and orders
him to work. Clearly, King has the better muse.

Yes, I like inspiration. I covet and court it. I find I cannot, however, keep it in stock. Discipline is a more stable element. When the
weeks slip by and no sacred fire falls from heaven to ignite my gray-
bound volume of *The Pulpit Commentary*, I still can search out and
express truth. It is not nearly as enjoyable as the white-heat of genius,
but it steadily yields content.

Quail preaching

A year after my crisis, as I evaluate my reevaluation, I find another
truth: it's always possible that everybody else may be wrong, and that
I may be right.

I can still recall the fateful interview with my parishioners. I
walked through the house to my bedroom and slumped into my easy
chair. Looking up, I saw my two-year-old son toddle into the room.
He didn't comprehend the details but knew that "someone had been
mean to Daddy." He pulled my hands away from my face and sol-
emnly intoned, "Daddy, don't listen to the hooty people!"

I'm uncertain where he got the adjective, but I know what he
meant. There are some hooty people in this world, some congenital
malcontents, who laugh at quails for not being hawks. I must listen
to criticism, but if my critics threaten to steal what is truly best in me,
I must steel myself to fight for what is uniquely mine.

In all this, I've learned that survival may be the greatest virtue.

Whether the critics are on-target or off-base (and especially while we're trying to decide which is the case), my best response is faithful perseverance.

Even in the depths, I didn't quit preaching. I have delivered sermons that I knew were unworthy. I have left the pulpit frustrated and embarrassed. But I know the only thing worse than bad preaching is no preaching at all.

27

Cacophony or Symphony?

*Combatants may win occasional battles or achieve some
gains as heroic martyrs, but they seldom
motivate lasting change.*

—Douglas Rumford

Some differences—between snowflakes, for instance, or symphony instruments—make us delight in diversity. Other differences, however, like those between vinegar and baking soda, combine to set off a furious reaction.

I learned the volatile nature of diversity in a church during an all-committee night. I had been pastor of the church for about a year and a half. The congregation was growing in its understanding and practice of Christian discipleship, but the growth was not without discord.

One committee was discussing spiritual qualifications for leadership. A young man was telling his fellow committee members that our increasing emphasis on a personal relationship with Jesus Christ was making us too narrow and restrictive.

"Look," said Jim, "none of us is a saint. If you don't have room for people who doubt and struggle and don't speak perfect theology, I won't be part of it."

A long, strained dialogue began. Over an hour later, we realized Jim was hearing one message—not intended by the others—and would not be convinced otherwise.

Meanwhile, in another committee, an older woman named Janice, who was new to our congregation, was calling for more evangelistic zeal. Later that night I learned she had said, "This church isn't really preaching the Bible. We're being too timid. The gospel is demanding!"

Others on the committee appreciated her desire to trumpet the high cost of discipleship a la Bonhoeffer. But they did not agree that our church wasn't preaching the gospel, and they differed on how to reach the goal of deeper commitment. The committee discussed the need to balance the demands of the gospel with the grace of the gospel—to meet people where they are. Janice felt they were soft-pedaling the gospel's demands.

I went home that night heartsick. I respected both Jim and Janice, yet now they were pulling hard in opposite directions. I visited each of them, but both concluded they could not continue as members.

The pain from that kind of conflict opens questions, challenges assumptions, and teaches lessons. I began to wrestle with the nature and expression of diverse opinion within the church. What is unity? When is total agreement in belief and practice essential? How can a diverse congregation move forward with harmony?

From my own limited experience and perspective, I have formulated some basic principles that are guiding me on my pastoral journey. I do not claim the authority of an expert. I simply offer my best reflections as an apprentice.

Kaleidoscopic ministry

Believers usually react negatively to the word *plurality*. We suppose that if we really love the Lord and each other, we will all agree. But do we always agree with our parents? Our spouse? Our best friend? Ourselves?

Differences and disagreements are part of the business of living. Common sense tells us these do not have to mean antagonism or division, yet many churches and individuals fear diversity is an evidence of disunity and even unfaithfulness.

Scripture supports the notion of diversity in the church. In Luke 9, for instance, the disciples wanted to forbid a man from casting out demons in Christ's name because he wasn't part of their group. But Jesus gently rebuked their intolerance and exclusivism: "He that is not against you is for you." We are left to speculate about the man's relationship to Jesus, but it is clear Jesus did not demand everyone meet a rigid set of external criteria.

Diversity is a fact of life for us pastors. The mobility of society means constant relocation of church members. Many cross denominational lines to join the church that most appeals to them. They bring to their new church different ideas and practices.

People coming to our church from a background of adult baptism, for example, struggle with our baptism of infants. Others never had women in leadership and find they must work through their theology and understanding of Paul's teaching. Some come to New England from regions of the country where churches are often more influential; they expect the church to take stronger stands in the community. Others come from churches where the style of worship is different, and they want that style here.

The tensions created by this diversity often make us uncomfortable. We desire to serve God in a pure, orderly way, and when diversity stirs disagreement, it's difficult to remind ourselves of its benefits.

But we need each person's viewpoint. We need those who reflect and those who act. We need the advocates of biblical literacy and those who hold forth compassion for the elderly, the poor, and the imprisoned as taught in Mattew 25.

The joy comes as we listen to, appreciate, and affirm each other. Yes, diversity causes friction, but that friction produces warmth.

Boiled-down basics

Does acceptance of diversity mean you open the door to any viewpoint of theology or ethics?

Certainly not!

In any object or activity we find a mixture of essentials and non-essentials. In church history, debate over what was *adiaphora*, or "indifferent and tolerable," frequently shook the church. Just as maple sap is boiled and reboiled to produce the delicacy of maple syrup, it's critical to distill the essential in order to set priorities and values. Certain central beliefs must be shared as the basis for a working relationship.

On one occasion a woman named Mary came to me to discuss church membership. She had served as a lay worker on several church staffs in other cities before moving to this area. She wanted to explore my view of Scripture and the historical Jesus. It soon became clear that our presuppositions were widely divergent on these central issues. At the risk of being simplistic, let me say that Mary's theology was much more liberal than mine. After more than forty-five minutes of intense, stimulating, and unsettling discussion, Mary made an insightful observation: "We speak all the same languages except for the mother tongue. We don't read or understand in common ways the one Book that was written to bind us together in living for God."

Mary then asked the critical question, "Is there room for this broad range of theological opinion in this church?" Neither of us wanted to say no, but we both knew the chasm was too wide. We parted as friends, yet did not begin a pastor/parishioner relationship. Because Mary and I knew the need for agreement in the basics, we saved ourselves the ongoing anguish that likely would have resulted had she and her family joined the church.

In addition to personal conversations with the pastor, a new-members class helps prospective members understand the basic viewpoint of a congregation. We call our class the "Explorations Class," with the understanding that participants are exploring what it means to be a Christian and a member of this congregation. The six-week class is required for membership, but people take the class with no obligation to join. We have found this an invaluable means of building a solid relational and theological foundation for church life.

Open channels

The leader's task in handling diversity can be likened to taking a picture. Two technical factors contribute to the taking of a fine photograph: light and focus. Too little light means the image will not register on the film. Incorrect focus produces a blurry image.

A primary means of bringing light and focus to a situation is conversation. When challenged, most people avoid a problem or react aggressively. Neither means resolves the problem. The leaders of the church need to open channels for communication, especially on highly charged issues.

At Session (church board) meetings, we regularly discuss letters and comments from the congregation. Congregational forums, group discussion, retreats, and newsletters also enable the dialogue that keeps diversity constructive.

One congregation had existed as a diverse, healthy congregation for many years under the leadership of its pastor. Following that pastor's call to another church, the newly called pastor ran into difficulties. People began taking sides, and close friendships were strained. Within a year, the new pastor left, and the congregation found it needed to work through some basic issues before it could call another pastor. The people held a series of congregation-wide forums on specific topics, and I was asked to lead one. After teaching on diversity, I asked them to do these things:

> —List three to five primary beliefs you think ought to be central to the life of this church.
> —List three to five issues you know are currently discussed that you personally consider less than central to your life in this fellowship.
> —List three to five areas of belief and/or practice in which you are unsure. What would help you resolve your uncertainty?

When the people answered these questions, they began to see their differences were not as great as they'd seemed, nor were they rooted in the essentials of the faith. As the study closed, one man said, "One of the gifts God has given me in this church is its diversity. It's helped me stretch further than I ever thought I would. Let's not lose it."

Appreciated experience

Many conflicts are aggravated because people fail to take seriously the emotions involved. Emotions arise from our experiences.

Following a special service one evening, Geri told me she objected to "guitar and campfire" songs in church. We fell into a good, hearty conversation. She was honest and caring enough to tell me her experience as a child at church summer camps had been rigid and emotionally manipulative. Contemporary praise choruses transported her back to those uncomfortable, frustrating days. The painful emotions of her experience clouded her view of nontraditional music.

I shared with her one principle that helped me keep an open mind about worship styles: in worship, God is the audience. The incident of Jesus blessing the children came to mind, perhaps because our children's choir had just sung.

"Geri," I said, "when we clapped for the children this evening, I thought of Jesus laying hands on the children. We appreciated the children's enthusiasm and overlooked the less-than-perfect presentation. Instinctively, we know that our Lord is honored by the gift of the heart, regardless of the sophistication of the form. After all, music is an offering to God, not entertainment for the congregation."

Geri smiled. "I guess the Lord likes all our songs," she replied, "as long as they're from the heart. But don't forget about those of us who've been burned."

We both grew from our conversation: I was reminded again of the need for sensitivity, and Geri learned she could praise God with six-string guitars as well as pipe organs.

Style and substance

Too often we mistake style for substance, rejecting or accepting both without distinguishing the two. Evangelism is a frequent victim of this. I often encounter resistance to evangelism based on a person's unpleasant experience with a particular evangelistic method. The way to soften resistance is to focus clearly on the substance of evangelism and be creative in the style it might take in a particular situation.

After three years at my present church, I wanted to provide the opportunity for people to respond publicly to a call to commitment. I discussed the idea with our worship committee. They were concerned that we not create a situation in which people would feel judged if they didn't respond in a certain way, and they gave helpful counsel on the most appropriate way to present the call and the mode of response. We agreed that I would precede the call with a careful explanation in order to avoid misunderstanding. On the worship committee's recommendation, the Session unanimously approved the plan.

On Easter Sunday as the sermon concluded, I prefaced the call to commitment and recommitment with a careful explanation. Nearly 10 percent of the congregation stood in response. Later, many expressed appreciation for the opportunity. One woman said, "I'm usually to-tally turned-off by something like an 'altar call,' but your explanation helped me see the value of a public response."

At our next Session meeting I learned that a few members ex-pressed concern that this activity was "un-Presbyterian." In conver-sation, I learned that "un-Presbyterian" meant it was outside their ex-perience in Presbyterian churches. Our Presbyterian *Book of Order*, however, says that during the worship service the people "should have an opportunity to give themselves to the Lord. An invitation may be given to individuals to respond . . . by making a personal profes-sion of faith in Jesus Christ."

This experience reminded me that biblical and theological edu-cation of the laity reduces the strains of diversity by helping people better understand the substance of their faith. The teaching of church history and tradition can broaden people's outlook and help them accept others' viewpoints and practices.

Combatants may win occasional battles or achieve some gains as heroic martyrs, but they seldom motivate lasting change. The critical need in situations of diversity is to reason clearly through issues and to care lovingly for people. Above all, we need to hang in there.

To use the photographic analogy, we must discern the indivi-dual's and the congregation's "speed" (i.e., sensitivity to light). Some are ASA 100, slow to absorb but still capable of giving a good picture. Others are ASA 400, quick to accept new things. We must be faithful with what we are given.

28

A Wounded Pastor's Rescue

*Sometimes it is the shepherd, not the sheep, who needs to be
returned to the fold.*

—Jim Amandus with Bob Moeller

I was putting away my sermon notes one night after the evening service when I noticed a light under the door of an elder's office. I wasn't surprised. As a volunteer staff member, this elder often put in long hours. I decided to pop my head in to say good-night.

When I opened the door, there sat the entire elder board, meeting in an unscheduled, secret session.

"Uh, hi," I said, groping for words.

Equally unnerved by my chance discovery of the meeting, the elders' faces blanched, conveying both embarrassment and guilt. After a few moments of awkward small talk, I excused myself and hurried out of the church. I knew my days in that church, and maybe in ministry, were coming to an end.

Straying sheep

I had accepted the call to this church with zeal and optimism. Recovering from the devastation of a pastor's moral lapse, this church, by the time I arrived, had shrunk from 800 to 175 members.

I threw myself into the work. My wife and I soon fell in love with the people. I was on an emotional high. The church began to reverse its course. Within four years, attendance reached 400, and the past wounds appeared to be healing.

About this time, two families began visiting from another church.

They were candid about the fact that the board of their previous church had asked them to leave. I didn't ask any questions. Looking back now, however, I wish I had.

At first the new families were supportive and enthusiastic. They seemed overjoyed to have found a church home that would love and accept them. They quickly volunteered to serve. Within one year both men were elected to the elder board.

I had felt a vague discomfort with each family. They seemed to have trouble accepting others' shortcomings. They displayed little patience or tolerance with those not meeting their standards.

One of the men in particular seemed to have trouble staying in the same job. A pattern of conflict seemed to appear with each of his employers. He would have an initial confrontation with a supervisor over what he claimed were ethical shortcuts or compromises. Refusing to yield to his boss's authority or company policy, he would eventually resign and move on. It was always *their* fault he left the company, never his.

As these men gained influence, the church atmosphere seemed to be marked by suspicion and tension. My wife was the first to see the implications of the rigidity creeping into the congregation.

"Jim, we're not going to last very long in this climate," she observed.

I shrugged off her comment, believing I could work out any problem that might arise. After all, we were all reasonable people committed to doing God's work in God's way.

During this time, a couple from our church had separated and, despite our efforts to bring reconciliation, filed for divorce. The wife left the church; the husband stayed on. Hurting and in need of fellowship, he turned to our singles group.

Immediately, one of the new elders objected.

"Our singles ministry is for people who have never married or are widowed," he argued, "not for people going through a divorce.

"Furthermore, I don't think he should be allowed to sing in the choir. If we expect God to bless our church, we've got to maintain our standards."

"Frank," I replied, "this person neither committed adultery nor deserted his spouse. I don't believe in divorce any more than you do. But he's a member of the body, and we need to reach out to him at this critical point in his life."

The elder was unyielding. He received support for his hard-line policy from the other new elder. The divorced man had to leave the singles group and the choir.

"I'm concerned about the purity of our church, aren't you, Pastor?" the second elder asked.

From that day forward, a hairline fracture emerged between those two elders and myself. It would eventually grow into a San Andreas Fault of distrust and acrimony.

These two men managed to convince the rest of the elders. I was instructed to relay the news to the divorced man that he could no longer attend the singles group or sing in the choir.

I felt caught in the middle. I had been spending significant time with the man trying to encourage him. But I also was accountable to the elder board. I balked at the thought of hitting him with such hard news with no warning. When I did meet with him, I softened the news by telling him that, due to his divorce, there were concerns about his church involvement. But I stopped short of saying he was forbidden from taking part in the two groups.

When I reported on my conversation, the two elders were upset. They insisted I meet with him again and tell him exactly what had been decided. I apologized for failing to communicate the elders' decision clearly.

"Forgiveness granted," one of them said.

At a nearby restaurant, I met the divorced man for coffee. I told him the elders' decision.

"They're saying I'm unclean," he said, his head bowed. "That hurts, Jim. I'm crushed."

I wished I had some words to say. After a long silence, he said, "Maybe it would be better if I attended another church."

"I hope you stay with us," I said, "but I can understand why you'd feel otherwise."

He did stop coming to our church, but my wife and I continued to invite him over to our house.

All appeared to be fine with the elders until three months later. During a meeting, one of the two men looked straight at me and said, "Jim, I'm concerned that you have a character problem."

"What is it?" I asked.

"I think you're a habitual liar," he said in a matter-of-fact voice.

"Not only that, I think your eight-year-old son may be picking it up from you."

I was flabbergasted. Though I didn't react outwardly, several minutes elapsed before I recovered my inner composure. I had never considered myself perfect, but this was the first time anyone had questioned my basic integrity.

I thought the situation three months earlier was resolved. But I could see it wasn't. While forgiveness had been granted, trust had not. I could understand the basis of the criticism against me, but the charge against my son was unfounded.

The seriousness of the situation began to sink in. These men were true to "the letter of the law," but knew nothing of grace, forgiveness, and love. I began to fear the future.

Parish prisoner

Only a few weeks after this traumatic confrontation, I stumbled onto a secret session of the elders. When we met for a scheduled meeting a week later, I expressed to them my deep hurt and disappointment over their action.

"Gentlemen," I began, "I've always believed that we could work out problems openly and honestly. Having a meeting without me lacked integrity."

The elders apologized. But our relationship became increasingly strained. I found myself analyzing my every word, whether in private conversation or from the pulpit. I documented everything from memos to announcements to telephone calls. Rightly or wrongly, I felt like a prisoner in my own church.

Sadly, the congregation knew little or nothing of this. And as tensions mounted, my passion for preaching diminished. I was too emotionally distracted to give my best to the congregation. I found it demeaning to sit in my office like a lonely soldier entrenched in hostile territory, keeping logs and checking records. The struggle to survive sapped my energy. Trying to protect myself from the next surprise attack on my character consumed my working and waking hours.

The siege mentality was taking its toll. I was losing my self-confidence and my desire to be a pastor.

My wife's response was blunt. "Jim, put your résumé together." Furious at the treatment I was receiving, and livid at the accusations made against our children, she was ready to pack our bags and leave. I stumbled on, though, hoping to find my way out of the stalemate.

The hammerblow

Though everyone agreed we should work through the problem, we were unable to find a solution. The trust level reached lows of Depression-era proportions when the elders requested I take a sabbatical—immediately.

The next Sunday one of the elders stood before the congregation and simply announced I would be taking a leave of absence. No further explanations were offered. No questions from the membership were allowed. One Sunday I was in the pulpit; the next Sunday I wasn't.

I remember thinking, *I'm being treated exactly like my divorced friend. It hurts to feel like an impurity.*

The next Saturday, sitting in the living room, the terrible reality struck. Turning to my wife, I said, "Lori, tomorrow's Sunday. Where are we going to go to church?"

Our forced exile had driven us from our spiritual home. We were no longer welcome among the people to whom we had given our lives for almost six years. We held each other and cried.

When individuals from the church would call and ask, "What's going on?" all I could say was, "A situation has arisen between the elders and me that we're trying to resolve. If you want more specifics, call them."

I didn't want to open myself to the charge I was talking behind the elders' backs.

Those who did call the elders were given little information. As a matter of policy, the elders had decided not to comment on the situation. If not for the Psalms, the stress of the situation would have crushed me. Those emotionally poetic words were my lifeline to God during those dark days. I grew in my empathy and understanding of David as I memorized many of his songs.

My pain was sometimes so intense I would repeat a particular Psalm at five-minute intervals throughout the entire day. That discipline kept me from giving in to the overpowering desire to retaliate, to vindicate myself.

In one last attempt to save the situation, we approached the leaders of a large and influential church that had ties to our congregation. We asked if they would be willing to act as mediators. They readily agreed and sent two men from their staff to meet with the elders and myself.

The two elders promptly listed their grievances. I didn't challenge their accusations but opted instead to take an open and conciliatory stance. I admitted I had mishandled the divorce controversy. I confessed that I had failed to follow the elders' instructions on my first visit. I asked for their forgiveness.

By approaching the situation with humility and openness, I had hoped a similar response from my antagonists would follow. I was wrong. After listening to both sides, the mediators promised to return with their recommendations in a few days. But when they handed down their verdict, I was stunned. They recommended I enter a probationary period for a year or so. They thought this would allow the elders to continue to observe me in order to rebuild trust. After the "cooling-off period," the elders and I could work together to decide my future at the church. Their decision was a crushing hammerblow. It felt as if they were swatting flies with two-by-fours.

I weighed my options. None appeared good. Either I could accept the probationary period and try staying on at the church, which meant submitting to the control of the two elders, or I could resign. Even if I did submit, there was no guarantee I could stay on. They had already warned me that my reinstatement would require a long period of observation before making a decision about my future at the church.

I responded by saying, "Gentlemen, I don't think there's anything I could do in a reasonable period of time to rebuild your trust in me. I've acknowledged my shortcomings, I've confessed my sins, and I've asked for forgiveness. I will honor your recommendation. But if we were going to turn a corner, I believe we would have done so by now. Even with a leave of absence, I don't sense there's any willingness from you to move on and rebuild the relationships."

I knew then that my ministry there was finished. At that point, I didn't really care. My wife, my children, and I were all out of gas. The gauge measuring our desire to remain in ministry was on empty.

As the "sabbatical" neared its end, I notified the elder board of my intention to resign. Their response surprised me. They asked me not to leave, which I thought strange, considering their lack of confidence in my ministry and character. The mediators also encouraged me not to leave. But my family and had had enough. We simply couldn't go on. I went ahead and gave official notice of my resignation.

In leaving I experienced the same emotions often felt at a funeral—loss, confusion, sorrow. Except in my case, no service was ever allowed for either ourselves or our friends to grieve. The elders refused my last request to share a farewell message with the congregation. They told me they couldn't take a chance on what I might say from the pulpit. So with little or no explanation, I disappeared from the congregation.

I lost more than a job. I had lost my place of worship, my friends, and my identity as a pastor all at once. It was a low point, perhaps the lowest of my entire life.

Our first decision after resigning was to put our house on the market. It sold the first day. Knowing that our time in the area was coming to an end, I decided to lift the news blackout. Meeting with close friends and supporters from the church, we relayed our ordeal. I made an attempt to be as objective as I could about what had gone on. I admitted that I was partially to blame. I shared that I had blind spots and weaknesses in my life. But I couldn't say I was a habitual liar. Deep in my soul, I knew it wasn't so.

See-saw

Now that I had resigned, I felt ripped down the middle. On the one hand, I still loved the people, I loved the congregation, and I loved God. But on the other hand, I couldn't stand the local church. In all the confusion and hurt that followed, I told myself I never wanted to pastor another church. My ambivalence became obvious in my search for a new job.

Though I would send out my resumé, as soon as I received a letter of interest, I would trash it. I just couldn't bring myself to fill out a questionnaire or return a telephone call from any search committee. I wasn't about to give anyone the right to scrutinize my life again. I painted all church leaders with one broad brush: pseudo-pious, judgmental, uncaring, hypocritical.

God continued to work in my life, however. My first, crucial step back to ministry was a heart-to-heart conversation with my father. We had moved in temporarily with my parents until we could locate new employment and housing.

"Jim, I know you've been hurt badly," he said. "But don't leave the ministry just yet. God has his hand on you. Your gifts, education, and talents are too great to be discarded. Give it some more time before you make a final decision."

I had always respected my father. His advice that day touched a responsive chord in my heart, broken as it was. Although apprehensive, I decided to give God a few more weeks to change my mind. If nothing happened, I would say goodbye to ministry.

Taking residence

A few days later, a close friend contacted me with a surprising proposal. His pastor, Chuck Wickman, was initiating a new program in their church—a "Pastor in Residence." It was targeted at restoring pastors who were disillusioned and hurting because of a bad church experience.

I wanted to know more, and within a few days Pastor Wickman called, inviting me to lunch. Chuck's easygoing, soft-spoken manner immediately resonated in my soul. Over lunch I learned that his interest in wounded pastors was more than theoretical. He himself had twice left the ministry after difficult parish experiences. His spirit, though, had been tenderized by those hard encounters. As we talked, I couldn't help but recall my father's prediction that God might still have a place for me in ministry.

Besides wanting to empathize with hurting pastors, however, Chuck had another motive. It grew out of one overriding conviction: A pastor is a terrible thing to waste.

He was grieved by crisis experiences, such as the one I endured, that drove so many ministers from the local church permanently.

"It's a tragic squandering of the resources of the kingdom of God," he said.

He had done extensive research in exploring the reasons why pastors leave the ministry. "My goal is to find a way to stop the hemorrhaging of talent, experience, and ability from the local church," he said. "I'm determined to reclaim highly trained, competent, and caring individuals for ministry." His invitation to enter the Pastor-in-Residence program was like oil poured on my wounds.

Less than three months after I had left my church—humiliated and bitter—I was preparing to reenter the ministry as a Pastor in Residence. I was, by no means, agreeing to accept another church if offered one, but I was taking the first step in that direction.

The way before me

I was nervous about visiting Chuck's church, Christ Community Church in Monrovia, California, for the first time. What would I say if people asked why I was there? Would I have to tell them about my past? Would I still be welcome if they knew the whole story?

Chuck had anticipated these questions. He assured me he would make the proper introductions and explanations. If any contact had to be made with my prior church, he promised to be the liaison between the two groups.

I had expected a church initiating a Pastor-in-Residence program to be much larger. But on a good Sunday, Christ Community ran no more than 150 people. They didn't own their own building; they rented the local YMCA.

My initial fears were unjustified. The whole atmosphere of the church, including the worship service, was casual and easygoing, like Chuck. After he introduced me that morning, the entire congregation broke out in spontaneous applause. The sound of their clapping overwhelmed me. Standing there, fighting back tears, I absorbed the love and acceptance I needed so badly. It was another significant healing moment.

Chuck did one more thing to prepare my way. He told the elder board they had only one responsibility toward me—to be my friend. I chose to share with them the circumstances behind my resignation. I discovered how therapeutic it was to articulate my pain to a group that accepted me. Most of them had come out of a church where they had witnessed conflict and infighting. They understood my sorrow and, without having to say so, gave me permission to grieve in their presence.

Snapping chains

The structure of the Pastor-in-Residence program was simple. I was asked to make a six-month to one-year commitment to the church. In addition, I was instructed to raise my own financial support. Chuck would assist me in sending out a fund-raising letter to my friends and family. Finally, I would serve as a member of the staff and meet with Chuck once a week.

Beyond that, I was not expected to carry any formal ministry responsibilities. My time was my own. If I needed help or counseling in any particular area, the church promised to match me with the appropriate resources. I was free to do as much or as little as I wished.

Because I had previous training in Christian education, I began by helping the Sunday school superintendent arrange classes and curriculum. Besides keeping me busy, it quietly reminded me that I still had something to offer the local church. But I realized I needed to deal with the unresolved anger I carried. Throwing resumés in the trash can was no long-term solution.

I sought the help of an individual in the church who was finishing his master's degree in counseling at a local seminary. He graciously took me on without charge. The fiery outrage still rumbling within slowly died out. The highest hurdle was forgiving the men who had hurt me. Part of me wanted to forgive them; another part wanted revenge. But over time, I released, bit by bit, the bitterness. As I did, the chains of resentment snapped. Jesus' words about pardoning someone seventy times seven took on special meaning. It was my duty to forgive my tormentors, even those who had labeled me a liar.

Heavyweight title

The Pastor-in-Residence program returned to me several things I had lost. First, and perhaps most important, was the integrity that goes with the title "pastor." When a pastor is stripped of office and forced to pursue other work, he can face a credibility problem. If a search committee asks, "What are you currently doing?" it's awkward to respond by saying, "I'm selling insurance," or, "I don't have a job." The title "Pastor in Residence" restored some dignity. I was a pastor applying for another pastorate, not an outcast trying to get a foot in the door.

Second, the Pastor-in-Residence program offered me a safe place to sort out my feelings toward the ministry. Chuck said, "Jim, I want to give you time to make a good decision about future local church ministry, not a decision based on financial pressures, isolation, or a sense that no one cares."

By sending out approximately forty letters, including a cover letter from Chuck, our financial needs were met. The support poured in. Each letter, each check, each note of encouragement was more than a financial gift. It was a vote that I should stay in the ministry. These votes felt like a landslide victory. The gifts from members of our former church meant the most to us. They affirmed that our ministry there had not been in vain. Since we had never had an official goodbye, it gave many people an opportunity to express their affection.

Christ Community also helped restore my sense of self-esteem. Little by little, I quit berating myself. People came alongside and said, "Jim, you are a pastor. You have a pastor's heart. You can do it."

After six months at Christ Community, I boarded a plane for a job interview. Because of my unique role at Christ Community Church, I was able to say to the search committee, "I'll be as open as you wish about my past situation. But if you feel you need more information, call Chuck Wickman. He knows the whole story, and he'll be glad to discuss any aspect of it with you." With nothing to hide and a strong reservoir of supporters back at the church, my confidence level rose dramatically.

Though that church proved not to be the right place for us, my wife and I, as we were flying home, looked at each other and said, "We did it. We actually went and interviewed for a church."

I likened the experience to having a cast removed from your arm after a football injury. Your first hit on the line tells you whether or not you're back in the game. After that first interview, I knew I was ready to play again. It felt good.

The final benefit of the Pastor-in-Residence program was the opportunity to improve my conflict-management skills. One day I said to Chuck, "I'm still an angry person. I believe part of it is that I've never been taught how to resolve conflict. I internalize problems and blame myself way too much."

Chuck directed me to a series of tapes on church conflict by the Alban Institute, with material prepared by Norman Shawchuck. I devoured the tapes. What was meant to take months to study, I completed in a week. The tapes showed me alternative ways to handle conflict, each of which has its own unique consequences.

Wounded healer

The day came when I was ready to leave the program. I accepted the call to my present church with newfound confidence. About a year after I was settled in, I realized there might be other ministers who had left the ministry who needed the Pastor-in-Residence program. When I met a pastor in the area whose story sounded remarkably similar to mine, I knew it was time to repay the favor that Chuck had done for me.

Not feeling the need to be original, I took Chuck's ideas and implemented them here.

When a skeptical board member asked, "How much is this Pastor-in-Residence program going to set us back?" the answer was, "Not a penny." And like Chuck's program, individuals can do as little or as much as they wish. We make available a number of personality inventories and tests to help them identify the emotional problems with which they may be struggling. If they feel the need for a counselor, we make certain they are matched with a caring, competent therapist. In addition, we make retreat centers available to a husband and wife where they can be alone with God and sort out the big questions.

The first man to go through our program decided to enter a different vocation. That was fine with me. I rejoiced that he was able to make that decision in a safe, caring environment. He's an evangelist at heart with incredible gifts in that area. His future plans may include bi-vocational ministry, and learning a trade is a first step in that direction.

While you can't program love, you can communicate love through a program. That's what the Pastor in Residency does. One fascinating, unforeseen side-effect of the program is that we now have five former pastors in our congregation. The word has gotten out that we are a safe place for hurting ministers to hang out and recover.

It took time for our board to learn why bad church experiences leave pastors devastated. They were accustomed to the business world, where losing and finding jobs are a way of life. I've helped them to see when a pastor loses his church, he loses more than a job. He loses his ministry, his identity, and his support system all at once. Our board members now have a sensitivity and compassion for pastors who go through that awful experience.

A *Christianity Today* Gallup poll revealed 30 percent of Protestant clergy think often about leaving the ministry. In his doctoral research, Chuck Wickman found that 48 percent of those who do leave the ministry want to return to it. My bottom line for continuing the program is this: it costs a church very little to restore a pastor who has so much already invested in him. He is the product of literally thousands of dollars spent on education, years in training, and invaluable years of experience.

Like Chuck, I too believe it is a terrible squandering of divine resources to waste a trained, gifted, and talented pastor. Sometimes it is the shepherd, not the sheep, who needs to be returned to the fold.

29

Reconciling Battling Members

Conflict resolution is more than a bleak necessity.

—Edward Dobson

One young man in our church, a fairly new believer employed by another member in our church, resigned his job with the understanding that the company owed him a sizable sum of money.

Months passed, and the owner, a long-standing member of our church, refused to pay. Finally, rather than sue, John lodged a complaint with the Restoration and Healing Committee of our church. After six months of mediation, both parties agreed to a settlement of 20 percent of the original sum.

Again, months passed, and we were told that the owner of the company would not pay up. So the church board got involved again. The committee voted to discipline the company owner, barring him from ministry in the church and placing his membership on hold.

Saturday, at 10:00 P.M., he called me at home and demanded to see me immediately.

Like it or not, pastors at times are firefighters. And it doesn't take a ten-alarm fire to scorch a pastor—a flickering match can inflict third-degree burns, and a smoldering mattress can kill through smoke inhalation.

Whether members feud over something as minor as Mary forgetting to invite Betty to her tea or something as major as thousands of dollars, the pastor risks hurting feelings, feeding opposing agendas, making enemies, and creating factions.

So why hazard it? Why not just let people handle their own problems?

Deciding factor

I'm not always a firefighter. In our church, the Committee for Restoration and Healing was established to handle cases including threatened divorce, business disputes, interpersonal strife. I'm not on that committee. They resolve most situations without my input (twelve to fifteen cases at any given time).

But not all. Though I had scrupulously avoided being sucked into the dispute described above, when the owner of the business phoned me on that Saturday night, I had to act.

When we met, he maintained, "I really don't owe him the money."

After some discussion, I replied, "You agreed to this settlement. You signed off on it, and you haven't met your commitment."

The following week he cut a check. Both men and their wives, formerly close friends, met with me. They apologized to each other, asked forgiveness, hugged, and prayed.

A pastor can sometimes be the deciding factor in such a resolution. Though he may not say or do anything differently than others, simply by his weight of position and spiritual authority, he breaks the deadlock. That can mean better spiritual health for the individuals involved and greater unity for the church. Such reconciliation doesn't happen automatically. I've learned a few things over the years, though, that make it more of a possibility.

Avoidable mistakes

I have found three mistakes that can turn peacemaking perilous:

To mediate alone. One member of our church filed for divorce against her husband, which automatically involved her with the Committee for Restoration and Healing. They met with her and her husband, and they concluded that the couple had no biblical basis for divorce.

They informed her of their decision, offered support and counseling services, and in accordance with church policy, said, "For the next twelve months, you will be an inactive member of the church. During that time you need to work toward a biblical resolution of this conflict. After twelve months, if you have not resolved it, the church will be forced to drop you from membership."

She aborted the process, withdrawing her membership. However, a year later she remarried and returned to the church. At that time we did something that in retrospect I think was unwise. The elders wrote her a letter: "You are not welcome here until you face up to the situation which was unresolved when you withdrew your membership." We didn't want her to divorce her new husband but simply to acknowledge, "Yes, I have strayed from God's will, and I'm sorry."

A week later we decided it had been a stupid move—that we were not prepared to try to stop people from attending. So the chairman of the board and I met with the couple. She defended her actions as biblical. We disagreed with her and said they could attend the church if she and her new husband wished, but we also told her we would not accept them into membership without an acknowledgment of wrongdoing.

She replied, "We still plan to come."

They attended for a while. Eventually they stopped, and the last I heard, she had retained an attorney and was considering suing us for discrimination against divorced people.

When predicaments like this arise, I'm always relieved I haven't tackled the dispute alone. Nothing can be more dangerous for a pastor. Group intervention is advisable for three reasons:

1. There's wisdom in a multitude of counselors. In this case, we determined our every step based on the wisdom of the group. One man would bring up a point, another a counterpoint, then a consensus would emerge. The group's collective wisdom surpassed anything I would have decided on my own.

2. There's protection in numbers. When situations get ugly, a pastor needs the legal protection of the board and the corporate status of the church.

3. Numbers dilute the possibility of the dispute narrowing into a personal conflict—me versus another person. The decisions made are decisions of the church, not mine. Sometimes the final agreement will be unfavorable to one or both parties, so one or both will be dissatisfied or bitter. The pastor who tackles it alone is in a no-win situation.

To take sides. One pastor I know made this mistake in marriage counseling. The husband and wife both were drinkers, but the woman was an alcoholic. In one session, after the husband had complained about how her drinking was weakening his commitment to the marriage and how their teenage kids detested their mother, the pastor took the side of the husband.

"If you don't get a hold of yourself," he said to her, "you may lose your family. You've got to take responsibility for your actions."

That may have been true, but the moment the words left his mouth, he realized he had blundered. The husband, who was no saint, felt justified, and the wife felt attacked from all sides. She never returned to counseling with that pastor.

Each side in a controversy desperately wants the pastor to be the judge (and to rule in their favor, of course). To such couples, I have learned to say, with Jesus, "Who appointed me a judge or an arbiter between you?" I assured them, "I am here to help *you* resolve this issue."

I or the committee can't resolve other people's conflicts. We can't agree for them. We can't forgive for them. If there is going to be true reconciliation and peace, the combatants must achieve it.

To rush into intervention. Although doing nothing can allow small fires to enlarge, a pastor rushing to resolve a conflict can cause equal or greater problems.

1. For small problems or petty conflicts, a pastor's intrusion can be threatening and heavy-handed. Knowing that the pastor will call every time they have a tiff may scare some people out of the church. Nobody wants a busybody for a pastor.

2. The pastor's involvement in a dispute can inflate a conflict between individuals into a church-wide problem. As leader of the church, anything I do or say has the potential to become a church issue, and thus a potentially divisive or polarizing issue. Others can perceive me as throwing my weight around or abusing power, giving ammunition to those who are already opponents of my leadership.

One pastor I know tried prematurely to resolve a conflict between four leaders in the women's group. The problem had smoldered as a personality conflict but ignited when they disagreed over program plans for their monthly meetings. When the pastor tried to settle the feud by publicly backing the decision of the leader, he suddenly found himself the enemy of the other three women. Soon their husbands also opposed him, and within months nearly every committed leader in his small church had left.

3. In a small church especially, if a pastor involves himself frequently in conflict resolution, he will find himself mediating more and more disputes. Even squabbling children instinctively know how to get clout on their side, running to their parents with tears in their eyes. The more pastors settle fights, the more they fan the flames of sibling rivalry, and the more they will be called on to referee.

4. Maturity involves learning to settle disputes we have with others. I'm not helping my people to grow in Christ if I jump in and try to help them solve each of their problems. They've got to learn to work these things out for themselves. I want to be there when things threaten to get out of hand; that, after all, is one of the purposes of the church—to be there in crises. But it's also a purpose of the church to help people to mature in faith. And that means, most of the time, letting people settle their conflicts themselves.

Intervention

Most disputes are complex, with combatants stubbornly crouching in their bunkers, so I have to coax people to the peace table in stages.

Determine whether intervention is necessary. Naturally, this is a judgment call. But, in general, if the dispute has been ongoing and is beginning to affect the church body, then it's time to try to intervene.

An argument between the Sunday school superintendent and a Sunday school teacher about the lack of crayons in the supply room is one thing. When the Sunday school teacher and the superintendent start telling other teachers about the stubbornness of the other, creating suspicion and anger in a whole department, then it's probably time to step in.

This applies whether or not the parties involved come to me or our committee. Just because someone approaches us with a conflict doesn't mean it's worth the committee's time. And just because people don't come to the committee doesn't mean we won't step in. It depends on how destructive the conflict could become.

This rule also applies to cases that don't directly involve other members. For instance, divorce proceedings may appear to be a private affair. But if the man or wife is involved in leadership, then the church's integrity is at stake. If the couple can't resolve their differences, then whether or not they approach the church, we will attempt to intervene.

See whether the parties are willing to end the fight. Just because we think intervention is necessary doesn't mean we will proceed with it. Our experience has shown that unless the parties involved are willing to end their fighting, there's no point in going through a resolution process. The antagonists need to admit that their dispute displeases God and that they need to do something about it. If they can't see that, there's no point in seeking resolution. Church discipline becomes the only option.

Negotiate a process agreeable to both parties. Although we offer some guidelines for a resolution process, the parties have to negotiate the process themselves. If we simply impose a process on them, they are much less likely to agree with the outcome.

The parties have to agree on what they are going to decide, what steps they'll take in deciding it, and who will help them decide. If either party is uncomfortable with one or more members of the restoration committee, we'll let them bring in a person they do trust. In other words, we're pretty flexible at this point, as long as the parties aren't stalling and are putting together a process they can both agree to.

In the case of the two men involved in the business dispute explained in the introduction, they agreed at this point that they would submit to the process of negotiation as well as abide by the recommendations that were made.

Require a commitment to submit to the process whatever the results. If the parties have agreed on the process, we assume they will submit to the results. But in any case, we want them to say so—it's another step of commitment to resolving the dispute. Saying this up front also reminds people that they better have been serious in negotiating the process—they are literally going to have to live with it.

In addition, we caution them, "You probably will not agree with everything decided, but since mature, biblically minded, and objective people will be mediating, the settlement will be as fair as possible. The only way to achieve reconciliation is through give-and-take on both sides. You can reconcile without agreeing on all the details."

It was only because we took this step that we were able to get the employer to pay his former employee. He reneged until I forcefully reminded him of his promise earlier in the negotiations.

Execute the mediation process. Sometimes this can take six months to a year. Along the way, each party may put roadblocks in the way. The process may require meeting with the aggrieved parties separately as well as together.

For example, recently an employer who is a member of our church dismissed one of his secretaries who is also a member of our church. She filed an age-discrimination suit against him with the local employment commission. She also notified the church of her actions.

We met with her and requested she remove her claim from the public forum and let the church mediate her situation. She agreed to do that, and her employer agreed to our mediation. It took several individual meetings before the parties were brought together and the problem solved. The mediation also included an expert on employee relations and the law.

Bring closure to the reconciliation. Beyond dousing the flames, we seek to restore the relationship. After the settlement, we encourage the former foes to join in Communion with the mediation committee. This may involve seeking forgiveness from each other. In some cases, it takes several hours to confess and resolve many hurts. When one conflict between two businessmen was resolved, they met together, asked forgiveness, cried, and hugged.

Doctor's role

An acquaintance of mine told me something a doctor told him: "Doctors don't heal the body; the body heals itself. Sometimes a disease or infection becomes more than the body can handle on its own. With the medication and procedures we use, we are trying to give the body a chance to heal itself."

In conflict mediation, I see my role in similar terms. I can't coerce people to reconcile. But just as a doctor can resort to ice packs for a sprained ankle and antibiotics for an infection, so I can bring factors to bear in a dispute that will encourage the disputing parties to seek their own healing. These are:

Scripture. Sometimes a pastor feels he or she exerts no more authority than the referee of a World Wrestling Federation match. However, while the WWF doesn't exactly stand behind its referees, God wholly backs up his Word.

Scripture is the strongest factor influencing people to begin and continue the painful process of reconciliation. God-fearing people, convinced that conflict and bitterness displease God, will swallow their pride and make peace with enemies. It doesn't take more than a few gentle reminders, especially from Ephesians, to encourage people to reconcile.

My use of Scripture, of course, depends on the clarity of the Scripture. When the verse under question is clear (for example, that stealing is wrong), I state my position unequivocally. When a verse is subject to two or more interpretations (on the divorce issue for example), I explain my interpretation and clearly label it as such. I don't try to strong-arm them into buying my interpretation, but rather insist that they decide what they think is right. I leave the issue between them and God, because that's where the issue ultimately rests (it's *their* conflict). I never get embroiled in an argument over correct interpretation.

Motivation. By approaching the parties in conflict and saying, "Let's try to work this out," I serve as an instigator of, and impetus to, reconciliation. Just as a preacher brings people, especially people who otherwise avoid that decision, to the point of faith with an "altar call," so I beckon adversaries with a "peacemaking call."

Productive communication. Until they start talking, rivals cannot reconcile. But when opponents try to communicate on their own, they often lock horns and do more goring than good. They accuse, threaten, and yell.

In the presence of a pastor, they are much less likely to behave in the same way. A church committee can perform this same service, but there's also something about the office of pastor that puts people on their best behavior. In some pastoral situations, that reality makes me squirm—I usually don't like people to put on a false front when I'm around. But when I stand between two angry people, I'm thankful for the forbearance that my office encourages.

Accountability. On occasion, I've had to warn warring mem-

bers that they were jeopardizing their opportunities and privileges in
the church by their ongoing strife. If they don't settle, I tell them,
they'll forfeit leadership roles, ministry functions (such as choir), and
ultimately church membership.

I'm not waving a stick at that time; I'm simply informing them of
the implications of their stubbornness. No one should minister whose
spiritual life is crippled by a refusal to restore relationships. No one
should continue as a member who blatantly ignores Scripture and
church leaders. And although committee members can bring others
to accountability in this way, sometimes it takes a word from the pastor to drive the point home.

Staff infection

Conflict between staff has many of the same dynamics as does
conflict between members. I see only a couple of things that need to
be kept in mind. In particular, most staff conflict is due to one of two
causes:

1. Lack of communication. Staff members assume what other staff
members may or may not be doing.

2. Getting cornered. Staff members take a position and then can't
gracefully back down.

One Sunday night the bathrooms were backed up by paper tow-
els in the commode. The custodians blamed the young people,
though they didn't have witnesses. They came to the youth pastor
and said, "You've got to control those kids."

"Did you see any young people even go in there?" he asked.

"No, we didn't see them."

Well, that led our business administrator to rekey every door in
the building. He restricted certain areas of the building to pastors'
access only, and to prevent kids from entering after their activities,
he denied the youth pastor a key to the front door of the building.
The result was mistrust and palpable animosity.

Finally, I convened our management team of seven people and
our ministry leaders and said, "This key stuff is a pain in the neck.
Let's talk it out."

In that setting everyone involved was more flexible, and we resolved the problem quickly.

I have found that most staff conflict can be solved by getting peo-

ple to sit down and talk by themselves. If they have tried and cannot
settle the dispute on their own, I offer to sit down with them and
mediate the problem.

In contrast to mediating with others in the church, I am much
more willing to mediate alone between staff members. For one thing,
I see that as part of my responsibility as head-of-staff. For another,
there are unique staff dynamics that should remain confidential.

I didn't enter the ministry to settle scuffles. I get frustrated when
I have to take time away from preaching, evangelism, and discipleship in order to hose down fires. But ministry boils down to relationships, to individuals working together in harmony. Positive, peaceful
relationships are the building blocks of a strong church. As a result,
conflict resolution is more than a bleak necessity: "Blessed are the
peacemakers, for they will be called sons of God."

30

Healing the War-Torn Church

*I must raise the church's sights to how mighty God
is, while lowering their view of the problems.*

—Michael Phillips

Only one week after I had candidated and been accepted as the
new pastor of a different church, my future congregants began
to call. Our conversations were not happy talk, not effusions of
"Things are going to be great." Rather, they dealt with the near, dark
past and the frightening future.

"Pastor, we heard so-and-so is leaving."

"Pastor, the church is going to fall apart."

After the first frantic call, I said to my wife, "We made a big mistake." In the days to come, two dozen more people called, intensi-
fying my regret and foreboding.

In my ministry, I have begun more than one pastorate on a scarred
battlefield. As new pastor in a civil-war-torn church, you face a frightening task. Though you gallop on the scene like a hero, with back-
slapping and cheers and words of encouragement, when you sit behind the desk the first week, the reality sets in—this church really has
been at bayonet points. Casualties litter the field. Snipers are still firing. Many combatants remain mortal enemies. Morale is low. The
church's reputation is in rags. Soldiers are slinking off in the night.

Each time I find myself facing the same questions: *How can I lead
this people into a new day? Will they follow? Will I fail and not only
stain the church's name but soil the lives of good people?*

In each setting, I've not only drawn increasingly on my experience, but I've sought the advice of battle-scarred but victorious pas-

tors to help me bring healing to a war-torn situation. Here are a few things I've learned.

Reconnaissance patrols

In a war-torn church, I first must appraise the situation. My first question is *What skirmishes are still begin fought?*

In one church, I did reconnaissance by arriving in town before my family and staying with some of the families in the church. I had asked the board to recommend some of the families of younger Christians—they wouldn't be so inclined to coat the past with pious veneer. They talked to me straight, telling me some of the whos, wheres, whens, whys, and hows of the battle.

The gathering of such information, though, requires diplomacy. In one situation a young mother spoke fondly of the former pastor's wife—and then unleashed a broadside against her.

In such awkward moments, I try to sympathize with the pain they feel, while showing neither approval nor disapproval of the cause. I responded, "Sounds like you feel confused. You sound loving and yet angry."

My approach seemed to help this woman. When we prayed, she voiced both her hurt and her love. In the months to follow, she played a central role in our church's recovery. The peace that resulted from her healing served as an antidote for others.

I generally tried to bring issues into the open. I decided if this church was going to get back on its feet, we couldn't play "Isn't Everything Rosy." People needed to know that I knew what went on. At one person's home I casually said, "I understand you used to be Sunday school superintendent. Is there a reason you aren't now?"

He wasn't offended by my question. "Yes, I would like to tell you why I resigned," he said. It turned out they were close to leaving the church because they were so devastated by a relatively minor problem.

I just listened, yet afterward he said, "I just needed to talk to somebody about this," and within a year he was back serving in leadership.

At one meal with the leaders I said, "I want to hear the stuff you probably decided never to tell me." They looked shocked for a few seconds, but then the board chairman mentioned two or three problems. Others filled in details that he didn't know. We talked till one in the morning.

This had a profound effect. It pulled down the "Aren't we the best congregation in the world" facade. Also it cleared the air—and made me a confidant. After that night they treated me as if I had been there for ten years, as if I had gone through this with them and could be a part of the solution.

I followed that evening up by going to individuals and saying, "I'm not here to condemn you or anything, but do you want to talk about what happened?" Generally they would. I didn't give them any answers; I just let them know I was aware.

Often a pastor can go two or three years before he knows all these things. I wanted to know them all in the first couple of months. I wanted to be armed with the past so I could deal with present reality.

The second question I want to answer during this early reconnaissance is *Who needs immediate rescue?*

By the time I arrived at my present church, most people were no longer in crisis. Some combatants had fled to other congregations; others had decided to stick it out. Most crucial to me, then, were those who were undecided where they stood with any church or even with God.

"Pastor," an elder confided one afternoon, "Mary and Bob are such fine people, but this has really confused them. Although they never used to miss services, I haven't seen them for three weeks."

This elder's concern was justified. I invited Mary and Bob to my house for dessert and learned they were looking at other churches. But they still loved the people at our church. We talked further, and I shared my vision for the days to come. Eventually they decided to stay with us.

In this phase of the church's recovery, I've also learned the necessity of dealing with those whom the church sinned against during the war. It was my conviction that if we were to receive God's blessing, the biblical patterns of confession, repentance, and reconciliation had to be followed.

During the time I pastored our church, a man I'll call Tom had never attended, but I knew his name well. His relatives and friends brought it up repeatedly.

Tom and members of his extended family had joined the church at the same time. Soon Tom's brother and sister-in-law became close friends with the senior pastor, and Tom's son with the youth pastor. But Tom, a widower, felt increasingly left out. The pastor would invite members of Tom's family to his home, yet leave him out. On one occasion the pastor called the rest of the family to the platform and honored them, while Tom sat unmentioned in the pew.

One day he beefed to an elder. "Am I really on the outs? Does the senior pastor hate me? Am I a problem to him? Maybe I should just leave the church." The elder informed the senior pastor. The pastor resented Tom's comments and began to talk him down to other leaders. Attendance, due to friction between the pastor and the church, began to decline.

Several leaders suggested that Tom had an evil spirit that caused division among members. Word filtered back to Tom. When he tried to confirm the rumor with the pastor, he was told, "You ought to leave the church if you aren't willing to change your attitude."

He left. But the tension between the church and the pastor escalated, and eventually the pastor himself marched off the battlefield.

After the dust had settled, most people in the church realized that Tom had been mistreated. He was simply a lonely fellow who perhaps had said the wrong thing to the wrong person at the wrong time.

I decided that even though I was not the pastor involved, I was now the church's representative and had a responsibility to approach him. After gaining approval from our ruling board, I went to Tom, confessed our sin, and asked forgiveness. We talked long into the afternoon, trying to piece together what had happened. We both wept. Later that week, several leaders went to Tom and confessed their part in the debacle. In the end, over thirty people did the same. Although he never did return to the church, I believe this set our church free for the future.

My third question is *How healthy are we?* And no matter the diagnosis, I have learned that the crucial tonics are teaching and preaching: I must raise the church's sights to how mighty God is, while lowering their view of the problems.

Certain themes are vital. In each church I have pastored, the first year of my preaching is devoted to the Gospel of Mark. It is perfect for a war-torn church; it emphasizes healing and deliverance, showing the magnificence of Jesus' miracle-working power. Several pastors who have successfully brought about major changes after a church disaster have told me they follow the same pattern: consistent preaching on healing themes, consistent teaching on God's power.

Also, the more pastors I observe during this crucial first year of recovery, the more the word *consistency* comes up. Major shifts in procedures or policies create an imbroglio of emotions that fuel the inferno. My policy is to honor the old maxim: change only what must be changed for practicality's sake. With one exception: let in wisps of creativity. Small innovations can open the window, if only a crack, and give that hint of fresh air that suggests a better future.

In one stagnant setting, I added a time in worship when individuals could talk and pray with another person.

In another church, we chose a triumphant theme hymn—"All Hail the Power of Jesus Name"—and sang it at the high point of every worship service.

Although none of these changes were monumental, they were all disproportionately effective. They eased people into thinking that more consequential changes were coming.

To raise the church's hopes, I've also developed slogans or theme verses to summarize the church's mission. In my present setting our watchword is "We Are a Hospital for the Soul." It has helped us to shake an old perception in town ("If you want to get beat up, go to that church").

In my experience, this early stage of reconnaissance and initial treatment has lasted a few months, sometimes up to a year. Then I move into a second phase of healing operations: getting the troops back into action.

Victory gardens

During World War II, one of the more inspiring innovations for the home front was the Victory Garden. In order to supply food needs both at home and the battlefield, people began to grow plots of corn, peas, potatoes, onions, with some turning their entire backyards into Victory Gardens.

The results were nothing short of miraculous. Older men and young children who felt left out of the crusade against evil could now support the cause in a tangible way. It boosted morale.

I have learned that Victory Gardens can also flourish in the war-torn church.

One hectic Friday afternoon, I received a call and soon wished I had left the receiver alone. "Pastor, I have a great idea," the caller began. "Can I come over and share it with you?"

On my pastoral radar, the blips in our conversation showed a familiar pattern. All I could think was *What do you want me to do, and how much time will it cost me?* Reluctantly I agreed to meet.

Was I in for a pleasant surprise.

"Pastor Mike, every year just south of town," the young woman began, "there is a rock festival, with drugs and alcohol everywhere. Sex and violence are common. God is telling me I should do something about it."

This already sounded like a lot of work. I began thinking of ways to let her down gently. But when I mentioned my time constraints, she interrupted, "Wait a minute, Pastor. Did I ask you to do anything?"

"Well . . . no. But I thought you were going to."

"No," she said. "I simply want to know if you think it's a good idea. I want to get a prayer team together. If you want to be a part of that, you are more than welcome."

Prayer is something I can easily commit to, so I gladly signed on. By the third meeting, a quarter of the church was on their knees in travail over the horrors of this festival. And soon an idea was born: Why not plant a rescue mission right in the center of the din and throng?

At first the idea sounded ludicrous. How could we expect to do any good with such evil around? But the more we thought about the scene, the more convinced we were that this was our calling. So began our Victory Garden.

The entire church got involved. People cooked food for the workers and for anyone who wandered into our camp. One man built a forty-foot cross to hang over our tent. We trained many in evangelism techniques and deliverance ministry. Others gathered first-aid supplies. We arranged a schedule so that six people could be at the camp at all times.

When the party began, however, we felt like a balloon at a porcupine reunion. Motorcycle gangs cruised through our plot of ground. Drugs were everywhere. A man in a Winnebago parked right by our tent and turned up his Led Zeppelin and Def Leppard so loud that we couldn't even hear ourselves talk. No one paid any attention as we attempted to hand out literature and strike up conversation. It seemed we were wasting our time.

So we prayed harder. Then about 5:00 P.M. on Saturday, some people carried a young man into our tent. He had fallen off his cycle and hit a tree. He was dead.

A crowd gathered. As friends and even strangers mourned, people from our church began to pray individually with them and talk about the Lord. In the hours to come, we led twenty people to Jesus. Our ministry to the rock festival had begun.

We have continued that outreach for the last six years, with significant results. More than two hundred have given their lives to Christ. At last count, seven of these have gone to Bible school, and most of the others are attending churches somewhere. It has also revolutionized our church, bringing spiritual excitement and a conviction that God's power is working through us.

Recovery signs

Improved morale is the first sign of recovery, but morale alone is not sufficient foundation to conclude recovery is complete. I also look for signs of maturity.

I am not a gardener nor the son of a gardener, but I do grow tomatoes for our salads. With minimal weeding and fertilizer, I've had pretty good success. Until last spring. The leaves of my plants were yellowing and falling off. Four of the ten plants withered and died. So I fertilized and watered like crazy, only to have two more plants turn critical.

Meanwhile, at the supermarket I overheard two ladies discussing their tomatoes. One remarked how wet the spring had been and how her tomatoes were suffering. She added, "But if I don't water them for a few weeks, they'll be fine."

I went home and turned off the sprinkler. Within a month, every plant greened. They doubled in height, and my mouth watered.

Similarly, after the congregation has begun to heal, I find that if I push people too hard for overly ambitious undertakings, they begin to yellow and fall away. Although a church has recovered its enthusiasm, it hasn't necessarily regained full maturity. I look for three signs that suggest maturity is keeping pace with morale.

The ability to overcome adversity. One of our church member's was arrested for sexually abusing his foster daughter. Reeling over this man's wrongdoing, many in the church wondered, "How can we love him? What do we do now?"

The man's sentence allowed him to occasionally attend our services, and I carefully watched to see how people reacted. Many hugged him tearfully; some maintained a cool distance. He had sought forgiveness from us for his crime, and many granted it personally. The elders each invited him over to their homes to talk and have prayer.

In short, there was love and grace and healthy caution—three grown-up reactions for a sprouting church. Their warmth and willingness to forgive showed me they had what it took to keep growing.

Spontaneous discipleship. In our ministry to those in the drug culture, I soon developed a wait-and-see attitude regarding the depth of a convert's commitment. One young woman, whom we'll call Laura, a new Christian of but a few months, concerned me. Laura phoned me one day to say that an old boyfriend, also an addict, had reentered her life. She requested prayer for him.

Then she missed three or four Sundays in a row. Unfortunately, because of a host of new attenders, I overlooked her absence. When I finally noticed, I arranged a visit.

When I arrived, a young woman opened the door. "Pastor, this is a great surprise!"

I, too, was surprised, for the person who had greeted me was one of our deaconesses. She and Laura were in the middle of prayer. I learned that they had been meeting three times a week to pray together, and just that week the old boyfriend had left for California. The crisis had passed, and she has been in church ever since. That kind of initiative at tracking fellow believers also signals maturity.

Concern beyond our four walls. After being sick, I can always tell when I'm getting better: the needs of others get as much attention as my own pain. This is also a sign that a church has recovered from the welter of war.

Before I came to one previously embattled church, another nearby church had made efforts to bring peace to our congregation. Instead, opinions and feelings were expressed between the churches, creating a brittle relationship. When I arrived, the other church remained aloof from me and the congregation.

I ignored the problem until several years later. Through no fault of their own, their church came under mammoth financial strain. Member churches in our denomination rallied to help—and we joined them. When I totaled our contribution, it exceeded one month of our budget.

This willingness to sacrifice continued in other ways. That year our missionary giving almost doubled. One whole service was devoted to intercession for the son of a pastor who lived hundreds of miles away. The church even volunteered to help in the program of a local church of another denomination.

First-love recovery

Recently I received a note from a member: "Pastor, I don't know what's happening in everyone else's life," it said, "but I sure feel safe and loved here." With her permission I read the letter to the congregation, and many others rose and reaffirmed her words.

That night signaled something else to me. Our grim civil war was history.

Some time ago, I read about a woman who discovered something remarkable while digging in her flower garden. With her trowel she jabbed what she thought was a piece of plastic. Then she realized it was a ring. She brought it into the house and polished it. It was her wedding ring, lost twenty years earlier.

The timing of her find was remarkable, coming the day before her fortieth wedding anniversary. That evening when her husband came home, she presented it to him. He picked it up, shed a few tears, and placed it on her finger, reciting again his marriage vows.

In many ways, as I've pastored war-torn churches, I feel as if I have had the privilege of helping them find long-lost rings.